THE CARE DILEMMA

THE CARE DILEMMA

*Caring Enough in the
Age of Sex Equality*

DAVID GOODHART

FORUM

FORUM

First published in Great Britain by Forum, an imprint of Swift Press 2024

1 3 5 7 9 8 6 4 2

Typeset by Tetragon, London
Printed and bound in Great Britain by CPI Group (UK) Ltd, Croydon, CR0 4YY

A CIP catalogue record for this book is available from the British Library

ISBN: 9781800753617
eISBN: 9781800753624

MIX
Paper | Supporting
responsible forestry
FSC
www.fsc.org FSC® C013604

In memory of my mother, Valerie, 1926–2014

CONTENTS

I

THE ROAD HOME

Freedom is a great horse to ride, but you have to know your destination.

Matthew Arnold

The domestic realm – the family, the household, our private lives – has undergone dramatic change in the past 60 years. That change has often pitched sex equality and care for the dependent young and old against one another. This book explores ways to reduce that tension not by pushing back against equality but by raising the status and value of the traditionally female realms of care.

To help think about the issue dispassionately, consider it an investment problem: how can we invest enough in the things we say we want (having and caring for children, and the best possible care for chronically ill and disabled people and the growing army of the elderly) while maximising the choices and opportunities open to men and especially women – including, in some cases, the right not to care?

This book touches on many big, often personal themes: the family, parenting, declining fertility, the epidemic of mental fragility, childcare, care of older people, the social care system. What links these themes is that they are all connected to an undervaluing of the domestic realm, and the aptitudes for care and attention associated with it.

Women's autonomy and financial independence has been the biggest step forward in human freedom in high income countries since 1945. This advance is of course welcome, but along with other more general advances in individual freedom it has had unintended consequences for family life.

There is no 'golden age' of family life to return to, but few people welcome the fact that by their early teens nearly half of children in the UK no longer live with both of their biological parents. Moreover, many women, and men, continue to derive great meaning and satisfaction from the domestic realm. They regret the fact that recent family policy has been focused on making it as easy as possible for both parents to spend more time at work.

This is an area of public policy with one of the biggest mismatches between the priorities of the political class and public opinion. As this book was going to press, the last UK government (with full support from the new one) was unrolling a big expansion of state support for childcare outside the home for children as young as nine months, at a cost of around £4 billion a year – a policy that will be especially valuable to families with two parents working full-time. But two parents working full-time while raising pre-school children is the preference of less than 10% of the British public.[1]

This tendency to undervalue the domestic realm is, to borrow the terminology of my last two books, an 'Anywhere' bias. In *The Road to Somewhere: The New Tribes Shaping British Politics*, my 2017 book on populism, I described an emerging divide in the world view of two 'ideal' types: highly educated (and often mobile) people who see the world from anywhere, and more rooted (and usually less well-educated) people who see the world from somewhere.

'Anywheres' tend to be comfortable with change, autonomy and openness. They find meaning and identity in educational and professional success. Though a minority, Anywheres have dominated British society since the 1990s. 'Somewheres', by contrast, have identities shaped more by geographical location and social group. They have been discomforted by many aspects of the Anywhere worldview and their resistance has contributed to disruptions in our recent politics, notably Brexit.

In a second book, *Head, Hand, Heart: The Struggle for Dignity and Status in the 21st Century* (2020), I described how the Anywhere focus on one form of human aptitude, analytical intelligence, has made the mainly non-graduate Somewheres, who often earn a living with their practical abilities or emotional intelligence, feel like second-class citizens. My claim is that the merit in meritocracy is too narrowly defined around cognitive contribution. There are other ways to live a successful life than academic higher education followed by professional work in the knowledge economy.

The Care Dilemma is the third book in my Anywhere–Somewhere trilogy. It can be read completely independently of the first two books but, like those earlier ones, it dwells on aspects of modern Britain that tend to be occluded by the public realm and career-orientated Anywhere world view.

To answer the implicit question in the subtitle about how we can care enough in the age of sex equality, I will explore four consequences of our reduced investment in nurture, both in the private and public realm. These are:

1. Less family stability and the consequent rising cost of the social state
2. The mental fragility epidemic among young people

3. The rapidly falling birth rate
4. The recruitment crisis in many face-to-face care jobs.

The first two themes – the less stable family and the mental fragility epidemic – feature strongly in the first five chapters, which focus on the family revolution and the fallout from it, while the other two themes, the falling birth rate and the recruitment crisis in care jobs, are covered in the two middle chapters. The final three chapters draw the threads together and offer some directions of travel.

I have also drawn inspiration from two quotations that have helped to frame my thinking, from, as it happens, two American women academics at different ends of the political spectrum. The first concerns the care versus sex equality tension and is expressed, in the cold language of economics, by conservative academic Amy Wax: 'Care is today undersupplied because more than most activities it generates "positive externalities" – that is, positive benefits for society – that do not flow to the caregiver. This creates a mismatch between effort and reward that used to be solved by restricting women's opportunities to do anything else. Having relaxed those restrictions, we do not have an alternative solution, and are today living with the consequences.'[2]

The second is from Anne-Marie Slaughter, former adviser to Hillary Clinton, who wants us to think about equality in a less public realm-focused way: 'My generation of feminists was raised to think the competitive work our fathers did was much more important than the caring work our mothers did… Women first had to gain power and independence by emulating men, but as we attain that power we must not automatically accept the traditional man's view, actually the view of a minority of men, about what matters.'[3]

I am aware that as a man I have limited direct experience of some of the things I am writing about. When it came to caring for my own four children when they were younger, or for my elderly parents before they died, I played a subordinate role to, respectively, my ex-wife and my female siblings. But these are issues that are central to the future of our society, and men are entitled to views about a better balance between the domestic and public spheres just as much as women are.

While writing this book I had an exchange with a well-known academic who premised her comments about an earlier draft of this introduction by saying: 'There is a really loud dog whistle that women should go back to hearth and home.' As a man I am bound to attract such comments. And writing about these themes partly from the outside does, indeed, require me to take careful note of what women, of many different opinions, write and say about them. But to be clear, I do not think women should be returned to 'hearth and home'. I don't want anybody to go back anywhere. This is a forward-looking book. And it will be obvious to readers who are familiar with their work that I have been influenced by unorthodox British feminists Louise Perry and Mary Harrington.

This is not an argument between today and the 1950s. It is an argument between a minority of people like my academic critic, whom I call the *care egalitarians*, and their main counterparts, the *care balancers*. Egalitarians believe that men and women are not only equal but fully interchangeable. They believe that family structure is largely irrelevant to people's life chances, the falling birth rate doesn't matter, and that the gender division of labour is an anachronism.

Balancers, on the other hand, embrace equality but worry more about the consequences – for women, men and especially children – of unstable family life, regret the diminished domestic sphere and the shrinking family, and want to reform rather than abolish the gender division of labour.

The future that might flow from the logic of our current arrangements is one of maximum individual freedom and minimum obligation to others. Reproduction, if it happens at all, will largely be left to technology, with sex differences dwindling. People will lead increasingly autonomous, screen-based lives, largely unencumbered by emotional connection.

There is a different future that re-embraces the strenuous joys of multiple-child families, better values face-to-face care work in the public economy, rewards nurturing work in the home and allows men and women to balance more fairly their respective contributions in both the private and public realms in a spirit of mutual obligation.

No, I replied to my academic acquaintance, I do not advocate a return to a pre-1960s world. However, I do want society to attach greater value to 'hearth and home'. This is not a dog whistle – the opinion data tells me that most women and men want this too.

DILEMMAS OF PROGRESS

'Freedom's just another word for nothing left to lose.' The refrain from 'Me and Bobby McGee', the Kris Kristofferson song made famous by Janis Joplin, is an unusually bleak and solipsistic interpretation of the spirit of the late 1960s. Wasn't it all meant to be about the emancipation from tradition and authority?

To Milan Kundera, the late Czech novelist, freedom is lightness, a realm of space and endless opportunity. He contrasts this with heaviness, which is earthbound and constrained. Yet, as Kundera recognised, lightness makes life whimsical, justifying irresponsibility and the breaking of contracts. Heaviness is grounded; it values duty and obligation.[4]

Sixty years on, Joplin's lament, and Kundera's contrasts, capture an important truth about the ambiguous legacy of the 1960s. Life in Britain today, as in almost any rich country, is lighter than it used to be. We are, on average, significantly richer, much better educated and far freer to choose our life course, especially if we are a woman, than we were back then. But we are also more likely to live alone, to suffer from depression, are less likely to have children and, if we are a child, much less likely to live in a stable family with both our biological parents.[5]

These are problems of a kind of success. That makes them hard to solve. Negative trends – increases in family breakdown, loss of family support for older people and mutual dependence between couples, unplanned childlessness, children's mental health stresses, disgruntled men who have lost their provider role but found nothing to replace it – are the unintended consequences of positive ones, such as the much greater freedom to leave broken relationships, the mass movement of women into jobs and careers, and the expansion of state and market support for care.

The successes of freedom have contributed to a *care and attention deficit* in rich countries. We do, of course, still care. The rhetoric of care has never been more ubiquitous, whether it's the caring corporation or self-care. Our smaller families are subject to more intense parenting than before: the image of the exhausted working mother, on what Arlie Russell Hochschild referred to as 'the second shift',[6] looking after children and old people when not at the office, is a modern cliché for a reason.

Yet the nature of care and connection has changed. Far more care is provided by the state or the market and far less by women in the family home. The state spends many times more on health and social welfare than it did 60 years ago, driven by an ageing population and also by the revolution in women's lives. Motherhood is now generally combined with paid work outside the home, including when children are of preschool age. This gives a new shape to the gender division of labour.

That little word, *care*, describes a host of different activities across the life course provided by different people in different contexts and with different impacts. Care for young children, especially your own, has greater effects on their life course than care for older people. It is generally experienced as more rewarding, too. But fewer women today are choosing face-to-face care work, whether in a nursery, care home or the home itself. Men have been picking up some of the slack at home, but less so in the public care economy. Care work has positive benefits for society, but is mainly low-wage and low-status. When you can choose any kind of work, why would you choose to do emotionally stressful and poorly paid care work?

Women are having fewer children, later in life. For most of history, society has, in a sense, free-ridden on women. They have borne most of the physical and emotional cost of delivering and raising babies. Today, thanks to reliable contraception and sex equality, having children is a choice in rich countries. Women are increasingly reluctant to pay the price now they have other options. As science writer Ellen Pasternack puts it, 'Now women are in a stronger bargaining position with their fertility than at any point in history. But the private incentives to have children are in decline. If we want fertility to stay high, we will have to offer better incentives than we currently do.'[7]

Most young women in the UK today still say they want children. More, in most cases, than they will end up having. They are put off by a host of factors, from housing to lack of a suitable partner. And having enjoyed a high degree of independence as young adults they are wary of the *dependence* that is usually a condition of motherhood.

Our challenge is this: how, in an era of sex equality, can women and men coordinate their priorities and interests to invest sufficiently in private and public care? And how can we do that when the historic institution for providing and coordinating care – the married family – has become much less reliable, especially in the bottom half of the income spectrum?

Family life in this country is almost unrecognisable compared with 1964: the family has shrunk, loosened and equalised, leaving us both happier and sadder, more relaxed and more stressed. Everyone reading this will have experienced the change. Whether one accentuates the positives or negatives probably depends on your age and your broader political outlook.

The family remains an irreplaceable institution for most of us. But the new reality of less permanent relationships, more mobility, later parenthood and smaller families, and most women as well as men working outside the home – combined with the decline of religion and the idea of a successful life now revolving around professional achievement – has meant a great transfer of energy from the domestic into the public sphere of paid work and public life.

For many (most?) this has been a friendly evolution, enabling women to enjoy a release from the often lonely business of caring for infants or old people at home. Yet what Mary Harrington calls the feminism of freedom, rather than the feminism of interdependence, promotes an obligation-free, individualistic idea of freedom that is incompatible with the experience of motherhood.[8] And the domestic sphere is often seen less as a haven and more as a launch pad or a place that women, and men, might 'step back' into when having a child before returning to where life really takes place.

These changes have benefited some human types and temperaments more than others. The mobile Anywheres have led the march

9

to finding meaning and purpose in the public sphere. The more rooted Somewheres, on the other hand, are more likely to regret the retreat of the domestic sphere. The extended family still plays a larger role in lower-income, more settled parts of the country (though low-income households are more likely to have non-traditional family arrangements). In the north-east of England 55% of people live within 15 minutes of their mother, compared with 15% in London.

The recent decline of the stable two-parent family (disproportionately in poorer communities), the fall in fertility rates, and an overdependence on the state to provide the support that was once the job of close kin does not seem to be making us happier. We have ended up prioritising paid work and somewhat arbitrary measures of GDP over health and well-being.

Moreover, the movement of women into paid work at all levels over the past 60 years has been the subject of an accounting sleight of hand. It tends to be registered as a simple plus to the workforce, to the income of our economies and families, and to women themselves. But we have not accounted on the other side of the ledger for the loss of work that was being done by women in the family and community in the old breadwinner–homemaker economy. The absence of parents with young children in the streets, parks and playgrounds, looking out for older people and each other, represents a real, but hard to quantify, loss to community life in many places.

The Treasury growth model provides a misleadingly partial picture of real life. Household income has risen, but it is too often accompanied by overstretched lives. Moreover, the steady movement of women into the paid workforce, from around 25% in the late 1950s to over 70% by the late 1990s, combined with the huge increase in the ownership of labour-saving devices in the home, provided a one-off boost to GDP that is not repeatable and exaggerates the growth story of those decades.

Controversial US entrepreneur Peter Thiel argues that much of the economic progress of recent decades has come from repackaging the value bundled up in family life: 'If you shift an economy from a single-income household with a homemaker to one with two breadwinners and a third person who's a childcarer, you have three jobs instead of one and therefore you have more GDP, and you will exaggerate the progress that's happened.'[9] And the new arrangements often rest on an old class divide, now with a female face, with the professional mother handing over her child each morning to the minimum-wage nursery worker.

There has been a long-standing interest in replacing GDP with more sensitive measures that better capture real increases in wealth and well-being, as well as real losses to both, and which include non-market wealth-creating activities such as domestic and childcare labour. When a forest is cut down, for example, it counts as a pure plus to GDP, without any recognition of the minuses from the loss of the functions it was performing, such as preventing flooding, sucking in carbon and producing oxygen. Similarly, a parent at home, usually the mother, was not doing nothing before she took up a paid job. A win for the formal GDP economy can be a loss for the informal. We understand this for the environment, so why not for the family? A more accurate metric for measuring social advance is needed.

Few people want to return to the breadwinner–homemaker model, which was, in any case, a historical anomaly. And, as many women argue, men need to do more to fill the care gap left by women both in the home and in the public economy.

Escaping the pressures of home life into more socially esteemed paid work is a relief for many mothers, and financial autonomy has become all too necessary thanks to the decline of marriage as a long-term economic contract in which partners pool and share resources. But the flip side of undervaluing the domestic realm is overvaluing the workplace. There are a lucky few whose jobs are creative and fulfilling but, as the saying goes, hardly anyone on their deathbed regrets not spending more time in the office.

Official surveys repeatedly show that many women feel things have slipped out of kilter. The need to prioritise paid employment outside the home, even for couples with young children, is bending them out of shape. In more than one third of households with preschool children both parents are working full-time, something supported by only 9% of the public according to the 2023 BSA (British Social Attitudes) survey.[10]

Society, it seems, has not figured out how the unpaid work in the home that used to be done mainly by women fits into the new model of dual-income households. Ellen Pasternack again: 'Because domestic labour is undervalued, there is a failure to recognise childcare as proper work unless it takes place in a designated workplace, by unrelated individuals who are employed to be there.'[11]

It is not a surprise that a political class still dominated by public realm-focused men has been eager to support the expansion of childcare provision to allow women to prioritise paid work in the way that men do. Yet the system has been oblivious to the appeals of more family-focused women – and men – who want to be able *not* to do paid work when children are very young and would be happy to do emotionally demanding hands-on care work in the public economy if the pay was not so poor.

THE CARE PARADOX

In rich countries we tend to flatter ourselves that we are more caring than ever before, both as individuals and societies. It is certainly true that we spend much more on health and welfare: in the mid 1950s the UK defence budget represented about 10% of GDP, compared to 3% for health, they have now swapped with healthcare spending just under 10% and defence just over 2%.[12] And the partial feminisation of politics and society has made a difference too. It is surely one factor behind the dramatically contrasting responses to the Spanish flu of 1918–19 and the far less deadly coronavirus.

Yet apparently we do not care enough to sign up for the actual work of hands-on care; there are well-established recruitment crises in many parts of the care economy in almost all rich countries, and fewer women and men are signing up for parenthood. We care in general, but not in particular.

This care paradox is the result of many factors – economic, political and psychological – and the trend is somewhat different in different countries. But hovering over this story are two meta-factors that I touched on earlier.

The first has to do with the conflict between care and equality. As any parent knows, children's interests are not always the same as theirs, particularly in this age of intensive parenting. Indeed, as academic Amy Wax argues, the point of traditional sex roles was partly to ensure a consistent level of investment in children.[13] But women, like men, are status-seeking animals, and if all of society's rewards derive from the public realm of paid work, and religious/patriarchal support for female altruism in the domestic realm has lost legitimacy (now relabelled as 'compulsory altruism'), it is no wonder that many women are on baby strike. A new social contract is required, consistent with both sex equality and sufficient investment in having and caring for babies.

The second meta-factor concerns those dilemmas of freedom. We live surrounded by a political and ideological force field that regards choice, autonomy and freedom as the highest goods: Kundera's lightness. Our prioritisation of freedom and satisfaction in the present, reinforced by TikTok and Instagram culture, means we tend only in retrospect to value the hard-to-quantify activities that give us satisfaction and create meaning over the longer term, such as watching children grow and mature. Past BSA surveys asked people whether they agreed with the statement 'Watching children grow is one of life's greatest joys.' It was one of few questions to receive 80% support, and this figure didn't decline over time. Perhaps significantly, it is no longer asked.

There is an undercurrent of regret in rich societies for some of the things we've lost on the way to achieving our contemporary freedoms. Some of those things belong to the cluster of sensibilities and priorities that were long considered primarily female. If a patriarchal society is one that undervalues the role and contribution of women, then the patriarchy is alive and well in the meagre pay packets of social care staff, the emptying maternity wards and the child clinging desperately to its parent as it is dropped off for a long day at nursery.

The pandemic is generally blamed for many of our current woes, but it may have also given us a glimpse of a better future. In the early days of lockdown, newspapers were full of stories about rising domestic abuse and women unfairly burdened with too much domestic work. But as the dust settled, the story in the UK was also one of people finding domestic life unexpectedly rewarding. The amount of time fathers spent on childcare increased, and many people reported an improvement, rather than a deterioration, in parent–child relationships. Moreover, the post-pandemic normalisation of working from home and the use of videoconferencing technology makes it easier for parents, men as well as women, to combine care responsibilities and paid work.

The overall retreat of the stable, two-parent family is in part an expression of the freedom to leave dysfunctional relationships, or not to start them in the first place. Yet it is also the result of the greater psychological strain placed on the nuclear family, since (out of both choice and financial necessity) most families now require two, often full-time, incomes.

This does not always benefit children, who generally thrive under conditions of secure attachment to a primary carer and plentiful attention in their early years. The work of John Bowlby, British pioneer of attachment theory, remains largely undisputed. Secure attachments can be created by a variety of primary carers and family forms, including single parents, yet the changes to family life described above have not, in general, been positive for such attachments.

The increasing mental stress felt by many young people has several causes, not least the social media 'rewiring' of childhood, according to American social psychologist Jonathan Haidt.[14] Yet according to many childcare experts, less secure attachments in childhood – with parents often splitting up and care delegated in part to a shifting cast of paid carers – must also take some of the blame. The impact on young children of institutional childcare is a contested field and is assessed in Chapter 3.

What is not contested is that unstable families are disproportionately found in the bottom half of the income spectrum, exacerbating inequality and weakening social mobility. The abandonment of marriage and long-term commitment began in the bohemian bedsits of the graduate class in the 1960s and 1970s but is now most practised in lower-income, less well-educated households. The well educated and affluent, those who have thrived in the era of more open, knowledge-based economies, generally get married and stay married. Those who have suffered most economically are also the most likely to abandon marriage.

The aim of this book is to persuade the reader that it is possible to raise the status of both the domestic realm and of public economy care work in an age of sex equality. The backdrop to both will be a concern about shortages: a shortage of babies and a shortage of nursing and care workers.

Policy should support both work-focused *and* family-focused mothers. Family-focused women are less visible in public life, and their preference for more state support to stay at home when children are young is eclipsed in the debate about family policy by the arguments about improved childcare, flexible working and the interests of those women who want to minimise the impact of motherhood on career progression. As author and podcaster Louise Perry has written, 'How can we support a woman's right to reject domesticity, without also devaluing an area of life which, for many people, both male and female, remains a central source of meaning and identity?'[15]

Although there is more family-friendly flexibility at work than in the recent past, the working day (like the school calendar) is still too often oblivious to family life. Capitalism has been happy to absorb women into the modern economy, but less keen to acknowledge that the end of the old model of male provider/female homemaker means that workers, especially mothers, must balance other priorities. People are expected to muddle through.

Imagine if we valued reproduction as much as we did production. There is an agenda here for any of the big political parties. But in recent years real family policy, addressing the stresses thrown up by developments described above, has been, for different reasons, an empty space for both main parties dominated by Anywhere public realm-orientated people.

The Conservatives, at least in office, have been afraid of saying anything that makes them sound too conservative, while Labour is dominated by an egalitarian reflex that is suspicious of the traditional family, wants as much socialisation of childcare as possible and sees female advancement outside the home as the key measure of family policy success. The more socially conservative family-first priorities of many 'red wall' voters seems to have made no impact at all on official Labour thinking, despite the great effort it made to appeal, once again, to such voters at the 2024 election.

That leaves a weak cross-party consensus around expanding subsidised childcare, essentially making it easier for both parents to spend less time in the family providing care. Neither party seems capable of addressing the issue of how family instability has a huge negative knock-on effect in all areas of social policy, from education to criminal justice.

The bill for family decline, including support for single parents and the cost of state funding for services once performed in the extended family, from childcare to care of older people, grows every year. Smaller and more dispersed families mean fewer grandparents to help with childcare and fewer siblings to help with grandparental and parental care. As we age unhealthily, with lower fertility levels creating more older dependants per worker as each year passes, we are slowly bankrupting the state. We think of Japan as having an efficient, productive economy but thanks to low fertility it has very high national debt, its debt-to-GDP ratio is 225%. The UK is around 100% but heading north.

Nobody wants to go back to the days of large families with mothers trapped in domestic drudgery into their 50s. Nevertheless, a norm of one-child families is a dismaying prospect, with unpredictable consequences on the national psyche. And few people will welcome living in societies that are dominated by the priorities of older people, with all the sclerosis that implies.

In 2022 in the UK there were around 900,000 people who turned 50, and about 630,000 babies were born. Even if AI sweeps up much of the routine work, will there be enough people to do the care work in dementia homes in 30 years' time?

Politics, it is sometimes said, is downstream of culture. And the broader culture is starting to wake up to the implications of the baby bust. The UK's actively anti-natalist policy framework, which does not properly recognise family responsibilities in the tax system and now restricts most benefits to two children, is increasingly an outlier among developed countries. But it seems highly unlikely that the Labour government will embrace pronatalism or do more to promote family stability, though a revitalised opposition Conservative party looking for a new direction might consider it.

The undervaluing of public and private care is a historical legacy derived from the fact that it used to be done by women for free in the home, and is now an unintended consequence of a raft of positive social trends, above all women's economic freedom. The revaluing of care advocated in this book can certainly coexist with these trends, and it can also help repair divisions in our society between those who have benefited most from them (the Anywheres) and those who have often felt left behind by them (the Somewheres). Not everyone has the cognitive ability, desire or opportunity to reach the higher rungs of the professional world. Nor does everyone have the patience, emotional intelligence and empathy to make a good carer or parent.

Both types of contribution are necessary to our society, but only one attracts high reward and recognition.

Traditionally, conservatives and liberals have been divided by the topics I discuss in this book. But they also have the potential to be bridging issues, partly because conservative goals often require liberal means. Increasing fertility is best achieved by giving parents more choice via decent, low-cost formal childcare or the option of staying at home when children are preschool, and a fairer sharing of domestic labour. Similarly, promoting more stable families (preferably ones in which parents are married to each other) in the bottom half of the income spectrum is only possible with more good jobs for non-graduate men and properly targeted support in the tax and welfare system.

Talking more honestly about the downsides of the shrinking family is a start. We are burning through our capital. It is a kind of civilisational short-termism. We maximise workforce, GDP and tax income today, but only by making it harder to create and raise the workers of the future. A fertility rate of below 1.5 today in the UK means fewer workers and less tax income to support the battalions of the retired in 30 years, unless we raise immigration levels even higher – something which is both unpopular and would require us to plunder much lower-income countries for care workers.

A flourishing society needs the right balance between lightness and heaviness. The following chapters provide some evidence about how we've lost that balance, why it matters, and suggest a few things that might be done about it.

2

A SHORT HISTORY OF THE
POST-WAR FAMILY

The 20th-century journey has taken us from the stark choice of having a family *or* a career to the possibility of having a career *and* a family. It has also been a journey to greater pay equity and couple equity. It is a complicated and multifaceted progression that is still unfolding.

Claudia Goldin, *Career and Family: Women's Century-Long Journey Toward Equity*

My mother married my father in 1950 and became a full-time mother and wife, with, eventually, seven children and a politician husband. She had only basic educational qualifications. My father played almost no role in our upbringings beyond financing them.

My four sisters, like my mother, all got married in their 20s. Unlike my mother, they worked in professional jobs, and three are graduates. They could afford to take long periods out to raise their children (my mother had 21 grandchildren) and in all cases placed family before professional advancement.

My two brothers and I married graduate women with professional careers and were far more involved in childcare and domestic life when our children were young than our father. Still, we played a largely subordinate role to our wives.

My two graduate daughters are in their early 30s and pursuing demanding full-time careers, as are their two younger brothers. All are unmarried and without children.

My family background is freakish in its fertility, and richer than most. It has also been somewhat more stable. Only two of us seven siblings have separated from our spouses. But in other respects that three-generation story is the story of families since 1945 in most rich countries: smaller, looser and more equal.

It is a messy story for both individuals and societies: a great emancipation with advances in choice, education and autonomy, especially for women, but a story, too, of losses and unintended consequences. The world of work has eaten aggressively into the domestic sphere, and the interests of young children have often taken second place to the freedoms and choices of adults. Almost half of children born in the UK at the start of this century have not lived with both biological parents throughout their childhoods. The rising tide of mental fragility of young people cannot be wholly disconnected from that rapid retreat of family stability and secure attachment in early childhood, as I will show in the next chapter.

But if our new domestic realities are producing new miseries, they are easing old ones. My mother, Valerie, was a pre-feminist woman who did not have the education or career that would have enabled her to leave my loving but unfaithful father, though she certainly thought about it. Her final years were marked by depression and heavy drinking. If she had been born a few years later she would, most likely, have had the education, earning potential and agency to make different choices. How many more stories of much greater misery than hers were buried under convention and coercion in the centuries before the reforms of the post-war period?

The changes to family and women's lives, especially since the 1960s, have been driven by a combination of shifting norms and technology. A rash of legal reforms in the 1960s and 1970s completed the political equality of the 1920s. Women now had legal and economic autonomy from men and from the traditional family – easier divorce, equal pay legislation, more state support for families and single mothers, and individual taxation of husbands and wives. However, it was only in 1975 that women could finally open a bank account without the signature of a husband or father, and marital rape was not outlawed until 1992.

The decline of heavy industry opened the way for mass female paid employment along with the growth of the services sector and the arrival of domestic appliances into ordinary homes. Meanwhile, the arrival of the pill and more accessible abortions led to smaller families and separated sex from marriage and long-term commitments.

The male breadwinner–female homemaker model limited women's possibilities. This was felt especially harshly by some of the 'Rosie the Riveter' generation, who had worked in demanding and responsible jobs during the Second World War and then, after the conflict, were subject to marriage bars, having to resign if they got married.

But the 'traditional' family of the breadwinner–homemaker kind was not very traditional. It lasted only a few generations, from the mid 19th century to the 1960s. Prior to industrialisation, most work took place in the home (the word 'economics' comes from the Greek *oikonomia*, meaning household management). Until 150 years ago most education did too. 'Productive, interdependent, and deeply collaborative, the household was society's grandest sphere... From a young age, children apprenticed with their mothers and fathers, respectively learning the gendered arts and crafts of the homestead,' writes American historian Erika Bachiochi, reflecting on the great home–work schism opened by industrialisation.[1]

The 19th-century women's movement, argues Bachiochi, sought a just response to most *paid* labour moving out of the home with men. It wanted proper recognition of the continuing *unpaid* labour being done in the household via marital and contract rights, as well as joint property ownership in marriage (something not established in the UK until 1888). Women usually worked outside the home for money in the new industries until marriage, and sometimes afterwards in the case of working-class women.[2]

In pre-industrial and early industrial times, raising children had usually been an extended family task. It also had to be combined with productive labour – hence the common image, still ubiquitous in developing countries, of a woman working in a field with a baby on her back.

As the home was stripped of its role in the money economy, and in the relatively brief period where the breadwinner–homemaker model was the norm, raising children (and caring for her husband) became the focus of the economically dependent wife and mother, not always with happy results.

The interwar women's movement saw men and women as equal but with different priorities, and pressed for the greater feminisation of society. This echoed the thinking of feminist pioneers like Mary Wollstonecraft, who thought education and independent-mindedness were necessary to be a good mother.

Some of this was also reflected in the first wave of post-war feminism. The 1966 Statement of Purpose of Betty Friedan's National Organization for Women called on the US to 'innovate new social institutions which will enable women to enjoy the true equality of opportunity and responsibility in society, without conflict with their responsibilities as mothers and homemakers'. The statement called for a 'true partnership between the sexes' and for greater recognition of the 'economic and social value of homemaking and child-care' proposing a national network of childcare centres and a GI Bill-type programme for retraining mothers after their caring days were over.[3]

But as so-called second-wave feminism found its voice in the late 1960s and 1970s, it became actively hostile to the domestic sphere and traditional female priorities, which it saw as suffocating and self-limiting. Women were said to be trapped in suburban palaces of consumption, passive and inert, while all the excitement, freedom and agency was found in the public sphere, the men's world. Gloria Steinem and other leading second-wave feminists argued that men and women are not only equal but more or less the same, whether in attitudes to sex or prioritising professional ambition.

Equality in the public sphere became the main marker of progress, with equal representation in all walks of life the default goal. Almost all other feminist 'waves' have taken an ideal of public sphere equality as their starting point, with raising the status of the domestic sphere coming a distant second.* The domestic sphere was also a place of male violence, one of the big themes of 1970s feminists, and in Chiswick, London in 1971 Erin Pizzey opened the first official women's refuge.

Ambivalence about the family – reinforced by the intellectual influence of Freudianism, with its stress on repression and neurosis – went hand in hand with the decline of religion, and also with the increasing economisation of public life. As Shirley Burggraf pointed out in *The Feminine Economy and Economic Man: Reviving the Role of the Family in the Postindustrial Age* (1998), orthodox feminists and orthodox economists overlapped in their view of the family as a place of diminished value. For the economists, this was because it did not

---

* The 1970s Wages for Housework movement was a partial exception. 'They say it is love. We say it is unwaged work,' said the 1974 manifesto.

contribute directly to GDP, and the feminists saw it as preventing women from contributing their full potential in the only sphere that mattered: the male-dominated public sphere.

Yet those housewives who for much of the 19th and 20th centuries had been raising children and holding together communities – from working-class matriarchs to grand country ladies – would be surprised to learn that they had been doing nothing of value. They were working for others, often expressing traditional 'female altruism', one of society's main adhesives since the beginning of time.

By the 1980s, it was sounding increasingly anachronistic to describe motherhood as a role with status and prestige that could be performed well or badly and something to which a woman of substance might aspire. The gender division of labour that it had been premised on was being swept away by technology and economics, and by a world view that saw the domestic realm as small and claustrophobic.

As Mary Harrington has put it, 'Feminists have long pointed to the unacknowledged foundation of altruistic care upon which the measurable GDP economy rests, and which that economy also renders second-class and largely invisible. But particularly since the second wave, the dominant feminist consensus has tacitly accepted this marginalisation of care.'[4]

The equality norm became mainstream in a remarkably short time. Fewer people are locked in failed marriages, women (or men) can bring up children on their own without stigma, and the public sphere now has much greater access to the brains and talents of the female half of the population. Younger women, and women without family responsibilities, are now more or less equal to men in education and workplace rewards. Indeed, highly educated women outperform men in both, except at the summit of business and earning power. (This creates its own problem for pairing and fertility, as we shall see in

Chapter 6; most women have, historically, been reluctant to partner with men below them in education and economic status.)

Yet there has been so much emphasis on greater autonomy for individual adults, and the central importance of work outside the home, that we have lost sight of two other important goals. One is how to create new forms of mutually beneficial interdependence between men and women in an era of sex equality. And, given what we know about its benefits to young children, the other is how to preserve the two-parent family, so far as possible, in an era of greater freedom.

The movement from a breadwinner–homemaker partnership to a double-breadwinner partnership is evidently still being digested, both by society as a whole and by the economy, with impacts on young children that are still unclear. A letter writer to an American magazine put it pithily: 'The workplace is bidding for and acquiring time once pledged to children and the children have no way to make a reasonable counteroffer.'[5]

It is a story of advances with unintended consequences, captured in my three-part frame for describing the key changes to family life since the 1960s: smaller, looser, more equal. These are all familiar enough changes to anyone who has been paying attention, but the speed and scale of the changes are still worth noting.

SMALLER

Human children are biologically and financially expensive, being completely dependent for several years after birth and then, in the developed world, somewhat dependent for at least two decades. So smaller families are generally a sign of progress in modern societies, freeing women up to do other things and allowing a greater concentration of time and resources on each child.

The nuclear family of two parents living with their own children is often seen as a recent development. But it seems to have been the dominant arrangement in England since the 13th century. Historian and anthropologist Alan Macfarlane has argued that one reason for England's early embrace of a market economy and, subsequently, industrialisation, is because the extended family was abandoned here earlier than elsewhere.[6]

Children generally left home as young adults to establish their own homes, and some services (such as clothes-making) that were performed inside the extended family in other places were, in England, increasingly bought for money in a public marketplace. This created a bigger social space outside the family – what we would now call civil society – that was governed by law, rather than patronage networks, which were governed by kinship.

According to historian Peter Laslett, the average household size in England and Wales was relatively constant, around 5 people, from the 16th to the 20th centuries.[7]

Average *family* size in the 20th century was more of a roller coaster. In 1900 the average number of children per woman was around 3.5, down from an average of 5 to 6 from the 1770s to the 1870s (when many still didn't survive childhood). There was then a continuous drop all the way down to a low point of 1.8 in the Depression years of the early 1930s, rising back up to around 2.8 at the end of the baby boom in the late 1960s.

By the mid 1970s fertility had fallen back to below 2 and bounced along between 1.6 and 1.8 between the 1980s and early 2000s, before rising again to almost 2 in 2012 (driven by the higher fertility of foreign-born mothers). It fell back to 1.58 in the pandemic year of 2020 and has since declined further to 1.49, the lowest level ever.

27

Although the UK, like many other rich countries, has had fertility below the replacement rate for more than 50 years and the 20th and 21st centuries have seen a general decline in birth rates, the rate is surprisingly variable, maybe providing some encouragement to those of us who would like to see a return to the replacement rate of 2.1.

One thing likely to make that a demanding goal is the likely increase in both intentionally and unintentionally childless women, with fertility technology only partly able to mitigate the postponement of childbearing. For much of the last century the proportion of childless women in the UK was relatively high. It hovered around or just below 20% for the first part of the century, but for those women born from the mid 1920s to the mid 1940s – the mothers of the baby boom generation – childlessness fell back to around 10%, before rising again to nearly 20% for women born in the mid 1960s. A woman born in 1965 was twice as likely to be childless as a woman born in 1945. Some surveys now find that one third of Millennial women (those born between 1981 and 1996) say they do not want children, though we will not know if this holds true until they complete their fertile years.

Childlessness used to be partly compensated for by a relatively high number of larger families, but the numbers of larger families have been in headlong decline since the 1960s. My own mother, with her seven children, was unusual. When she was the same age as I am at the time of writing, 67, she already had 12 grandchildren. I have none.[*]

The typical British household today of 2.4 people has considerably less noise and bustle than it did 50 years ago. This is not just because

---

[*] One in six women born in 1942 had four children or more. For a woman born in 1969, giving birth in the 1990s and 2000s, the number having four children or more had fallen to one in ten.

of fewer babies and smaller families. It's also thanks to higher rates of divorce and separation, and more people living on their own. Of the UK's 28 million households around 30% are single-person ones, double the rate in the mid 1960s, and the split is almost even between those over and those under 65. This family fragmentation is another factor behind the pressure on housing supply.[8]

Of the 8.2 million households with dependent children, the commonest type is now a one-child household (3,575,000), though some of those one-child households will gain a second child in time. Just 1.2 million households have three or more children.[*] For UK women born in 1975, now past childbearing age, easily the most common number of children was two 37% – with 27% having three or more, 17% having just one child and 18% having none.

Women having either one child or none is now on a sharply rising trajectory, thanks in part to the older age of women both getting married and having their first child. The average age for marriage in 1981 was 23 for a woman and 25 for a man. It is now 36 for a woman and 38 for a man. The average age of a first child for a woman in 1981 was 25; it is now 31.

According to a midwife in a hospital in Kingston, London, the *average* age of a first-time mother in her hospital last year was 37, with women in their 40s being commonplace and the oldest being 52. That hospital is probably an outlier, but it might be an outlier that speaks to our future. In 2016, births by women over 40 overtook births for those under 20 for the first time since 1947.[†]

---

[*] Across the EU as a whole, the proportion of households with dependent children that are just one-child households is now around 50%. The percentage is slightly lower in the UK.

[†] 1998 was the peak year for teenage pregnancies, but a successful public health campaign cut the number in half over the next 25 years.

LOOSER

Marriage is now not just happening later but also much less frequently, and more than half of all children in the UK are born to either cohabiting or single parents.

For families with dependent children today, 61% are still married, 16% are cohabiters and 24% are single parents. But a majority of children are now born outside marriage. Of the 625,000 births registered in 2021 in England and Wales, 304,000 were to a married couple (or one in a civil partnership) and 321,000 were outside marriage, around 70% to cohabiters and 30% to parents not living together.

The shift in norms that prioritised individual happiness and weakened the social stigma that used to reinforce traditional sex roles and sexual restraint is usually associated with the arrival of the contraceptive pill and the 'permissive society' of the 1960s. In fact, the emancipation and experimentation associated with the 1960s was mainly the preserve of a youth culture, while mainstream society remained largely untouched.

But the legal changes of the late 1960s and early 1970s – divorce reform, legal abortion, the decriminalisation of homosexuality and, slightly later, sex equality laws – usually linked with the reforming Labour Home Secretary, Roy Jenkins, and driven by changing attitudes among the highly educated, trickled down fast. The 1970s, and even more so the 1980s and 1990s, saw the rapid normalisation of cohabitation, divorce, and births outside marriage.

Those decades are now most associated with the free market economics of Margaret Thatcher, but we should see the liberalisation of economies and the liberalisation of individual behaviour as part of the same broad move away from a sociocentric to a more individualcentric society. In economics this trend weakened the state and strengthened market actors. In social norms, it weakened tradition and authority and empowered individual rights and desires. The political right was associated with the first and the political left the second. But there was more that connected the two transformations than either side would like to admit.

Birth outside marriage, cohabitation, premarital pregnancy and marriage breakdown had long, semi-hidden histories in Britain prior to the 1960s. Their existence was often tacitly acknowledged and accepted by people and even by the law. But, as historian Pat Thane writes, there was a taboo against open disclosure of such personal details, which were often closely guarded family secrets: 'Such secrecy was not confined to sexual matters but to other highly personal aspects of life. The death, even of close relatives, was regularly hidden from children.... Mental illness was widely treated as a secret family shame... what occurred from the 1960s was the disappearance of much of the secrecy and shame that had for so long surrounded many aspects of personal behaviour.'[9]

As a somewhat rebellious baby boomer coming of age in the 1970s, I can recall the sense of exhilaration, and embarrassment, as family secrets tumbled out of the closet: my father's affairs, the great uncle who turned out to have killed himself over a woman rather than his finances, the lesbian aunt. Many readers over 60 will be able to recall how the private realm became more visible and contested as the authority of the old rules, and of parents, was weakened.

Most people writing about this shift in norms tend to see only a surge of freedom, tolerance and openness. But, as with the central theme of this book – sex equality and the underinvestment in care and the domestic realm – positive and negative trends are inter-twined. The *overall* change was a net gain for human freedom, but the other side of the coin was a loss of family obligation, a reduction in commitment between spouses and a loss of stability for many children.

The divorce rate grew rapidly after the change in the law in 1969, which allowed couples to divorce after two years of living apart if both partners agreed and five years if only one was in favour. Divorce petitions rose from about 55,000 a year in 1966–70, rising to 165,000 in 1993 before declining sharply between 2005 and 2018, reflecting the fact that a smaller, more committed, proportion of people were getting married. In the 'peak divorce' era of the 1980s and early 1990s wives were almost twice as likely to petition for divorce than husbands, but that has now evened out.

In absolute numbers, about 400,000 people per year got married in the early 1970s compared with about 250,000 in 2015 (despite a rising population).* Of those marrying in 1963, less than one quarter were divorced before their 25th anniversary, while of those marrying in 1996 41% were divorced before that landmark.† Harry Benson, of the Marriage Foundation, estimates that 35% of couples marrying today will divorce, down from a peak of 44% in the mid-1980s and back to the rate of 1972.[10]

It was the normalisation of cohabitation and births outside marriage, however, that delivered the blow to traditional ideas of marriage and family. Before the 1970s, cohabitation was relatively rare, and cohabitee parenthood even more so. In 1960 a mere 2% of couples cohabited before they married, and I am old enough to remember

---

* The number of marriages in England and Wales slumped to just 86,000 in the Covid year of 2020, though it bounced back to 247,000 in 2023.

† Only 10% of those who married in 1965 failed to reach their 10th anniversary, compared to 25% of those marrying in 1995, though that number has fallen to 18% for those marrying in 2011 (the most recent cohort to reach the anniversary for which there is data).

the sense of glamour and disapproval surrounding a female cousin in the early 1970s who was 'living in sin' with a photographer. By 1998, three quarters of couples who married had cohabited beforehand, a kind of trial marriage for many.

The number of live births registered outside marriage was 5% in 1960, rising to 33% in 1993, and is now just over half. Sexual behaviour changed too. In the 1970s, nearly two thirds of women were either virgins or had experienced sex only with their future husband when they got married, and only 2% reported having had ten or more sexual partners before marriage. Today, less than one third of women have had only one sexual partner before marrying, and nearly 20% of women report ten or more sexual partners before settling down.

'Illegitimate' was removed as a term from official discourse, including official statistics, by the Family Law Reform Act 1987. And, more significantly, from the 1970s onwards a growing proportion of such births were jointly registered by unmarried parents, indicating a relatively stable relationship – from 49% in 1975 to nearly 80% in 1996.

With this rise came social acceptability. According to the BSA survey, in the late 1980s nearly three quarters of people still thought couples with children should be married. Today it is less than one quarter. The BBC radio drama *The Archers* is sometimes thought of as a barometer of national sentiment, and back in the late 1960s it was a big scandal when Jennifer Aldridge had a baby outside marriage. When, in 2011, her niece Helen Archer had an IVF baby when not married, it was completely uncontroversial.[11]

But since cohabitation became commonplace, cohabiting couples with children have on average always been younger, poorer and less well educated than married couples and, perhaps partly for those reasons, more likely to break up. Cohabitation is an inherently unsteady state, with a large majority of cohabiters going on either to split or to marry.

Only one in ten married couples split before their child's fifth birthday, compared with one third of unmarried couples. And it is the affluent and better educated, and some ethnic minorities, who have generally stuck with the institution of marriage.

It is worth stressing how rapid many of these changes have been. Among children born in 1958, just 9% had experienced parental separation by the age of 16, for those born in 1970 it was 21%, and for those born in 2005 it was 46%.[12] Families today are dramatically more diverse, fragile and complex than when I was born in 1956. As well as a dwindling plurality of married parents living with their children, there are stepfamilies (blended families), cohabiting parents, single parents, couples living apart, civil partnerships and same-sex couples married and unmarried with and without children.* The variety and fragility is more marked in the UK than comparable European countries, with higher rates of divorce, parental separation and more children born to lone parents (though the high rate of children born outside marriage is similar to many European countries).

State support for families, including single-parent families, has grown steadily since Eleanor Rathbone's Family Allowances Act of 1945 provided five shillings a week (the equivalent of £8 today) for families with more than one child. In 1977 this became child benefit, payable direct to mothers – now £102 a month for a first child and £68 for subsequent children – up to the child turning 16 (20 if in full-time education). Parents, including single parents, who are not

---

* There are now about 280,000 people in married same-sex couples (and 133,000 in civil partnerships) in England and Wales, with about 30,000 same-sex couples raising children together.

working or on low incomes can claim extra support via Universal Credit, Housing Benefit, council tax reduction, free school meals and other benefits.

But the big changes in law, attitudes and state support that underpinned these looser family arrangements have come at a price. Single-parent households are hugely over-represented in the poverty statistics. On average, the children of single parents perform poorly on almost all indicators, from education to mental health and criminal justice. Parental separation has a significantly negative effect on life chances. Even children from comfortable backgrounds have, on average, lower educational attainment and incomes later in life if their parents separate when they are young.

I will describe the price of the family revolution in more detail in some of the following chapters. But there is a positive side too, so first, here is the story of the changing position of women.

MORE EQUAL

The last 70 years have seen a rapid shift from the breadwinner/homemaker couple in the 1950s and 1960s – though most women still worked outside the home at some stage – to the breadwinner/part-timer couple of the later 20th century, then to the majority double full-time breadwinner model of today.

Women's autonomy has been increased by the arrival of the dual-income household, and this arrangement has somewhat equalised the time devoted to domestic labour. But it has also made the mother's 'second shift' and childcare responsibilities an intimate point of stress and conflict for couples. In the case of nursery-based childcare outside the home, it has created a new arm of the welfare state (albeit mainly delivered by the private sector).

The early post-war period, with the end of rationing and the arrival of the affluent society, saw, if anything, a short-term retreat for equality. In 1960, according to historian Stephanie Spencer, 26.4 % of girls were married before their 20th birthday, compared to just 11.4 % in 1936–40. Young brides were mainly from working-class backgrounds, but the trend transcended class and was one reason why the age of majority was reduced from 21 to 18 in 1969.[13]

In the US this was the era disparaged by the elders of second-wave feminism such as Kate Millett and Betty Friedan, with the latter describing the stay-at-home mother trapped in 'a comfortable concentration camp'. There was almost no use of the phrase 'sex discrimination' in the *New York Times* in the 1960s; its use exploded in the 1970s.

Encouraged by post-war labour shortages in the UK, many women expected to return to the labour market after they had raised a family in the 1950s and 1960s. Female employment rose from around half in 1971 to 72% in 2023. The even bigger social and psychological change was the rise in working mothers with dependent children, including preschool children. Only 25% of women with children under 5 worked in 1973, by 1993 that had risen to 43%, and today it stands at 72%. There has been a corresponding decline in stay-at-home mothers, from around 50% in 1975 to less than 20% today. The year 2020 was the first on record in which families with children with two full-time working parents outnumbered those with a man working full-time and a woman working part-time, even though that is still comfortably the public's most popular option.[14]

As women's educational leapfrogging of boys and men, starting in the early 1980s, worked its way through the pipeline, women became increasingly visible in higher-paid professional employment. There are now significant educational attainment gaps favouring girls at age five, seven and eleven. Girls then outperform boys at GCSEs by almost ten percentage points, and 63% of young women achieve three A levels, compared with 51% of young men. In the UK women have outnumbered men in higher education since 1996, and in the US since 1978. In both countries higher education has moved from being a majority male institution to a majority female one. Slightly more women than men are now classified as working in professional occupations, though they still lag behind men, just, in the official classification of the top two social classes (professional and managerial class, higher and lower), with 38% of men and 33% of women found there.

For 12 years, between 1982 and 1994, I had a moderately successful career as a newspaper journalist on the *Financial Times* (before leaving to set up my own magazine in my late 30s). I climbed the career ladder at a favourable time for a man. There was a substantial minority of women on the paper, but men occupied most senior positions. From the editor down that is not the case today.

This huge change to the experience of the average woman *outside* the home meant big changes *inside* the home too. In the language of economics, the opportunity cost for mothers from child-rearing, especially for professional mothers, has increased sharply. And much of family/women's policy and feminist advocacy in the past 40 years has been about trying to reduce that cost.

Protecting a woman's job during maternity leave, now a year long, arrived with the 1975 Sex Discrimination Act. And maternity pay, for any woman employed for more than six months, now lasts 39 weeks, albeit at a low level (six weeks at 90% of their average weekly earnings and the rest at just over £184 a week). Since 2003 men have been entitled to two weeks' paid paternity leave and since 2015 have had the right to share up to 50 weeks of maternity leave, but only 5%

choose to do so. To care egalitarians wanting to abolish rather than reform the gender division of labour, this is a big disappointment.

Meanwhile, the share of all unpaid work in the home by men has risen from 27% to around 40% since the 1970s. This partly reflects the fact that women on average spend *less* time on cooking, cleaning and clothes care than they used to, thanks to more use of domestic appliances (and, for richer women, the use of cleaners). Women and men now spend about the same amount of time working, in paid and unpaid work combined, though men on average still work more paid hours.

Women and men together actually spend more time on 'home production' in general than in the recent past. Ideals of intensive parenting and involved fathering have spread widely since the 1990s, especially among the highly educated: nearly two thirds of all fathers in most developed countries are now classified as involved fathers, spending an average of almost two hours a day on childcare.

I might have just about qualified as an involved father, though two hours a day sounds like a stretch. As often happens, especially in professional homes, the early years of my four children overlapped with the most intense period of professional work I ever experienced – launching and establishing a new magazine. I guiltily remember falling asleep while reading my children a bedtime story and playing in the park but thinking only about the next cover story.

Now, I look back on that time as happy, stressed years, and we had probably the best arrangements possible. My ex-wife, Lucy, worked three days a week in a prestigious job as a newspaper columnist and we could afford to hire a live-out nanny, who stayed with us for 15 years. We also had Lucy's parents living around the corner. For those reasons the stereotypical conflict between exhausted mother and deficient father over the working woman's second shift – which became such a cultural staple from the 1990s – was played out more gently in my home than many others.

I was content to play second fiddle in a domestic sphere, shaped and dominated by Lucy. Parenting roles in my home, as in most, were set early on thanks both to biology (breastfeeding and the bigger changes to women's bodies and brains resulting from pregnancy and childbirth) and that large gap between maternity and paternity leave (which didn't exist in my days as a young father). It feels natural for a mother to take on more of the housework and child management during maternity leave, and that pattern then tends to persist, with the mother focused on managing the household and the father focused on maximising earnings at work and acting as backup and support at home. To the great frustration of academics such as Tina Miller, who complain of the 'essentialism' in this gendered division of labour, women retain the primary responsibility for childcare and housework in most Western countries.[15] This clearly has implications for the motherhood pay gap and the relative under-representation of women at the top of most professional hierarchies.

When children arrive, women on average cut their paid work hours by at least 25% and see their incomes from paid work stagnate. This happens even in most households where the woman earns more than the man – which included mine, at least after I left a well-paid job to set up an unprofitable magazine. This is unfair on those many women who love their children *and* their careers, who often end up suffering the maternity pay and promotion gap and smaller pensions. And most state support for childcare, until the 2024 expansion, only kicked in two years after the end of maternity leave, a hangover from the time when most mothers stayed at home for much longer.

Sociologist Catherine Hakim has classified British women as divided between the 15–20% who are mainly work-centred, a similar proportion mainly family-centred, and 60–70% who are 'adaptive', meaning encompassing both work and family but focusing more on the latter when children are young, and increasing paid work as children become more self-sufficient.[16]

Mothers' conversations ring with complaints about the 'mental load' – what Miller calls the '24/7 thinking responsibility' for children – especially when combined with a stressful full-time job: living with a child's failures and successes, their social logistics, the family's clothing needs and so on. But, as Miller's research shows, many 'gatekeeper' mothers also find it hard to share the primary carer/decision maker role.[17] Some mothers report higher anxiety when men take more than 40% of the childcare,[18] I was certainly not doing 40% of the childcare, but I was aware of Lucy's reluctance to devolve some of the work, combined with resentment at my limited involvement. I called it control freak/martyr syndrome, which she was fair-minded enough to recognise in herself.

The second shift does bear more heavily on women's careers than men's, and without a partner who is ready to take on half or more of the domestic burden the idea of 'having it all' will always be an unattainable goal – or at least having it all *at the same time*. Even with a fairer sharing of domestic labour, combining parenting with a demanding job is bound to be more stressful than focusing on one role or the other, even if the combination can be highly rewarding in the long run.

Nonetheless, big strides have been made towards a better balance. As American economist Claudia Goldin, recently the first solo woman to be awarded the Nobel Prize for economics, put it: 'Every generation of women in the 20th century took another step along this journey, while a host of advances in the home, the firm, the school, and in contraception paved the way for this progress... The journey has taken us from the stark choice of having a family *or* a career to the possibility of having a career *and* a family. It has also been a journey to greater pay equity and couple equity. It is a complicated and multifaceted progression that is still unfolding.'[19]

If you take median hourly earnings of men and women *working full-time* as the measure, the gender pay gap – more accurately seen now as a motherhood pay gap – has fallen by more than half, to 7.7% in the UK in the last 25 years, and for those under 40 it is just over 3%. But if you look at men and women as a whole (including the fact that more women don't do paid work at all, and many more work part-time, and for fewer hours than men), it is possible to arrive at a pay gap number as high as 40%. An Institute for Fiscal Studies (IFS) report found that the average pay gap for 1991–2015 between mothers and fathers was 10% before the birth of a first child but widened to 30% when the child was 13.

Yet Goldin is optimistic about the future. Not only because norms are shifting in the direction of more couple equality, but also because technology and job design is making it easier for women, and men, to combine family and career even when competing at the top. And there has, indeed, been a sharp increase in women on company boards and in public appointments in the past decade in the UK.

But the more equal story sketched out above has a twist in the tale. While men and women in the workplace, and to a lesser extent the home, have been converging, work and life experiences *among women* have been diverging since the 1960s. Alison Wolf puts it like this: 'Until recently all women's lives, whether rich or poor, have been dominated by the same experiences and pressures. Today, elite and highly educated women have become a class apart... They are now more like the men of the family than ever before. It is from other women that they have drawn away.'[20]

41

In recent decades the professional labour market has been largely desegregated by gender, but at the lower end of the labour market many women still work in female-majority jobs, and men in male-majority sectors. Women without degrees still dominate in some of the least well-paid occupations, such as care and cleaning, usually combining these with care responsibilities at home. And many women, particularly those in their mid 40s to late 50s, end up in a corridor of double care looking after both children and older relatives. Around 25% of women work in low-paid jobs, compared with 15% of men, reflecting also the fact that women are far more likely to work part-time.

Better-paid professional women have fewer caring responsibilities than lower-paid women, and the IFS found that during the pandemic lower-paid mothers did double the amount of housework than before while higher-paid mothers, who are also more likely to be married, did just 6% more.

Professional women are also the main users of formal paid-for childcare, which has helped to propel the issue up the list of politicians' concerns in recent years. Nurseries and nannies have long been used by richer women, but it was not until 2001 that Labour brought in 12.5 hours of free nursery care for 33 weeks a year for 4-year-olds, soon extended to 3-year-olds in 2004, and to 38 weeks per year in 2006. Then in 2010 the offer was extended to 15 hours a week free nursery care for 3- and 4-year-olds, rising to 30 hours in 2017 if both parents were working (and for two-year-olds from disadvantaged homes). The current expansion, announced in the 2023 budget, extends the 30 free hours to 2-year-olds and, in 2025, will apply to infants from 9 months old.

This latest extension is popular with many mothers in professional careers, but will not be relevant to many others. Only about one third of families currently use any formal childcare for children under two, with either the mother (or more rarely father) staying at home or grandparents and friends helping out. And according to the Department for Education, two thirds of working mothers with children under four would rather work fewer hours if they could afford it, and one third not at all.

Many women want (or need) to work outside the home even when children are of preschool age. But, as I will show in Chapter 4, most women also want a better balance between home and work, with more time at home, especially in the first couple of years of motherhood. In most cases, it is not that women are looking after their own children because childcare is too expensive; rather it is that looking after their own children is too expensive, given the family's financial needs, so they have to go out to work.[21]

It is sometimes argued that the need for two full-time incomes is related to the disappearance of a family wage paid to the man. But even by the 1950s and 1960s the old union demand for a family wage to maintain a man, and his wife and children, had given way to the 'social wage' (brainchild of Jack Jones, the great union leader of the 1960s and 1970s), which was more about pensions and benefits than family income.

In the 1950s and 1960s wages in fact grew faster than at almost any time before or since. Real per capita income in the 1960s rose about 25% in the UK, so it seems improbable that employers were slyly undermining male wages by employing more women. There was plenty of work for everyone. The real reduction in working-class male wages came two decades later, thanks to more global trade and automation, along with the loss of the Married Man's Tax Allowance.

The need for two incomes was driven by a combination of mothers' desire for financial independence, expectations created by rising living standards, and, in some parts of the country, rising housing costs. House price data from the 1960s suggests that the price of the average house went up about 60% in the decade at a time when home ownership was rising fast and overall prices rose only 45%. In later decades this evolved into an 'arms race': two-income couples could bid more for desirable housing, so prices for homes went up, so more women had to work full-time to be able to afford them. The 1980s saw the biggest increase in home ownership of any decade, driven partly by dual-income mortgages, which were first allowed in the early 1980s.

Greater opportunities for most women since the early 1960s have not, by and large, come at the expense of men. There are some exceptions to that; for example, social mobility has been more limited for men with only basic education because of the big increase in graduate women moving into professional jobs. There has also been a sharp overall fall in employment for men both here and in the US – in 1971 the employment rate for working-age men in the UK and US was respectively 95% and 80%, while today it is 79% and 66% – which will be partly a function of some men staying in education for longer but also due to the increased demand for the soft skills that women tend to excel at and reduced demand for low-skill, male-dominated manual jobs.

Women's greater freedom to leave disagreeable men or not to partner with them at all is also a factor in the increase in men who are neither working nor looking for work. Some are lost to the system. Why some men have given up and how other men are contributing to a new gender division of labour is something I will consider in Chapter 5. But first, after my whistle-stop tour of the past sixty years in family life – smaller, looser, more equal – I will consider some of the fallout.

3

THE FALLOUT: INSECURE CHILDREN AND MISERABLE MOTHERS

The traditional family is breaking down because individuals are investing their time and money elsewhere, but the social need for many of the family's traditional services remains. How can individual decisions and society's needs be reconciled?

Shirley Burggraf, *The Feminine Economy and Economic Man*.

The freedoms of the family revolution described in the previous chapter, and the onward march of individual choice and autonomy, are part of the air we breathe. But, as Kundera knew, lightness comes at a price. This chapter will consider the price: the overwhelming evidence that family instability has a negative impact on children's life chances and is also a big, and under-examined, factor behind the epidemic of mental fragility. It will review, too, the impact of formal childcare on preschool infants and the strains of modern parenting, especially on mothers.

Families can be places of unhappiness and conflict. Even violence. For those of us lucky enough to have had largely positive experiences of family life, the word conjures up something benign and comforting. For others, the associations are more ambivalent. But few families are immune from the mental stresses of modern life.

Former equalities chief Trevor Phillips wrote the following, reflecting on the death aged 36 of his daughter Sushila after a 20-year battle with anorexia nervosa: 'I would want to ask more questions about the effect of sweeping social changes in developed nations; not because I want to turn the clock back to some earlier golden age, but to ask whether we are being honest with ourselves about the impact of those changes and whether we have invested the resources necessary to offset the downsides that have come with social progress.' He pointed to one aspect of the family revolution: 'Could the dramatic increase in homes where both parents have to work be taking its toll on the millennial children born between 1980 and 1995?'[1]

Across the developed world, the one quality-of-life indicator that is relentlessly declining is mental health. And this decline appears to go hand in hand with looser and smaller families, themselves the product of a culture that has elevated freedom and individual autonomy without the traditional balancing forces of religion, community obligation and moral stigma that once provided the handrails of structure and guidance.

Looser family structures are not only implicated in mental health, but in the whole way we relate to each other. Sociologist Anthony Giddens has pointed to the fact that a high divorce society, with the message that family relationships are impermanent, creates a culture of perpetual negotiation and conditionality, saying that whereas in the past 'kinship relations used to be a taken for granted basis of trust, now trust has to be negotiated and bargained for'.[2]

FAMILY STRUCTURE MATTERS

The big picture is clear. A little more than half of all children in England and Wales are now born to parents who are not married (compared with 8% in 1971 and 30% in 1991), and just under half of those children (46%) do not live with both biological parents by the time they are 14.[3] This means that many of them will need to establish new relationships both with their parents' new partners and also with new half- and step-siblings. Only about half of children in separated families see their non-resident parent frequently.[4]

There is also a clear social class dividing line in family structure: 71% of parents in high-earning households are married, compared with 34% in low-earning households. The divide is even greater by educational attainment: 68% of graduates are married, compared with 17% of those with only basic education.[5] Economically secure parents, usually with degrees or equivalent, tend to delay childbearing, have children within marriage, marry similar people and tend to stay married to them, and can (notwithstanding the inevitable ups and downs of life) provide the stability, resources and character formation that allow children to flourish.

By contrast, those with fewer resources and qualifications are more likely to have children younger, within cohabiting relationships or outside a partnership entirely, and are more likely to separate and have unstable family lives. This class divide in family structure means that most people in politics, academia and journalism have limited direct experience of the scale of family instability. Just ask a teacher who works at a school or further education college in an economically deprived area. Most will have dozens of stories of young people from broken homes in which addiction and even abuse are common.*

---

* Abuse is much more likely from step-parents. According to one study of sexual abuse, 1 in 6 girls living with a stepfather experience sexual abuse, compared to 1 in 40 living with a biological father. See Diana E. H. Russell, 'The prevalence and seriousness of incestuous abuse: stepfathers versus biological fathers', *Child Abuse & Neglect*, 8/1 (1984), 15–22.

A stable childhood often starts with the simple fact of being expected and wanted. Among married couples three quarters of births are planned, compared with only half among cohabiting couples and 16% among single mothers. Single mothers are much less likely to breastfeed, much more likely to smoke through pregnancy, and much more prone to experience postnatal depression than partnered women.

The proportion of single-parent households with dependent children in the UK, about 24%, is much higher than in the rest of Europe, where it averages around 13%, and is much higher in poorer, post-industrial places like Hartlepool (30%) than richer places like Winchester (7%). Over 40% of families with children in the London boroughs of Southwark, Lambeth and Islington are lone-parent families.

And the true figures are even higher than those snapshot numbers suggest. Looked at over a six-year period, as many as 33% of families with children have been a lone-parent family at some point. The revolving-door template of relationships has been shown to be the most damaging of all to young children, with frequently disrupted attachments.[6] According to the authoritative IFS Deaton Review into inequality in the UK, *Families and Inequalities*, single parenthood 'may now be embedded in the local culture' in some places. It is a similar story in the US, as is the class divide over marriage.

Single mothers – or more rarely fathers – can of course be excellent, loving parents. One emotionally focused parent is better than two detached or abusive ones. Many children of single parents turn into happy, well-balanced adults, and sometimes high-achieving ones, like prominent Labour politicians Bridget Phillipson and Wes Streeting, not to mention Bill Clinton and Barack Obama. It should also be noted that many people classified as coming from a single-parent household will have had loving substitute fathers or mothers.

But average outcomes matter. It is no disrespect to struggling single parents, usually mothers, to highlight the fact that the lower level of family resources and parental time in single-parent households, compared with two-parent families, can have negative consequences. Such households are generally more fragile: when a single parent loses their job, it has a much bigger impact.

Of the 30% of all children living in income poverty at age five – meaning below 60% of median income before housing costs – about three quarters of these are from single-parent families. 50% of single parents receive means-tested state support of some kind, compared with 12% of cohabiters and 6% of married parents.

It is often argued that a lack of resources *causes* less secure relationships, and there is some truth in that. But the average family was much poorer 50 years ago and yet, thanks to different norms, far more likely to stay together. Similarly, people from Pakistani and Bangladeshi backgrounds are the poorest groups in the UK but have the most traditional family arrangements (which brings its own problems behind firmly closed doors). We also know that children flourish in stable families with good, conscientious parenting, whatever the income or education level of their parents.

Family stability is not merely a function of income and education levels. For children born to *cohabiting* parents in the first part of the 21st century, the likelihood of seeing their parents split before the child turned 12 was 53%, 60% and 66% for high, medium and low education levels respectively, while for those with *married* parents it was 27%, 31% and 39%. In other words, married parents with low education levels are significantly more likely to stay together than cohabiting parents with even the highest education levels.

Resources clearly matter to families, but stability is an *independent* factor and one that is easier to cultivate in a secure, two-parent partnership in which both parents feel committed to each other and to their children for the long term. A child who is read to regularly will do better in cognitive tests no matter what their background, and children are more likely to be read to in married families.*

A large body of research across many countries has established beyond doubt that children whose parents separate are more likely to be disadvantaged on a range of childhood, adolescent and adult outcomes, including psychological health, education and later labour market outcomes, and in their own family lives in adulthood.† The children of separated or divorced parents are significantly more likely to see their own marriage or long-term childbearing relationship break down: almost 30% of children from broken homes experienced the breakdown of their own family, compared with 16% of those from intact families. Social class makes no difference to this pattern.[7]

Immediately following separation, both parents usually suffer a big drop in income: about 20–30%. Women lose more financially in the longer run, though usually with less disruption in their housing situation (almost 40% of parents with child maintenance obligations fail to pay anything at all).[8] Both men and women suffer worse mental health as a result of relationship breakdown, but while this is often

---

* Nearly half of British adults say they were never or only occasionally read to by a parent. See 'Why Family Matters: A Comprehensive Analysis of the Consequences of Family Breakdown', Centre for Social Justice, Mar. 2019. The Deaton Review says that for those born in 1970 in the UK, the children of highly educated parents who separated had a 13% lower probability of going to university.

† American psychologist Rob Henderson, who grew up partly in foster homes, says that an orderly or disorderly early environment has more impact than wealth or poverty. He points to the fact that while about 35% of young Americans graduate from college, 11% of children from the poorest families do so and just 3% of foster children. See Rob Henderson's Newsletter, 21 Jan 2024.

a short-term effect for adults, for many children the impact is more long-lasting.

In the short term, children often go through a flurry of bad behaviour when parents separate, as confusion reigns and unconditional relationships suddenly become conditional. Boys tend to act out and girls become more anxious and introverted.

People often wonder whether the impact of parental separation on children is worse than living in a family with persistent conflict. The answer seems to be that in high-conflict families where the parents have separated, the outcomes *are* slightly better for children. But in low-conflict families they are worse, presumably because this dramatic change is unexpected and bemusing to a young child. And, counter-intuitively, it appears that the vast majority of break-ups involve low-conflict couples. Harry Benson of the Marriage Foundation found that in answers to survey questions about happiness and quarrels, couples that split are almost indistinguishable from couples that remain together: of married couples who split only 9% are classified as high-conflict, while among cohabiters it is a tiny 4%.[9] A study of five-year-olds using the UK Millennium Cohort Study found that 'the dissolution of high-quality parental unions has the most harmful effect on children.'[10]

The IFS report *Families and Inequalities* does not shy away from the impact of looser family forms: 'Parental separation lowers the economic and psychological well-being of parents and diminishes the resources available to children, as parental time, engagement and money are spread more thinly across households, which has legacies that reverberate into adulthood.'

Yet the IFS authors do *not* draw the obvious conclusion from this and stress the importance of promoting the stable two-parent family. Instead, they fall back on the standard demands for more public spending on early education and mental health services, reduction in child poverty, and – the nearest they get to promoting more stable families – more parenting and relationship support.

The researchers at the IFS are merely reflecting the majority view among the UK's political class that choice and autonomy, and the fear of stigmatising single-parent families, must trump any concerted attempt to incentivise more stable, two-parent families, which is deemed a private matter beyond the reach of policy. But, for the sake of children, we need to show more respect for this data and find ways of acting on it.

THE MENTAL FRAGILITY EPIDEMIC

A recent surge in the mental fragility of young people has been widely reported. A less secure start in life for many of today's children, including the higher probability of living through parental separation or the stresses of single parenthood, must be a contributing factor.

It is important, first, to put the epidemic into perspective. Something significant is happening, yet Simon Wessely, past president of the Royal College of Psychiatrists, tells me that there has been only a small increase in the population rates of *serious mental illness* – schizophrenia, bipolar, severe depression – over recent decades. Indeed, the number of people admitted as inpatients following contact with NHS mental health services has been falling in recent years.[11]

'But,' says Wessely, 'there has been one change in the recent period that is significant, and that is the rise in common mental disorders (CMDs) – basically anxiety disorders, lower-level depressive disorders – and particularly among young women.' The rise in CMDs among women aged between 18 and 24 rose from 28% to 41% between 2010 and 2021.[12]

This evidence, in part from self-reporting surveys, begs the question of how real the increase is. The language of mental illness has expanded to encompass everything from serious depression to stress at work. Some psychologists, such as Lucy Foulkes, are pushing back against the medicalisation of ordinary variations in human behaviour and mood and suggesting that mental health awareness campaigns are contributing to a social contagion and becoming counterproductive.* The 'worried well' are also adding to even longer waits to be seen by the under-pressure Child and Adolescent Mental Health Services for those who really need it (mental illness is said to make up 28% of the UK's disease burden, but it receives only 13% of NHS funding).[13]

Nevertheless, both self-reported survey results and increased use of NHS mental health services signify something. The Mental Health of Children and Young People in England survey reports mental disorders among 5- to 15-year-olds almost doubling between 1999 and 2022, to 18%. It also found 23.9% of girls aged 17–19 reporting mental disorders, with fully half of those saying they have self-harmed.[14] (Hospital admissions for self-harm among young women rose 40% in the decade between 2012 and 2022 but have subsequently *fallen back* to 2012 levels.)

---

* See Lucy Foulkes, 'Can the UK Afford a Mental Health Crisis?', BBC Radio 4 Analysis (6 Nov. 2023). How (and to whom) questions are framed in surveys can make a big difference, according to a 2013 paper by academics at King's College London. Far higher rates of stress and mental disorder were reported when people were asked questions in their occupational role rather than just as ordinary citizens. The academics' General Health Questionnaire (GHQ) found 14–17% of the population suffering from CMDs, but when people filled in the same questionnaire in their professional capacity as police officers, teachers, etc., the proportion suffering from CMDs rose to 30% (https://journals.plos.org/plosone/article?id=10.1371/journal.pone.0078693).

And this is not just an issue for teenage girls: the NHS Mental Health Bulletin mentioned above reports a sharp rise in the overall population that had contact with NHS mental health services in the six years to 2021–2, rising from 3.4% to 5.8%. There are now more than 8 million people in England taking antidepressants, with 2 million taking the drugs for more than 5 years, and the Office for National Statistics (ONS) says that 7.1 million people in England and Wales self-report a mental health condition.

Around one quarter of the 2.7 million people of working age who are economically inactive for health reasons give a mental health issue as their main condition, an increase of 15% since 2019.[15] Meanwhile, the proportion of school-age children with SEN (special educational needs) is 17%, with the more serious cases, those supported by an EHC (Education, Health and Care) plan, up to 4.3% in 2023. This is a 64% increase since 2016.

There are several good reasons why the number might be rising sharply, as well as some less good reasons. One of the good reasons is a greater understanding of autism and attention deficit hyperactivity disorder (ADHD), and the relabelling of people who were previously classified as suffering from speech/language disorders or mental retardation (which have seen some corresponding declines in diagnoses). Autism is estimated to affect between 1% and 2% of the population and ADHD 3% to 4%. There has also been a more expansive definition of autism which has picked up more people, especially girls and women, at the less severe end of the spectrum.* And it is possible that

---

* Since 1952 the number of mental health conditions that can be diagnosed has grown from 106 to more than 400, and a 2022 academic paper found a nearly 800% increase in diagnoses of autism in the 20 years up to 2018 (Ginny Russell et al., 'Time Trends in Autism Diagnosis over 20 Years a UK Population-Based Cohort Study', *Journal of Child Psychology and Psychiatry*, 63/6 (2022), 674–82).

various environmental or social factors are increasing the incidence: the Royal College of Speech and Language Therapists, noting the disproportionate connection between a SEN diagnosis and pupils from poorer families, said that some of the correlation is likely to do with 'smoking and consuming alcohol during pregnancy, parental stress and family breakdown'.[16]

But a doubling in just six years of those prescribed medication for ADHD, to 235,000, suggests to Simon Wessely that there has been some 'diagnostic creep'. He says that with sharp increases in referrals for autism and ADHD many people are being diverted to private providers 'who seem to make the diagnosis incredibly easy'.[17] More than half of teachers in a recent survey said that too many children are being wrongly diagnosed with SEN, providing them with an excuse to behave badly or underperform.[18]

One child psychiatrist I know tells me that at the start of his career most parents did not want their child diagnosed with any kind of mental condition, and that now many parents demand a diagnosis, as it can help to fund extra support at school – which schools encourage – and might also exonerate parents from blame for a badly behaved child.* Some adolescents and young adults, meanwhile, now wear a neurodiverse diagnosis as a badge of honour.

The epidemic, then, evidently has an element of cultural amplification, but it is also something real. And almost all the reports on rising mental fragility quoted above *explicitly connect it with family insecurity*. The NHS Mental Health of Children and Young People survey states that 'children with a mental disorder were more likely

---

* There can also be an economic incentive. The Centre for Social Justice (CSJ) has estimated that a single unemployed parent can increase their income from £20,000 to £33,000 if they and one child have an ADHD diagnosis. CSJ, *Two Nations* (Dec. 2023), 75.

than those without one to have experienced certain types of adversity in their lives, like parental separation.'[19] It also finds that nearly 40% of children in families classified as the 'least healthy functioning' had a mental disorder. A major Department of Health mental health survey in 2022, meanwhile, found that easily the biggest single influence on people's mental health and quality of life was family relationships.[20]

Similarly, the NHS Digital survey of young people aged between 11 and 16 in 2021 found that those with a probable mental disorder were twice as likely to report problems with family functioning.[21] The ONS report of 2019 titled 'Children Whose Families Struggle to Get on Are More Likely to Have Mental Disorders' found that 25% of 11- to 16-year-olds from the least healthy-functioning families suffer a mental disorder compared with 11% from healthy-functioning families, while suffering from a mental disorder was more than twice as likely in lone-parent families then married households (27% compared with 12%).

The most thorough analysis of the link between family breakdown and teenage mental disorders comes from Harry Benson of the Marriage Foundation, who looked at mental health problems among 10,929 14-year-old children whose mothers took part in the Millennium Cohort Study. He found that 20% of 14-year-olds in intact married families and 27% among intact cohabiters had mental problems, while among divorced families 32% had problems compared with 38% among separated cohabiters.[22] He says that what children really want and notice is stability and commitment in their parents' relationship. This is something that is invariably lower in cohabiting relationships.[23]

It is not possible to prove definitively that greater family insecurity is a prime mover in the mental fragility epidemic. Nevertheless, even if less secure family life is not directly contributing to higher levels of mental fragility, it definitely reduces the ability to cope with it. If you are a young woman struck by depression who is married, living close to extended family, and with a strong network of friends you are more likely to be able to cope with it than if you are a single young woman living away from the place you were raised, with only a few work colleagues to help.

Sceptics can point to the fact that the big increase in family loosening began in the 1980s/1990s, while the sharp rise in childhood mental disorders is a more recent phenomenon. Nevertheless, the proportion of children experiencing parental separation by their early teens more than doubled, from 21% to 46%, between the 1980s and early 2000s. And for a minority of those children who experience family breakdown, the discovery that relationships with the primary providers of love and protection are unstable and conditional might have echoes of a previous sense of insecurity when, as infants, their daytime care was delegated to nursery staff. The next section will consider the evidence.

INSECURE ATTACHMENT AND MODERN PARENTING

Despite the achievements of modern science and technology there are still many important areas of life where there is no expert consensus. Diet, beyond a few basics, is one example. Parenting is another. And a subset of parenting that remains a subject of significant controversy is the impact on preschool children of formal childcare outside the home.

My own experience of such care will be sadly familiar to many conflicted parents. When my ex-wife Lucy returned to working three days a week, after six months of maternity leave, it was my job to take our firstborn, Rose, to the nursery a few miles away. I remember having to peel her off my shoulder as she screamed in protest at being left with those kindly strangers. This repeated itself day after day. The screaming did relent somewhat but she never properly settled and so, after her sister Maud arrived, we decided to explore the alternative of a part-time, live-out nanny.

There are now many millions of people walking the earth who were placed in childcare for long periods from as early as a few months old. After initial unhappiness like Rose's, they settled into the new care regime and have grown into happy, secure adults. But there is also a lot of evidence to suggest that this is not the best start for many children, or parents, and that the precautionary principle is being discarded by an insistence that the interests of small children and parents with careers cannot possibly conflict.

But what if they do conflict? One of the foundation stones of modern psychology is attachment theory, developed by John Bowlby and Mary Ainsworth in the 1950s and 1960s. It is based on the idea that proper bonding between an infant and its primary caregiver, usually its mother, is required in the early months and years of life to enable normal social and emotional development.[*]

This starts in the preverbal phase, with the baby's intense interest in facial movements and the mutual mirroring and smile responses between the baby and an attentive caregiver. After a few weeks the baby starts to discriminate between its primary carer and others. But the crucial attachment period is between six months, when the baby first develops stranger anxiety, and two years. In this period, when

---

[*] A taxonomy of attachment types was developed by Mary Ainsworth as a result of her experimental observation of infant distress, when a mother leaves her one-year-old child on their own, or with a stranger, for a few minutes. Originally three, and later four, main types of response were noted: secure attachment, insecure-avoidant, insecure-ambivalent and insecure-disorganised.

the brain is doubling in size, babies begin to use attachment figures as a secure base to explore the world and return to.

Attachment theory has evolved from Bowlby and Ainsworth's day and is constantly being rediscovered. In popular versions it is often reduced to three styles: the securely attached, who are generally open and trusting; the anxiously attached, who long for connection and can be noisy attention-seekers but fear abandonment and thus commitment; and the avoidantly attached, who are the withdrawn and easily bruised who also fear abandonment and keep others at arm's length.[24]

The theory has also had an enormous influence both on mainstream psychiatry and public policy. In the late 1940s and early 1950s hospitalised children with serious illnesses, like TB, endured prolonged separation from parents. A social worker, James Robertson, in collaboration with Bowlby, observed the damaging effect of the emotional deprivation on the youngest children, and thanks to their lobbying hospital policy was changed.

Even more significantly, the UK used to have thousands of children's homes for orphans and children from troubled homes, but in the 1950s there was a major shift from institutionalised care to foster homes. Bowlby's work on attachment theory and the importance of stable relationships for young children came after the initial legislation promoting fostering, but it provided a justification for the shift. His work has had other important effects, ranging from a greater concern for maternal mental health to the turn against sending children away to boarding schools when very young.

Attachment theory has also had many critics, both within psychiatry and in wider society. The feminist critique in the 1970s insisted that Bowlby placed too much emphasis on the mother and maternal deprivation, and that exclusive dependence on the mother alone can be damaging for both mother and child. Many such

59

critics like to quote the African proverb 'It takes a whole village to raise a child.'

There is also what might be called the common sense, or 'Oliver Twist', critique, based on the observation that children have been subject to an extraordinary variety of maternal attachment regimes yet have often grown up secure and well balanced from apparently unpromising starts. For example, in 19th-century Britain upper-class children often had wet nurses and could then be sent away to board at the age of five or six, while many working-class children from large families suffered neglect and violence from an early age. Even many of the Romanian orphans who suffered in miserable institutional nurseries at the end of the Ceaușescu regime became happy adults after adoption, according to some of the research studies that followed their progress.

Bowlby was a man of his times. In the immediate post-war period, there was a tendency to sentimentalise the mother–child relationship after the disruption and deprivation of war. (In 1950 he was commissioned by the World Health Organization to write a report on children orphaned or separated from parents during the war, and this report reinforced his belief in the negative impact of maternal deprivation.) But his theory has evolved. Attachment types are not set in stone. There is now a greater emphasis on so-called neuroplasticity and how behaviour patterns are working models that can be updated by subsequent interactions. Bowlby himself said that he may have overstated the importance of maternal separation. And a small child's attachments should be thought of as a hierarchy with, usually, the mother at the apex, closely followed by the father, grandparents, older siblings, childminders, primary carers in a nursery and so on.

Every child is a unique combination of genetic and environmental influences, and anyone who has had more than one child knows how even children of the same sex raised in broadly the same way in the same family often develop very differently. What might be shrugged off by one child could be damaging to the emotional development in another one. Because the orphan Oliver Twist survived and, in the end, flourished, does not mean that all children who experience cold or uncaring parenting, or all those Romanian orphans, have done so.

Attachment theory, to my untutored eye, seems to be a mixture of good sense and speculation. But more recent work in neuroscience and brain imaging confirms the importance of the mother relationship in the preverbal state. According to the leading scholar in this field, Dr Allan Schore, 'the right brain of the mother becomes the right brain of the child.'[25] The right brain, the main seat of emotion and unconscious processes, develops more rapidly than the left in the first three years of life. Schore sees maternal responsiveness as key to the brain's developing habits and to the infant learning emotional self-regulation. And the more emotionally nourished the child, the better its prefrontal cortex executive brain functions are likely to develop. At birth the baby's brain is only about 25% the size of an adult brain, but by age three it is 80%, with a final growth spurt in adolescence.

Given this, it seems possible that exposing a child to long hours of formal childcare, especially under the age of two, might in some cases be a cause for concern. Extended separation from a primary caregiver can be highly stressful for a baby and leads to the production of abnormal levels of cortisol, which can have negative, long-lasting effects on emotional development.[26]

But the public policy mind is subject to cognitive dissonance on this subject. It accepts the continuing importance of attachment theory in theory but not in practice, where it conflicts with the priority of maximising the employment of mothers. The contradiction is resolved, in Whitehall and elsewhere, by the assumption that formal childcare has been granted a clean bill of health by research into its impact on small children.

The reality, judging by the many academic papers on the subject, is not so accommodating to adult priorities. Child development is an 'elaborate dance',* with a huge number of variables that interact in complex ways, such as the age of the child, the length of exposure to formal care, the quality of that care and the nature of the home that the child is coming from. (Not to mention all the other potential influences on a child's development such as genetics, breastfeeding, maternal mental health, nutrition, air quality and so on.)

Then there is the issue of the outcomes that researchers are trying to measure and how long they persist: cognitive advance is, in principle, relatively straightforward to gauge, but non-cognitive emotional and behavioural development is more elusive.

Finally, this is a highly contentious and politicised field of research in which people on both sides of the debate are driven by motivated reasoning and tempted to find facts that suit them. Moreover, as policymakers in most Western countries are already heavily committed to formal childcare, they are likely to be biased towards research that retrospectively justifies their decisions.

So there is no expert consensus. There are, however, some mainstream assumptions. A comprehensive review of 45 major research papers by Maria Lyons – including four literature reviews and the official research by the US's National Institute for Child Health and Human Development and the UK's Department for Education – reached five main conclusions.[27]

First, the most important factor in preschool children's educational and socio-emotional development is parenting and the home

---

* The phrase of psychologist Noam Shpancer.

environment. Second, the impact of nursery care depends on the quality of the care provided relative to the quality of care provided in the home. Third, findings on the impact of nursery on children's cognitive development are mixed, with mostly positive and some neutral results. Fourth, findings on the impact of nursery on children's socio-emotional development are mixed, with mostly negative, some positive and some neutral results. Fifth, the long-term impact of nursery on children's development remains largely unknown.

Critical Science, an influential website, provided an overview of the literature (drawing on many of the same papers as Lyons) in 2021 that was more prescriptive in its conclusions.[28] For a child exposed to between 15 and 30 hours per week of nursery care, he (or she) concluded the following: under the age of one, nursery care was damaging for almost all children both cognitively and behaviourally. From one to two nursery may improve cognitive skills a little but has negative effects on behaviour. Age two is the best age to start for boosting cognitive skills but children are more likely to act out when they reach school. At age three and above nursery care is broadly positive for most children.

However, formal care of over 30 hours before the age of four, says Critical Science, is not recommended for any child as 'that much time in daycare has about two-thirds the negative effect on behavior of having "a moderately depressed mother".' Cognitive benefits, Critical Science observes, are both more likely to fade and are also easier for parents to replicate at home by, for example, regular reading to children, whereas behavioural problems tend to persist. Non-cognitive skills, like self-control and the ability to concentrate, are also key to acquiring cognitive skills.

Several of the papers reviewed, by both Lyons and Critical Science, point to the fact that the normal pattern of cortisol levels starting high in the morning and declining during the day does not happen for children in nursery care – instead, levels rise continuously during the day as stress rises. And formal care settings do not generally allow for prolonged *physical* intimacy with infants in ways that might relieve the stress.

None of this research is conclusive, and like most social science it is dealing in correlations rather than clear causal links, and the usual experimental requirements of randomisation and control groups are hard to achieve. Few experts are comfortable about long exposure to formal childcare before the age of one but thereafter there tends to be a political divergence, with a conservative expert such as Erica Komisar opposing formal care before the age of three and a more liberal expert like Emily Oster comfortable with anything after eighteen months (which is around the time most formal care starts in Sweden and other Nordic countries).

Some of the papers do also point to beneficial outcomes for some young children, especially if they are over three years old and the pro-grammes are focused on disadvantaged families. The Perry Preschool and Abecedarian projects in the US are targeted schemes that have produced mainly positive outcomes. There is some evidence too of good results from the Ark Start nurseries in deprived parts of South London.

But there is one recent real-time social experiment on the effects of formal childcare that should be better known. A heavily subsidised universal nursery care project was launched by the Canadian province of Quebec in 1996 to encourage more mothers back into jobs. It was widely used, and by the year 2000 the programme was extended to babies a few weeks old. A 2015 paper tracking the outcomes and comparing them with peers in other Canadian provinces found that a disproportionate number of the Quebec children suffered higher aggression and anxiety and hyperactivity in primary school and into their teens.

Criminal activity, mainly among boys, was 20% higher. Full-time nursery care predicted more teacher conflict, worse parent–child relationships and high-risk behaviours.[29] The academic paper laying all of this out has been criticised on methodological grounds, but most follow-up studies have broadly confirmed it.

According to a 2022 survey for the UK Department for Education, around half of children aged four and under had used formal childcare in the previous week, the majority in nurseries but with some using childminders. Only 4% of children under one use nurseries, but that rises to 27% of one-year-olds, 45% of two-year-olds and 64% of three-year-olds. They spend on average 23 hours a week in formal childcare, with these hours rising with age.[30]

Although non-parental childcare in many different forms is as old as the hills, it has usually involved other individuals known to the children – siblings, grandparents, nannies. The mass institutionalisation of nursery care is a recent phenomenon which dates, in the UK, from the last decades of the 20th century. The state only became involved at the end of the 20th century as a regulator, and later as a direct subsidiser of nursery care. It is still an experiment in progress.

When in the UK budget of 2023 the Conservative government announced a big increase in free childcare hours starting with infants as young as nine months old it was strongly supported by the opposition parties – who promised to better it – as well as most of the media. Yet the Lyons paper finds no solid support for any of the four claims that are usually made by the childcare lobbyists applauding that planned extension: that it promotes infants' educational and emotional development, narrows the attainment gap, boosts the economy, and empowers women. The government's own most recent research found limited evidence of cognitive benefit and mainly negative evidence for socio-emotional development,[31] while Lyons found that 12 out of 14 international studies looking at emotional development for those under three years of age found negative effects.

Lyons is a stay-at-home mother and admits to her own personal bias. Still, it is hard to gainsay her conclusion: 'The push to culturally normalise non-maternal childcare rests on the beliefs that childcare can be shifted from the home to the market with no adverse consequences for children, mothers or society; that a mother's attachment to the labour market is more important than her attachment to her children and family; and that paid employment is both empowering and personally rewarding for women whereas homemaking and child-rearing are not. While these beliefs are influential in academic and political circles, evidence suggests that they are not representative of the values and beliefs of the general population.'

Every child is different, and many clearly thrive in formal care. Several friends of mine who have relied heavily on such care for children a few months old are understandably defensive about any claim that they might have been risking the emotional health of their own children and point to their well-balanced, successful sons or daughters as evidence to the contrary. But saving the feelings of parents who have used nurseries from a young age is a bad reason to not investigate the cohort-wide outcomes of the childcare experiment with an open mind.

Family breakdown and premature exposure to formal childcare are not the only potential causes of the mental fragility epidemic. Psychologists have long argued that post-pubescent girls and young women are more sensitive to negative emotion and thus more susceptible to anxiety and depression, something which has clearly been exacerbated by social media.* Carl Newport has also argued convincingly that excessive screen time reduces the opportunity to establish the real human bonds that people need. Meanwhile, much of the most persuasive literature on modern parenting points to a paradoxical combination of under and over attentiveness: some infants are handed over to formal care in the first few months of life prior to establishing secure attachment with a primary caregiver and then, as they grow into a young child and teenager, overprotected from risk.

Jonathan Haidt argues in his book *The Anxious Generation* that we have overprotected children in the real world, where they need a lot of free play, and under-protected them online, where they are not ready for much of what happens to them. A phone-based childhood has replaced a play-based one. The psychiatrist Simon Wessely, quoted earlier, believes that Haidt focuses too much on phones and social media but agrees about parenting: 'If I was a betting man I would say the main issue with the rise of mental disorders is modern parent-ing. I have always been impressed with those studies that show the shrinkage of the distance that parents allow their children to play away from them... which has shown a dramatic decline in a generation.'[32]

The proportion of children of 12 or under who are allowed to walk to school in the UK has fallen sharply, from 86% in 1970 to

---

* See Jonathan Haidt's 'After Babel' Substack (https://www.afterbabel.com/) and Jean Twenge's book *iGen: Why Today's Super-Connected Kids Are Growing Up Less Rebellious, More Tolerant, Less Happy and Completely Unprepared for Adulthood* (Atria Books, 2017). They argue that the arrival of social media platforms, around 2012, on which adolescents are encouraged to curate their own lives for several hours a day, is the prime mover behind the sharp rise in anxiety, depression and self-harm, especially among girls and especially in the Anglosphere and Nordic countries. Critics complain that the negative impact is less dramatic than claimed (and too reliant on self-report surveys), too focused on a single cause, and oblivious to some of the benefits of social media.

25% in 2010.[33] On a non-school day in 1975 boys spent an average 75 minutes playing outside and girls 58 minutes, while the respective figures in 2015 were 19 and 17.*

Coddling can start in the formal childcare setting, where risk-taking is not encouraged. As Mary Harrington writes, 'One crucial difference between how my daughter was able to explore the world as a toddler in daycare, compared with the home setting, was in the risk-aversion unavoidable in childcare settings. I would happily allow her to take physical risks, under my watchful eye, that would be unthinkable for a busy day-care worker with multiple charges, insurance liabilities and a business reputation to preserve... it is striking that bureaucratically managed physical and emotional "safety" has become a key political demand for young adults, around two decades after the rapid spread of nursery-based childcare.'[34] So, not enough cuddling in nurseries, as noted earlier, but too much coddling by parents and nursery staff.

The language of therapy that would have been known only to specialists in the 1970s is now part of everyone's vocabulary. An educational psychologist I know says she often meets teenagers both in the course of her work and around her own North London kitchen table who say they cannot apply for this or join that activity 'because of my anxiety'. And according to American journalist Abigail Shrier, more than 40% of Americans under the age of 25 have both been in therapy and have a mental health diagnosis. She blames the 'therapeutic parenting' of the generation raised in the 1970s and 1980s, at the height of the big wave of family breakdown, who felt in many cases that their own childhoods were full of pain and distress and

---

* The NSPCC insists that children should not be left alone until they are 12 years of age.

wanted something more supportive and nurturing for their own children. The problem, Shrier argues in her book *Bad Therapy*, is that this has cultivated an emotional hypochondria promoting introspection instead of resilience.

Large families are a natural antidote to this kind of overparenting but are now rare. I was lucky enough to grow up with many brothers and sisters and a large garden, and a parenting principle of benign neglect. To anyone who grew up with several siblings, a safe space is laughable. By contrast, a single child in a small flat under constant supervision has every aspect of their environment controlled for their first two decades.

Middle-aged people writing about parenting or family life almost always unfavourably compare today's childhoods with their own experiences from the 1960s and 1970s. No doubt nostalgia plays a role, yet here is a typical reflection from writer Decca Aitkenhead: 'My mother had four children in the early 1970s, but more spare time than I, with just two children, can dream of. She didn't have a job, whereas three quarters of mothers in the UK today do... But, much more important than that, my mother used to give us one bath and one fresh set of clothes a week, and mostly baked potatoes to eat. Bedding was seldom changed, activities seldom supervised; we roamed the local valley alone as soon as we learnt to walk. If I practised my mother's parenting today, the neighbours would call social services.'[35]

Sociologist Killian Mullan's research shows changes in children's time use going back to the 1970s.[36] It tracks the rise of more intensive parenting but shows that it is characterised as much by *not being outside* as by the patient work of instilling the virtues of self-control, conscientiousness, sharing and so on, into truculent young people. Children have been playing less outside the home, doing more homework, spending less time on hobbies and spending a lot more time on screens (for boys that generally means playing video games), than they did 40 years ago.*

According to a report by the Children's Commissioner, the share of parents reading to their children has held stable over the last ten years, at least for those with children aged three to five, but for children aged eight, there was a sharp drop between 2011/12 and 2020/21, perhaps because screens have taken the place of books.[37] Since the turn of the century there has also been an increase in what Mullan calls 'alone together' time – when the kids are in their rooms but the adults are downstairs. His most telling statistic is that during two fifths of the time parents spend with their child, either one or the other is looking at a screen.

There is, rightly, much focus on the excessive exposure of young people to screens and social media at a tender age, and the frequent use of this media by harassed parents as a babysitting device. There is less focus, however, on how screens and phones distract parents themselves from giving children the undivided attention they want and need for healthy development in the early years.

Too stifling, or too free range? Too authoritarian, or too permissive? These are the eternal dilemmas of parenting in search of that authoritative middle way between love and boundaries. We know that a small child needs to feel safe, loved and understood and that a teenager needs space to grow. The increasingly common combination

---

* Boys spend on average 2 hours 50 minutes in front of a screen per day, with girls a few minutes less. The time spent rises with age: 8- to 11-year-olds spend on average 1 hour 30 minutes per day, rising to 3 hours and 55 minutes for 16- to 18-year-olds. The older they get, the more time they spend alone with their screens: 8–11-year-olds spend 20 minutes alone on average per day, compared to 107 minutes for 16- to 18-year-olds.

of formal childcare for infants and over-supervision of housebound teenagers is a suboptimal combination. But what about mothers?

THE MOTHERLOAD

Is raising a child a job for society or for mothers? For the past few hundred years, in a country like the UK, raising a child was self-evidently primarily the mother's job, with help from her kin. But with more focus on the welfare of mothers, the health of the overall population and, in recent decades, the fact that women have wanted and needed to combine motherhood with paid employment, society has stepped in to play a bigger role.

Motherhood, however, is an institution caught in the crossfire of modern life. It can be both too demanding – thanks to an economy that still doesn't properly make space for it – and insufficiently rewarding for many women raised in a secular, individualist culture that no longer properly values it. No wonder the popular literature on motherhood is a litany of complaint.

Here is Justine Roberts, founder of Mumsnet: 'Parenthood is glorious and life-changing, but for many, meeting the needs of young children can feel like the domestic equivalent of painting the Forth Bridge, if the Forth Bridge was covered in mashed peas and refused to put its shoes on. Heading off to a workplace and being paid can affirm mothers' sense of themselves as capable, valued, intelligent adults.'[38]

Roberts also hastens to add in the same piece that 'the minority of women on Mumsnet who don't work outside the home feel quite a lot of angst and even anger at the portrayal of "stay-at-home" mothers as dim-witted and cloistered.' It is, however, professional working mothers who have dominated the public conversation about what women want.

And what they want is complicated. Ambivalence and guilt is built into modern motherhood. Even in the early weeks many mothers report feeling the need for time away from their babies, to reconnect with their old self, and yet also don't want to be separated. And after a few months the issue of returning to work – or not – produces guilt whichever choices are made.

'I felt guilty when I ate a Brie sandwich while pregnant. I felt guilty when I had an epidural for my first baby, and an elective caesarean for my second. I felt guilty when I had my six-week-old baby looked after for six hours a week while I wrote a book. I feel guilty when I sneak off for a quick scroll through Twitter when my children are at home, or peek at the paper while they're trying to tell me something detailed about Lego cards. And most of all, I feel guilty when I lose my temper... Too often the discontent that mothers feel is not directed at society, but at themselves.' So writes Eliane Glaser in *Motherhood*.[39] It is a familiar lament, especially from highly educated women, and often aimed at an indistinct culprit: the media, society, the patriarchy, men, other women, or some combination of all of these.

The conflicted mother is a product of the new choices and freedoms that women now enjoy. For the first time in history the average woman in a high-income country having her first child is likely to have spent ten or fifteen years as a relatively independent agent, with her own career and living space. To be plunged into an elemental physical world of childbirth and breastfeeding has always been a shock, but it must be a greater one for a modern woman: the wrenching loss of autonomy, the disappearance into a wormhole of nappies and feeding times, and the loss of personal status derived from the public world of work, all mingling with exhaustion and anxiety about whether the baby is developing as it should. Most women get baby blues of some kind and are often on the edge of tears in the first few days and weeks even if they have support from the father, parents and health visitors. (Some women get more than the blues: postnatal depression is said to afflict as many as 20% of mothers, and is more likely in those without partners.)

These unavoidable shocks of becoming a mother for the first time are exacerbated by the lack of the 'lying-in' period and the partial loss in recent decades of a broader culture of support during early motherhood, or merely the fact that grandmothers might live far away and can only come to help for a few days. As a recent report on childcare noted, 'High rates of postnatal depression should not be understood purely as a medical matter, but also partly as a product of this profoundly unnatural and unkind expectation placed on new mothers. Low levels of social support before and immediately following childbirth have been directly identified as a risk factor for developing postnatal depression.'[40]

Lying-in, or post-partum confinement, used to be common in the UK and other European countries. The mother would enjoy bed rest, for up to a month after birth, to deal with any post-birth complications and to enable her to build up her strength. The baby and mother would usually be looked after by female relatives, who would pass on their experience and knowledge.

I remember what felt like a long gap between the announcement of the arrival of yet another of my siblings in the 1960s and the return home of my mother. Until the 1970s the NHS used to provide about ten days in hospital after birth with help from experienced nurses, usually mothers themselves, on breastfeeding and the basics of baby care. The baby was often taken to a nursery overnight so a mother could sleep properly. Today, mother and baby are usually home within a few hours.

For the shrinking number of mothers who then stay at home for a few years it is increasingly rare to have a network of other mothers around you, partly because childbirth has simply become rarer and full-time mothers rarer still, but also because our friendships and families tend not to be as local as they used to be. There is, perhaps, a friend or two from NCT (National Childbirth Trust) or other antenatal classes, and there is now the digital world of Mumsnet (and similar platforms for new mothers such as Peanut, Mush, Mumsmeetup, Happity), but many new mothers report being exhausted and lonely in equal measure.

Then for an increasing number of mothers, a few months later comes the return to work: welcomed with relief by some and faced with dread by others who do not want to be separated from their baby. And a Pandora's box of conflicts and anxieties can then open up over whether fathers are stepping up sufficiently, and whether gatekeeping mothers are allowing them to. Moreover, are you now a less good worker *and* a less good mother?

Glaser recommends the work of British paediatrician Donald Winnicott, with his understanding of maternal ambivalence and his belief in the 'good enough' mother as an antidote to hard-to-live-up-to parenting fashions.[41] Winnicott was also keen to stress that much child development happens by itself. In a radio broadcast, quoted by Glaser, he says: 'Some people seem to think of a child as clay in the hands of a potter. They feel responsible for the result... and feel weighed down by this. But think of the baby as a "going concern" and you will then enjoy responding to the baby's development.'*

---

* Similarly, American psychologist Alison Gopnik says that parents should aspire to be gardeners, cultivating conditions for independent growth, rather than carpenters who aspire to construct their children.

In the last few years the concept of the 'mental load', the constant mental effort required to manage a household, usually disproportionately carried by women, has become a social media meme and even crops up in divorce cases, along with the supposed 'weaponised incompetence' of men (when they do things deliberately badly so they won't be asked to do them again). An influential academic paper from 2014 asked 500 couples in middle-class dual-earner households in the US to record what they were thinking about throughout the day and found that 'although men and women in dual-earner families have relatively similar workloads... on paid and unpaid labour combined... employed mothers experience substantially greater burden and emotional stress than employed fathers.'[42]

A successful female entrepreneur I know talks about the 'head bounce' required of mothers who are also in senior professional positions, having to switch from writing a business strategy paper one moment to thinking about a child's swimming lesson the next. There is an element of 'First World problems' about some of these complaints from the group that has done better, relatively speaking, than any other in Western societies in the last couple of decades: middle-class graduate women. Or perhaps it is a matter of 'be careful what you wish for'. The many women who have grasped the opportunity to combine motherhood and career surely understand that it will be more stressful than doing just one or the other. And men have stepped up more than is often recognised in the literature and newspaper columns of complaint (see Chapter 5).

It is also worth noting that this story of conflicted mothers is playing out differently among some ethnic minorities, especially Muslim and South Asian groups, where more traditional gender norms still prevail. Only around half of Pakistani and Bangladeshi women worked outside the home in 2023, though the number is closer to the national average of 72% for Indian women (70%) and Black women (66%).*

We should remember, though, that the reality of nearly three quarters of mothers with preschool children being in work is a *very* recent one. Some of today's work–life balance frictions are transitional and better balances will be found with experience. For example, Glaser talks about her creative professional female peers, some of whom, after their second child, threw themselves into full-time motherhood 'but then had a slow-motion crisis when their children didn't need them as much'[43]. She says they wish someone had told them that baby madness is temporary, that you should keep irons in the fire for when you want to be in the public world again. These things will, surely, be better understood over time.

It is also possible that the role of stay-at-home mother could be reinvented to provide it with sufficient standing to attract even educated women as an alternative to the sometimes illusory rewards of the public world status ladder. The rediscovery of the home-based cottage industry has been much discussed, something made easier by the internet and videoconferencing.

The middle-class stay-at-home mother who is raising several children but is also a magistrate and a school governor and a player in local voluntary organisations was still common in the 1970s but barely exists today. My mother had too many children and perhaps too little confidence to be such a woman, but she had friends, many with university degrees, who seemed to have busy and fulfilled lives playing that role. Being a full-time mother remained a respectable role

---

* Single parenthood is lower than average among most minorities, though it is higher among Black Caribbeans (just over half of all families) and Black Africans (just under half).

for a capable and intelligent woman in the 1970s. 'Then something happened in the 1980s and by the 1990s it was no longer something that a self-respecting, educated woman would admit to,' says Carole Ulanowsky, who wrote a PhD on the changing image of motherhood in those decades.[44] Full-time mothers came to dread the moment at the middle-class dinner party when someone asked them what they did.

Many women in well-paid professional jobs today, whose mothers were full-time housewives, would see such a role as a giant step backwards; but many others, especially if they have good marriages and sufficient income, would welcome such a role as potentially providing more variety and stimulation – with all the benefits of modern connectivity – than a conventional job.

The gain for the GDP economy from women's energy and brains has been a loss not only for the domestic sphere but also for volunteering. A paper by Laura Tiehen on the US story found that if married women's employment had remained at its 1965 rate, their volunteer participation rate would have been almost one third higher in 1993.[45]

Tiehen's evidence came from time diary studies, and the same time use studies in the UK confirm how rushed and harassed people feel today, especially mothers on the second shift. Feeling rushed is higher among professionals than people doing middling or routine jobs and somewhat higher for women. The worst levels are found, as one might expect, among high-status dual-career households with children, where feeling rushed is also often a badge of honour.

Average hours worked by individuals have been gradually falling over recent decades, but because of the increase in women's employment the total hours worked outside the home by the average couple is actually *up* 15% over the past 40 years.

According to many surveys, happiness levels in the US and some other Western countries have been declining for women, and more sharply than for men. Change can be painful, and women's lives have probably changed more than men's in recent decades. Many men are disgruntled too, as we shall see in Chapter 5, but we hear less about their complaints because they tend to be concentrated in the bottom part of society, while some of the most disgruntled women are in the most influential upper professional strata of society.

So, a more stressful environment for young working mothers, a greater reliance on formal childcare for infants, higher levels of family breakdown combined with overprotective parenting, appear, together, to be playing a significant role in the mental fragility epidemic and a more general decline in family well-being. How are people – and how is politics – responding to these mainly unintended costs of the sexual and family revolutions? That is the subject of the next chapter.

4

POLITICS OF THE FAMILY

The unintended consequence of instability in our family lives is a raft of social problems that we are now almost powerless to fix with traditional policy levers… social policy gains are actively reversed by the collapse in our home lives.

Edward Davies, policy adviser

No, I haven't written about the family, it's too fraught a topic.

Anonymous leading social policy commentator

The pandemic reminded many people that they still like, and need, the family. When called upon it turned out to have mutated but not dissolved, contrary to the fears of some conservatives. The haven in a heartless world still embraced us. Grown-up children returned to parents, grandparents were worried about and (so far as possible) looked after. Like millions of other families, one of my siblings created a WhatsApp group to bring the seven of us together, which still exists, and the established WhatsApp group connecting me to my children pinged as never before.

There were plenty of negatives, too: the struggles of parents with young children imprisoned in small flats; the extra load on mothers suddenly expected to homeschool their children while also continuing to work. But when the dust settled most people seemed to feel more grateful for the previously taken-for-granted institution than they expected, with fathers more involved in domestic life and 25% of parents reporting an improvement in relations with children compared with just 5% reporting a deterioration.[1]

Some economists noted an initial post-pandemic 'Great Resignation' thanks to long Covid and longer NHS waiting lists. Others have registered a 'Great Reassessment', with a high number of mothers and fathers wanting more flexible work and a better work–life balance after the extended experience of domestic life.

Commentators such as Eliza Filby have discerned a more general family revival in recent years, citing the virtual disappearance of teen pregnancy, a drop in divorce rates among younger married couples, the increasing use of grandparents in childcare, and a sharp rise in multigenerational households (defined as more than one adult generation living under the same roof) to nearly one third. She even claims that a large minority of Generation Z young people are spending at least some time every week looking after their grandparents.[2] For an ageing society, a revival of family responsibility would be very welcome given pressures on the health and social care systems. 5% of UK households are already said to be equipped with a granny annexe, with another 7% planning to add one.[3] As Filby asks, if you had space for a pram, why not a wheelchair?

But, alas, the main reason for the increase in the multigenerational household is the result of grown-up children, often with student debt, failing to get a foot on the property ladder. The three-generation household of parents and children *and* grandparents remains rare, at just 2.1% of all households in England and Wales (although it is higher among some minorities, especially South Asians).*

A robust politics of the family will still be needed to create a more welcoming framework for long-term family life to counter the trends described in Chapter 3. There is currently no strong current in British politics willing to back such reforms. Indeed, later in this chapter I will show how both major political parties, and the political class more generally, have since the 1990s been drawing a veil over the enormous impact of family insecurity and consistently placing the labour market before the family. The idea of strengthening the domestic realm and returning some aspects of care to the family has been seen as regressive.

CARE EGALITARIANS V CARE BALANCERS

The main political argument about the family revolution is conducted, as I summarised in Chapter 1, between two competing narratives I have labelled *care egalitarians* and *care balancers*. Every individual is different, and many readers will feel they don't fit either of these ideal types, but it is perhaps a useful lens through which to view some of the more intractable value conflicts in this book.

The *care egalitarian* narrative sees a world in which men and women are essentially identical, and any differences in priorities or attitudes are the result of social conditioning. This is a world in which formal childcare from when children are a few months old is a self-evident good not only for the mother released into the labour market

---

* A majority of people like the idea of three-generation households and one-third believe it should be incentivised by the state: see polling in the Legal and General research report, 'Under One Roof', https://www.legalandgeneral.com/insurance/over-50-life-insurance/under-one-roof/.

but for children too, who kick-start their education early, contributing to improved life chances.[4]

This world view sees family structure as largely irrelevant to life chances, and anyone who disagrees as probably hostile to single parents, as implied by the then Shadow Secretary of State for Education, Bridget Phillipson, in a 2023 speech: 'My childhood taught me that what matters about families is not the shape they are, or the size they have, but the love they give.'[5]

In this narrative, almost all gender differences in pay and all departures from equal representation in institutions are the result of direct or indirect discrimination, or at best the 'constrained' preferences – choices heavily guided by social norms – expressed by women. It looks positively on the shift to double full-time breadwinner households but believes we are barely halfway to equality. It is a radically androgynous, public sphere-centric worldview with an individualistic bias that sees men and women as autonomous, transferable units and largely discounts the possibility of somewhat distinct roles within a marriage or partnership as part of a long-term economic contract in which resources are pooled and shared.[6]

It is also significantly at odds with mainstream opinion, especially on male–female differences, family structure and attitudes to childcare outside the home. Yet since the 1990s it has come to dominate not just academia and parts of the media but much government policy, regardless of which party is in power, and the policies and assumptions of public bodies.

Sometimes it is claimed that egalitarians provide a necessary counterweight to a conservative counter-revolution that wants to roll back the changes since the 1960s. But the conservative world view has only narrow support and, at least in the UK, almost no influence at all in our politics: only 9% of British people agree with the statement that 'a man's job is to earn money and a woman's is to look after the home and family' (down from 48% in 1987).* In the US the figure is slightly higher but is also on a sharp downward trajectory.

There is, however, a larger, probably majority, body of opinion, male and female, behind the *care balancer narrative,* which welcomes most of the changes of recent decades but worries about some of the unintended consequences and overshoots, and wants to protect the domestic sphere from market encroachment and better value the care work done there.

Care balancers want to look without prejudgement at the facts about the impact of formal childcare on very young children and family breakdown on all children, as well as the impact on the quality of care for older, disabled and ill people when this is increasingly done by underpaid strangers. They are also aware that women are not a single bloc with shared interests across all issues, and that the concerns of less educated women doing jobs can diverge from those of graduate women with careers, who are often their employers.

Most care balancers want men and women to divide childcare and domestic work more fairly but do not believe it is a form of false consciousness for a woman to put family first and to want to stay at home and raise children, especially before school age, or for both parents to reduce their paid hours to avoid having to place a child in

---

* There is, in fact, a conservative group (one might call them *care traditionalists*) who are quietly living the life of traditional married couples, with a wife at home and husband at work. They are often religious people, Christians, or people from pious ethnic minorities, particularly South Asian Muslims from Pakistan and Bangladesh. The number in this group is likely to grow in the coming years, as those minorities grow, but their political profile will probably remain low as they are, generally, not trying to promote their preferences to anyone else.

formal care. In other words, they want to gradually reform the gender division of labour rather than abolish it.

With many of the equality battles in the *public* realm won, care balancers want to see the work of caring for dependants in the *private* realm valued and supported more, and want more political heft behind helping two-parent families to form and then stay together.

The difference between the two world views echoes the distinction between supporters of equality of outcome, usually on the political left, and the less prescriptive equality of opportunity associated with the right and centre. But the two groups do find some common cause in concerns about violence against women, occupational gender segregation and the undervaluing of public economy care work, though balancers recognise that gender preferences can diverge and are not dogmatic about 50:50 targets.

Another area of common ground between the two world views is a shared impatience at the continuing failure of the modern economy to accommodate the shift from a breadwinner–homemaker model to a double breadwinner model, and a need for more family-friendly work for mothers and fathers, both at the local supermarket and in the multinational boardroom.

Over the past 60 years the UK, like most rich countries, has evolved from a society with a rigid sexual division of labour to one with a more equal and flexible version of it. But to the frustration of many egalitarians, gender norms are shifting but not disappearing. Nowhere is this more evident than in the motherhood pay penalty.

To academic researchers concerned with maximising income both for couples and for the national economy, and who regard men and women as perfectly substitutable, it is wholly irrational for women who earn about the same as or more than their male partners not to return to work as soon as possible after childbirth. As noted, in fact, women who earn as much or more than their partners (now more than 30% of all couples) tend to reduce their hours of work by the same as lower-earning women – about 20% over the decade after childbirth, with similar falls in earnings.[7]

A recent report by the IFS on women and men at work seethes with frustration at this failure by women to behave efficiently (as does almost all the academic work in this area). The paper argues that higher-earning women would have to be 'orders of magnitude' better than their partners at childcare and other domestic work to make it worthwhile to stay at home. Yet 'we do not have any evidence that men and women differ in their productivity at childcare and domestic work,' says the report. And any differences that do exist are likely to be the result of differences in acquired experience. The fact that men and women may, on average, have somewhat different preferences does not fit the economic model.[8]

The Fawcett Society, similarly, in a magnificently blinkered analysis of why British Pakistani and Bangladeshi women do not take up their full quota of free childcare hours, attributes it to 'lack of cultural awareness and inclusivity' on the part of childcare providers. The idea that not everybody in the world shares the care egalitarian assumptions of the Fawcett Society seems impossible to imagine.[9]

SEX DIFFERENCES

Are men and women completely interchangeable? This is obviously an enormous subject, with many dimensions and nuances. One side in the debate, the egalitarians, generally see biological differences as relatively unimportant and the big differences in behaviour as largely the product of social conditioning, reinforced by powerful norms, and therefore reformable.

The balancers, on the other hand, accept that differences are strongly reinforced by culture but argue that our different evolutionary roles have also bequeathed us some important innate differences. Women have babies and men don't. Men are on average bigger and stronger than women. These two differences alone have a powerful influence on average behaviours.

Men and women have been under many of the same, but also many different, selection pressures over the course of history, and their bodies have evolved to do somewhat different things, as Caroline Criado Perez points out in her 2019 book *Invisible Women: Exposing Data Bias in a World Designed for Men*, her critique of a world designed for the male body. Men are typically more aggressive, more risk-taking and have a stronger sex drive than women. Men are a bit more interested in *things* and women in *people*. Sex differences in spatial intelligence are real, though not enormous. All these things should not be controversial, especially when one introduces the important caveat that they are also 'dimorphic' differences, meaning different but overlapping, rather than binary. Think of two overlapping bell curves, side by side.

Although men are on average more aggressive than women in aggregate, some individual women are more aggressive than some individual men. But also bear in mind that relatively modest *average* differences are often associated with much larger differences at the extremes. There are many more very aggressive men, who are disproportionately represented in prison and among domestic abusers, than very aggressive women.

Aggression differences are substantially driven by the hormone testosterone, which men have more of than women, as Harvard biologist Carole Hooven explains in her 2019 book *Testosterone: The Story of the Hormone that Dominates and Divides Us*. It is also well established that levels of testosterone and aggression track each other over a lifetime, with both spiking in young adulthood and then trailing away. She notes, too, that women who transition to being men and who take testosterone as part of their transition report that they have higher sex drives and don't cry as easily.

There are physiological differences everywhere in the body, including in the brain, which generally matures earlier in girls – one reason for the gender gap in education. And it is from these differences that some different behavioural traits arise. For example, two common female traits are higher levels of anxiety and greater agreeableness, and both are thought to stem from the basic one of women's greater physical vulnerability.[10]

The sex trade is another often-cited indicator of a big average difference, with around 99% of buyers of sex with strangers being men. This points to higher levels of socio-sexuality in men, meaning a desire for sexual variety and a greater ease of separating sex from emotional attachment.

In his discussion of sex differences in his book *Of Boys and Men: Why the Modern Male Is Struggling, Why It Matters, and What to Do About It*, Richard Reeves has a useful three-point list of how to think about these differences in an era of sex equality, embracing equality while acknowledging difference where relevant.

First, even if differences are innate (in the sense of arising from a physical difference), they can be magnified or muted by culture. And, indeed, the impact of sex differences on our comfortable, technology-enhanced lives in the 21st century is diminishing: traditional masculine virtues such as physical courage and stoicism are less required in a mainly peaceful, post-industrial society, and women's nurturing qualities count for less if they are not having children and are exercising a much wider range of emotions and aptitudes.

Second, many of the differences are only modest. On spatial intelligence, perhaps the most clearly established sex difference in all cognitive abilities, 70% of men are better than the average woman (meaning that 30% of men are worse than the average woman).

Third, average differences should not colour our view of individuals. Even if women are on average hardwired to be more nurturing than men – as they are – that does not prevent my youngest son from being a caring primary school teacher, and there are some women I know with no interest in children at all.

What does all this mean? Bearing in mind that there are only trivial differences on some of the most important things, like IQ, it is nevertheless the case that masculine traits can be more useful in some contexts and female ones in others.*

It also implies that there are limits to how far sex differences can simply be ignored. Young women should certainly continue to be encouraged into STEM (science, technology, engineering and maths) jobs as there may well be cultural norms that cause under-representation, and also advantages in including women's perspectives in those roles (given that girls do just as well if not better than boys in maths exams). However, that does not necessarily mean that a 50:50 balance is either possible or even desirable. The situation is similar for men moving into female-majority care jobs.

The same principle of openness to women should apply to all jobs requiring a high degree of typical male traits such as aggression and risk-taking. American economist Claudia Goldin says that even though 'there is lots of evidence that women on average take fewer risks and are less pushy' than men, there are more

---

* On IQ there are more men found at the tails of stupidity and genius, with women clustering more around the middle.

women who are now competitive in high-risk financial market-type jobs.[11]

Reasonable people will disagree about when the barriers to equality have been sufficiently removed. In the UK, even when girls get good A-level grades in maths and physics, they are still much less likely than boys to study them at university, while young women are hugely over-represented in the 'caring' sciences: almost two thirds of medical students are now women, almost all veterinary students and about 80% of psychology students.

The so-called gender equality paradox reinforces this point. The paradox states that in societies with more gender equality norms, especially Nordic countries like Sweden, women are more likely to choose caring professions and less likely to be well represented in STEM disciplines. Highly patriarchal countries like Algeria, Tunisia and Turkey have a higher percentage of female STEM graduates (around 40%) than the Nordic countries (25% or less).

A famous paper by Gijsbert Stoet and David Geary found that looking at test scores across 67 countries girls performed just as well in science as boys, but in relative performance boys performed better in science overall compared with other subjects whereas girls were even stronger in their other subjects. Stoet and Geary argue that countries that empower women also empower them to pick whatever career they will enjoy most and perform best in.[12]

The Stoet/Geary paper and, indeed, the idea that low STEM representation is an expression of women's true preferences, has not gone unchallenged. Critics argue that gender norms remain strong even in egalitarian places like Sweden and that bright young women in poorer countries are more motivated to maximise income on behalf of families and hence choose higher-paying STEM careers.

But in Sweden there is sharp gender segregation not only in

STEM versus care professions but also in the private sector, which is heavily male, versus the public sector, which is 75% female. The story is similar in other Nordic countries. By 2035 only 6 out of 35 Swedish professions are expected to be gender balanced. Swedish politics, at most levels, has an almost equal representation of men and women, but in leadership positions in the private sector women are much rarer. The US has a much higher share of female senior managers (43%) than the Nordic countries (31%).

Claudia Goldin, who is also one of the leading researchers of persistent labour market disadvantage for women, reckons that only about 20% of the continuing pay gap is down to discrimination, with most of it based on women's choices, reflecting the fact that they often choose jobs and careers that are better suited to combining with motherhood (part-time or easier to travel to) or offer more intrinsic satisfaction but lower pay.[13]

In any case, this evidence supports a less dogmatic care balancer approach to the gender division of labour. What matters is not whether different choices are driven by innate differences or sociali-sation but the democratic honouring of people's actual expressed pref-erences. No choices are completely free from social norms, but choices are not delegitimised simply because they are always constrained in some way. The alternative is a kind of Leninist assumption that care egalitarian policymakers know your true interests better than you do.

And there is a tension in the justifications for aiming for equal representation. Is it because men and women are the same, or is it because they are different? Is it that sex differences are irrelevant for almost all human functions so equal representation should be the natural state of affairs in a world without discrimination? Or, on the contrary, is it that women have a distinctively different perspective that is needed from the boardroom to the battlefield?

Both of these equality claims can be true in different contexts. But in other contexts neither of them are convincing and a gender divide still makes some sense. No one is campaigning for a gender balance among refuse collectors or prisoners. Likewise, there is no distinctively female approach to quantity surveying or nuclear engineering.

Gender roles, based on sex differences, have evidently become more elastic in recent decades, but they still exist. Most people experience them as positive things, as welcome parts of their identity. Some people at the most atypical end of their sex's common characteristics are more likely to feel them as oppressive, most notoriously in the case of those who wish to transition. But this reinforces the case for flexibility in the way that gender roles are perceived, not for pretending they don't (or shouldn't) exist.

Sociologist Catherine Hakim's three types of women (work-centred, home-centred and adaptive), discussed in Chapter 2, have different priorities, and probably different views of how to be a woman, but they have all benefited from greater opportunities and the shift in the balance of power and authority.

Patriarchy in the technical anthropological sense, meaning male control over women's fertility and sexual behaviour, has not existed in a country like the UK for many generations. And in the more everyday sense of men having more power than women in the public sphere, we are probably in a transitional phase out of patriarchy. Finnish demographer Anna Rotkirch describes this transition: 'Traditional patriarchal societies are characterized by early and universal marriage, early and high fertility, and deference of the younger generations to the older generations and of women to men... More liberal and indi-vidualised societies have later and lower rates of marriage, later and lower fertility, more equality between both the generations and the two sexes, and much greater leeway for individual sexual behaviours and gender identities. These changes in power relations... shape the lives of many contemporary couples.'[14]

Is it appropriate to talk about a shifting balance of power between men and women? Maybe a tangled dance of love and conflict, dependence and autonomy, is closer to the perplexing reality. Conservative feminist writer Louise Perry argues that because women (on average) are weaker and temperamentally more agreeable than men, there will always be a need for a women's movement to protect their interests. After all, the most brutal form of power of men over women is evident in the murder and rape statistics. But Perry also says that even before the big increase in female presence in the public realm in recent decades women have always wielded a kind of parallel power in the domestic realm. As one guest on her podcast put it: 'Was your grandmother really powerless?'[15]

As a young reporter on the *York Evening Press* in the early 1980s, one of my favourite jobs was interviewing older couples for the golden wedding anniversary page. These couples had married in the early 1930s, a few years after women had achieved political equality, and it was fascinating hearing their stories of courtship in the Depression years and then, often, wartime separation when children were young. They lived in an era of very different public gender norms and more constrained opportunities for ordinary women, but in most cases it was the woman who spoke for the couple and more often than not seemed the dominant (and certainly the most articulate) figure in the household. That may have been partly because the men, by then in their mid 70s, were often the physically weaker of the two. But abstract questions of gender power, while not irrelevant, seemed too crude to apply to such couples; they invariably agreed, in response to my stock question, that the secret of a long marriage was 'give and take on both sides'.

Power or authority or agency in the private realm is rarely taken into account in discussions of gender power, maybe partly because it is harder to quantify than, say, the number of women in Parliament or FTSE 100 boardrooms. But after the initial surge of women into positions of power in the professional world in recent decades, the next wave can, perhaps, weigh up the options more objectively and appreciate that what often accompanies the under-esteeming of the domestic realm is the *over-esteeming* of the workplace. Eliza Filby runs regular focus groups and finds that young women in their 20s, Generation Z, are increasingly shunning the committed career paths that their professional mothers took.[16]

And here is Jess Butcher, a tech entrepreneur in her early 40s, speaking in a TED Talk: 'I am seeing a number of the highest professional flyers in my circle quietly "leaning out" of ambitions of "making partner"... so as not to miss out on those precious early years of family life. Two years ago after losing two close friends to cancer I realised too that if I wasn't careful I was going to miss those early years too, years I will never get back. So I made the decision to step back from the day-to-day-running of my business.'[17]

Why does this seem an unusual, even countercultural thing to do? It is partly because most of the women who have dominated the public conversation about what women want are strongly public realm-orientated. Here is Joeli Brearley, founder of lobby group Pregnant then Screwed: 'Maternity leave can be desperately, achingly lonely... And at times being stuck at home with a tiny baby who needs you 24/7 can feel like staring straight into despair.'[18] She cites a Pregnant then Screwed survey that found 19% of mothers wish they had gone back to work earlier, a proportion roughly coinciding with Catherine Hakim's work-focused women. This is an attitude that many male politicians can easily identify with.

But Louise Perry again: 'Women with more masculine temperaments, women who are less inclined to have children, who are less
agreeable and so on, are more likely to end up in senior positions in
politics. And there is, therefore, a tendency to assume that this is a
universal tendency among women and to make decisions accordingly.
But it isn't.'[19] Many of the most successful female politicians are
childless, as are about half of female academics.[20]

Many women, in the words of podcaster Chris Williamson, have
been encouraged to 'work like your father and have sex like your
brother'.[21] This tendency of the dominant strand of feminism to
promote more traditionally masculine traits like aggression and
competitiveness and to downplay traditionally female traits such as
nurture and agreeableness, has been noted by many feminist writers
including Ruby Warrington and Camille Paglia. It seems to suit some
women, but not all of them.

Perry now also regrets the libertarian turn that feminism took in
the 1970s and sees aspects of the sexual revolution as regressive. The
arrival of the pill in the 1960s, as a safe and secure way for women
to control their own fertility, was, at the time, seen as a great step
forward. It led to a big expansion in female professional employment,
especially in the US, as college-educated women began to push back
their age of marriage (which was still 23 in 1960) and could establish
themselves in careers before marrying and having children.

However, as author Mary Eberstadt has pointed out, the pill also
made pregnancy a woman's responsibility rather than a joint responsibility.[22] The old norms (that generally disapproved of sex separated from
long-term commitment) existed in part to protect women from the
risk asymmetry in sexual intercourse – the fact that it has much bigger
potential consequences for a woman than a man – and locked in men, via
the shotgun wedding, to mutual responsibility if a child was conceived.

After the pill, and as part of the wider idea that obstacles to sexual pleasure belonged to a repressive *ancien régime*, the norms were turned upside down. As women became, potentially, always available for consequence-free sex, so long as the principle of consent was respected, it reduced their bargaining power in the mating game. It also led to an increase in both abortion – around 30% of conceptions in the UK led to an abortion in the UK in 2022[23] – and single parenthood, as men declined to take responsibility for children that, in their view, women could have prevented. Separating sex even more from marriage and family meant that men no longer had to be at least potentially responsible providers to get sex.

This pill-driven shift in norms helped to tilt society further in the direction of the hook-up culture and away from the harder-won happiness of committed relationships, towards Milan Kundera's lightness: living, like one of his unfaithful characters, for fleeting moments of passion and beauty.

When 1970s progressives were battling for women's equality in the workplace and the home, this is not what they had in mind. Those progressives might be happier when surveying the feminisation of the public realm, though some would note with dismay that the traditional areas of female concern in the family, childcare, and care work more generally, remain of low status and visibility.

HOW THE FAMILY BECAME INVISIBLE

Margaret Thatcher is normally regarded as a social conservative who felt uneasy about many changes to modern life. Yet in some respects she was an unheralded second-wave feminist, reflecting and promoting ideas about freedom and autonomy, especially for women, that dominated public policy in the 1980s and 1990s.

This is not how she appeared in 1979 to my feminist activist university friends, who found her intolerable despite the positive example she was obviously setting to women who aspired to rise to the pinnacle of the public realm. But it was her lack of concern for stay-at-home mothers and her willingness to dismantle the only significant support in the tax system for the married family in the UK which ought to win her at least the grudging respect of some freedom feminists.

Individual taxation of husbands and wives was introduced in 1990, with hardly a dissenting voice, as another small step in the movement towards greater autonomy and agency for married women – something my own mother just missed out on. At the same time, it was proposed that a transferable tax allowance between married couples should be introduced to replace the old Married Man's Tax Allowance, which was 50% higher than a single person's allowance in order to reflect the extra costs of raising a family.

This tax allowance to support families, common today in most rich countries in some form, never happened. Instead, a less generous Married Couple's Allowance was introduced, which was gradually reduced in value by successive Tory chancellors and then closed to new entrants by Gordon Brown in 2000. According to Nigel Lawson, the Chancellor who introduced independent taxation and was keen to couple it with a transferable allowance, he was only able to get half the job done because Thatcher 'had a pronounced lack of sympathy for mothers who stayed at home to look after their young children rather than going out to work'.*

---

* Don Draper and Leonard Beighton, 'Independent Taxation – 25 Years On: Does It Meet Today's Needs?', CARE research paper, Sep. 2013. The principle of the transferable allowance, allowing a spouse who is not working at all or only earning a small amount to transfer their allowance for tax-free income to their partner, was

Thatcher certainly didn't enjoy it herself, telling a Conservative publication in 1954 – in words similar to those of Joeli Brearley 70 years later – that being at home with children and doing the house-work made her feel like a drudge: 'I had little to talk about when my husband came home in the evening, and all the time I was looking forward to... getting back to work, and using some of the mental resources which I had been expressly trained to use.'[24]

One reason for Thatcher's lack of sympathy for stay-at-home mothers may stem from her own experience trying to find a safe Conservative seat. In 1957 she was interviewed for the Beckenham seat in South London, by a panel of mainly women, who asked her how she intended to represent the people of Beckenham and look after her young twins at the same time. The same question was not asked of one of her rivals, Philip Goodhart, who months earlier had become the father of a third child – me – and who went on to win the nomination and then the seat.

Thatcher's ambivalence is emblematic of Conservative family politics from the 1980s to the present. The party has long claimed the mantle of 'the party of the family', yet back in the 1980s and 1990s it presided over a huge shift in attitudes and family structure. Many Conservatives may have felt uncomfortable about what was happening, but the liberalising drift was too powerful to resist. There were occasional attempts to push back: Peter Lilley's famous attack on single mothers in his 1993 party conference speech, or John Major's 'back to basics' campaign for traditional family values. But the first came across as spiteful and the second disappeared

---

finally accepted in 2014, but it only allows for the transfer of 10% of an unused tax allowance, with a maximum of £250 a year, and only applies to married couples who are not higher-rate taxpayers.

under a tide of revelations about the promiscuous lives of Tory politicians.

More recently, David Cameron in 2014 talked about a 'family test', meaning that all policy would have to be judged against its impact on the family: 'Nothing matters more than the family. It's at the centre of my life and the heart of my politics.'[25] Rishi Sunak has said similar things.* Conservatives might also point to the Family Hubs and Troubled Families and Reducing Parental Conflict programmes as evidence of their support for family life. But valuable though these interventions might be for some of the most disadvantaged families, they do not ease the pressure on the average family in the way that proper recognition of family in the tax system (or making it easier for one parent to stay at home when children are of preschool age) would.

The lack of political support for such policies bears out the observation that, starting in the 1980s, the right won the economic argument but progressives won the social and cultural arguments. Labour from the 1970s onwards came to see itself as the party of feminist reform, celebrating the non-traditional family and the welfare support that enabled it, and promoting paid work, including for single parents, as liberating for women and beneficial for economic growth.

Accordingly, when New Labour came to power in 1997 one of its first acts was to cut lone-parent benefits, even for stay-at-home single mothers with young children, and introduce tax credits for working families with children, declaring work to be the best form of welfare. It also promoted state intervention in childcare, especially for families regarded as vulnerable, and launched the Sure Start early

---

* In rolling out the Family Hubs scheme in January 2023, Sunak said: 'Strong, supportive families make for more stable communities and happier individuals.' He often talks about the importance of his own family to him.

intervention strategy, with some promising initial results. It did not, however, become an advocate for the stable two-parent family. A few years later, Jon Cruddas, the socially conservative Labour MP who was charged with drafting the party's 2015 manifesto, found that almost all his references to the importance of family life in that manifesto were subsequently struck out.

These days the party is no longer shy about using the word *family* – Bridget Phillipson, when Shadow Secretary of State for Education, talked about Labour being 'the party of the family' in several speeches – and a priority in government will be reversing some of the benefit cuts to families with children. But, as noted earlier, Phillipson was not inviting a debate about the importance of the two-parent family, nor proposing a family-friendly tax system or subsidies for stay-at-home parents.

From the mid 1990s hardly anybody in the UK with significant authority in mainstream politics – with the possible exception of the *Daily Mail* – was left advocating for the importance of the domestic realm or marriage, or even the two-parent family, and, after Major's 'back to basics' failure, politicians of all stripes became allergic to making judgements about how others should lead their lives.

MPs themselves have higher rates of sexual infidelity and divorce than the population as a whole, and saying one thing and doing another is less acceptable today than it was 50 years ago.* Indeed, welcoming the loosening of the family and changes to sexual morality has become a kind of proof, over recent decades, of how comfortable a politician feels about modern Britain. Support for the traditional

---

* About 40% of the 2010 intake of MPs have experienced marital break-up, according to Dominic Lawson: 'Our Contempt for MPs is Lazy and Dangerous,' *Sunday Times* (2 Jun. 2024).

family thus became a largely untouchable subject, and stigma has been itself stigmatised. The UK is now top of the European ladder for family breakdown and bottom for family support in the tax system.

The Conservatives' semi-reluctant acquiescence in the face of these enormous changes also reflects the perennial conflict within centre-right parties of wanting the individual freedoms that make possible a dynamic capitalist economy but recoiling from the permanent, disruptive change that such an economy often generates for established ways of life.

One such change from the 1980s onwards has been the loss of decently paid jobs for men without much formal education. That, combined with greater state support and loss of stigma about single motherhood, has been a key factor, especially in the UK and US, in the decline of marriage and partnership at the bottom of the income spectrum. According to one UK analysis, the fall in male employment in deindustrialising areas explained between 40% and 60% of the 1.16 million increase in lone-parent families between 1971 and 2001.[26] The reluctantly autonomous single mother gives rise to the absent single father. This is what sociologist William Julius Wilson has called the 'marriageable men hypothesis', which states that men don't offer enough relative to what the state provides single mothers, meaning that partnership in itself is not seen as worthwhile.

In the US, economist Melissa Kearney nails down some of the evidence for this in her 2023 book *The Two-Parent Privilege*.[27] She quotes a study of US manufacturing towns after China entered the World Trade Organization in 2000 showing that the trade-induced reduction in men's earnings led to lower levels of marriage and more unmarried mothers living in poverty. She also looks at the impact of recent *increases* in well-paid manual jobs in the US in places benefiting from the fracking boom and finds that there was an increase in the number of babies born but not an increase in marriage, unlike in similar booms in coalfield towns 40 years ago, where both babies and marriage rates spiked. This suggests, as in parts of the UK, that the marriage habit has been broken in the bottom part of the income spectrum. Kearney argues that better economic conditions over a longish period of time for non-college-educated men are a necessary condition of restoring the economic promise of marriage as a long-term economic contract to share and pool resources in the project of raising children.

Similarly, it is the loss of marriage and stable family life, rather than poverty or inequality, that Angus Deaton and Anne Case see as one of the main causes of the increase in suicide and drug and alcohol deaths in the US, especially for white men aged between 45 and 55 – the so-called 'deaths of despair'.[28] Men who have no family to return to in the evening, no sense of contribution or achievement at work, and no religion to protect them from despair, are its victims. The rate of male suicide is lower in the UK, a bit less than 4,000 a year, and the rate has risen only slightly in recent years, but it is also concentrated on lower-income white men aged 40–50 and is twice as high for those who are single or separated compared with those in a partnership.

The knowledge economy has increased the pay and status gap between the better educated and the rest, creating more stable economic conditions for family life among the highly educated. Yet even here family life has been affected by the increased mobility of the professional class – thanks to leaving home for university and then congregating in a few metropolitan centres – who often live apart from siblings and older parents. This means that such professionals are often unable to help care for parents when they become infirm and lose out on grandparent care for their children when their parents are still vigorous.[*]

A modern liberal society can, and should, accommodate many different forms of family life. But that is not a reason to avoid addressing the problems created by the new arrangements. The Tory party, especially in the Cameron/Osborne era, preferred to largely bypass the subject for fear of appearing either hypocritical or out of touch, like members of Theresa May's 'nasty party'. Cameron himself is a partial exception to this rule. He did, as mentioned, talk about marriage as prime minister – and not only in the context of legislating for same-sex marriage in 2014, which he claimed as one of his proudest achievements.

Frank Young, a family policy veteran in various London think tanks, believes that Cameron struck an unofficial bargain with the social conservatives in the Tory party: they would mute their objections to same-sex marriage in return for a more vigorous promotion of the institution of marriage. 'But,' Young told me, 'even with marriage liberalised in this way, the second half of the bargain was never delivered… If the Conservative Party ever wants to get back to a position where it is not just managing the state, but reducing the need for ever more state, then it will need to get serious about family and marriage.'[†]

There has been, as noted, little serious thinking in either main political party, or the political class as a whole, about the overshoots and unintended consequences of the family and sexual revolutions. The subject has been on the fringes of politics, often the concern

---

* See the 2023 Richard Bean play *To Have and to Hold* on this theme.

† Some Conservative political insiders argue that Brexit killed Cameron's promise. There was a package of marriage promotion ready to be launched after the Brexit referendum had been successfully negotiated. Marriage promotion is said to be one of the few issues that divided David Cameron and George Osborne. .

of committed Christians and other religious believers. But public opinion, as we will see, is strikingly ambivalent about many of the consequences and would surely welcome thoughtful initiatives to mitigate the most damaging consequences of change.

Those initiatives might include a serious attempt to reduce the disincentives to long-term family formation in the benefit and tax system. Currently, if a woman has a child and does not work but the father does, there is a double *dis*incentive to marriage or officially living together: the woman would lose her benefits and the man would receive only minimal tax benefits from partnership.

'A welfare system that was originally designed to compensate men for loss of earnings is being slowly and messily redesigned to compensate women for the loss of men,' David Willetts pointed out in his book *The Pinch*.[29] And it often compensates in a manner that perpetuates single parenthood. The system discourages single parents from creating stable new couple relationships, or being honest about them, by withdrawing almost all benefits as soon as a new household is formed with an earner. If it was possible to retain some or all of single-parent benefits for a period after forming a new relationship it would make it less financially risky.

Meanwhile, the result of not recognising households and family responsibilities properly in the tax system means that a single childless adult earning £50,000 a year, will have disposable income placing them in the top 10% of the income distribution. If the same adult has children and a non-working partner, they would be in the bottom half of this distribution.

Or take a single-earner family with one person on £60,000 a year and a double-earner family with both parents on £30,000. Take-home pay for the first household is £43,843 while for the second it is £5,000 more. The first household also loses some child benefit payments, worth around £2,000 a year to the second household if they have two children under 20. The second household might also qualify for certain aspects of Universal Credit.

A real family policy is not cost-free, but nor is a status quo that means ever-growing demands on the state. Using public policy and the persuasive power of politics to encourage marriage and greater relationship stability, especially among people in the bottom part of the income spectrum, is good economics, good politics and popular. The private realm of the conventional family is anachronistically associated in the minds of many liberal-minded people with traditional gender roles and the subordination of women, yet in the real world society has moved on.

Actual family policy in recent decades has been largely reduced to sex equality-meets-employment promotion: some improvements to parental leave; more flexibility at work for parents; encouraging more mothers, including single mothers, back to work; more subsidised childcare. These are all reasonable goals, but they are scarcely a *family* policy. Whitehall has no interest, and the civil service elite is disproportionately made up of public realm-focused youngish people without family responsibilities. The Treasury is primarily interested in getting women back into the labour market, while the Department for Education is focused on reducing educational gaps. Both see more institutional childcare as promoting their main purpose. Nobody speaks for the child or the stay-at-home parent.

Second-wave feminism's perspective on women and work still often presents itself as a challenge to the status quo, but it has long been the *establishment* ideology in the UK. Caroline Dinenage, then a Conservative minister, could have been speaking for any of the UK's major political parties, addressing a UN conference in 2016, when she said that she agreed with Gloria Steinem, the leading American feminist of the 1970s, about her priority being to maximise women's opportunities in the workplace. George Osborne, when Chancellor, said that stay-at-home mothers were making a lifestyle choice and should not expect any help from the state. He also introduced the two-child cap on most welfare benefits.

Both main parties – notwithstanding Cameron and Sunak's words – have embraced something close to a care egalitarian world view, and this minority perspective is set to become even more influential under the Labour government. Meanwhile, the married couple family is rendered semi-invisible in both public policy and the wider public culture. You can see this in everyday dealings with the state or local authorities or the NHS. The language of 'husband and wife', even 'father and mother', has largely disappeared from official documents. Instead we have organised society increasingly not around the family but around a single person living alone, devoid of wider duties and relationships – a British version of Sweden's statist individualism.*

As Danny Kruger MP has written: 'Treating people as solitary units is simpler for the state… Policy aimed at individuals can pretend a neutrality about lifestyles and culture, and avoid the need to make invidious choices about how to help people in complicated personal circumstances; the state simply arrives after the event, like the cleaner or the ambulance, without judgement on the situation it is there to clear up.'[30]

Women's autonomy is not in principle in conflict with the persistent majority ideals of mutual dependence, and pooling of resources, that a good couple relationship is built on. Mutual dependence

---

* Even the British royal family have succumbed. In many tweets from the Princess of Wales about the 2023 'Together at Christmas' carol service celebrating people who work with small children, the word *mother* never appeared.

informed the old Married Man's Tax Allowance and the pooling of tax relief on mortgages (also phased out by Gordon Brown). Yet joint bank accounts are now so rare that I hesitated the other day when asked to pay into one – despite the fact that experiments have shown that joint accounts are associated with higher relationship security and satisfaction. We now seem to acknowledge partnership *interdependence* only retrospectively, in divorce settlements.*

Much of the charity sector, too, looks past the conventional family. A big children's charity would regularly approach a friend of mine who worked for a Westminster think tank to offer significant sums for research, but would exclude anything that focused on marriage and the importance of family stability. The NSPCC used to publish data showing that child abuse was much less likely in married homes with two biological parents, but it stopped publishing the figure some years ago so as not to stigmatise stepfamilies.[31]

This bias blinds our politicians to the pervasive role of family instability in so many areas of life. Think tanker and former policy adviser Edward Davies points out that many of Britain's biggest social problems have family instability in the background and that 'social policy gains are now actively reversed by the collapse in our home lives.'[32]

Poverty: single parents are hugely over-represented in the poverty statistics and among food bank users, while two-parent families are largely absent from long-term poverty numbers. Poverty can also, of course, be a *cause* of family instability. But affluent children from broken homes with neglectful parenting are likely to underperform

---

* One exception to this is the advertising industry, which still presents an idealised 'happy families' picture, especially in the case of building societies and holiday companies.

social class expectations, while poorer children from stable homes with good parenting are likely to outperform those expectations.

Housing and homelessness: according to the ONS, the main reason for experiencing housing problems was a breakdown in relationships, cited in almost half of all cases.

Education and young people: educational attainment is hugely dependent on people's home and neighbourhood background. Those who experience family breakdown before the age of 18 are twice as likely to be homeless, get in trouble with the police, underachieve educationally and experience family breakdown themselves.[33]

Criminal justice: there are massively disproportionate levels of family breakdown among persistent offenders and gang members. However, according to the recent Farmer review, regular prison visits by family members can significantly reduce reoffending.

Racial inequality: attainment rates by race in education and the economy are strongly correlated with stable family structures, with Indian and Chinese families with high marriage rates at one end of the success spectrum and Black Caribbean and white working-class people with high rates of single parenthood and family instability at the other. The latter are the two groups most likely to be excluded from school.

Inequality and social mobility: all of the above contribute significantly to higher inequality, usually correlated with lower social mobility. The high proportion of single-parent families in both the UK and the US is one reason for those countries having such relatively high inequality (along with outsized financial sectors).

While I was writing this chapter I read a *New Statesman* interview with Sam Freedman, the influential blogger and policy commentator, who in the course of 2023 produced a series of excoriating analyses of policy failure in housing, welfare benefits, criminal justice, housing and more. He described some of the problems, as he sees it, in his specialist area of education: 'Schools have a huge problem with mental health. They've got huge problems with children in poverty. We have too many kids who just aren't able to learn because there are so many other issues going on. If you're a teacher in a school in a lower-income area, you're doing a lot of... knocking on people's doors to try and get absent kids to come into school. You're dealing with huge numbers of social services cases, and abuse cases. And that is so draining if what you wanted to do is be a teacher.'[34]

Yet it did not occur to Freedman or his interviewer that many of the problems he describes, in education and elsewhere, are significantly connected to the weakening of family structures. A few days after reading the *New Statesman* article I met another prominent commentator I know, who had recently written a big piece on social policy that, similarly, failed to mention the word family. I asked him why not, and he replied that it was a 'fraught' topic and 'I haven't done any work on it', which is code for 'I don't like the conclusions I might uncover.'

It was reported in early 2024 that the Treasury was looking for measures to reduce the surging disability bill, and in particular the recent rise in mental illness as a reason for being off work. There was speculation about tax breaks for companies to hire therapists, but no interest in the role of family and family breakdown in the new melancholia. Or consider this from highly respected health analyst Jennifer Dixon, head of the Health Foundation: 'The dials on mental health, chronic pain, obesity and inequality are all going in the wrong direction, leaving the NHS to pick up the pieces. But the root causes lie in wider issues such as poverty, stress, poor-quality work, housing and education.'[35] Nothing on how a weaker family contributes to loneliness, declining mental health or less support for the old.

Post-2010 austerity has certainly not helped – cutting local authority funding by 40% from 2009 to 2019 – but the reflex of the political class, especially the centre-left section of it, is to blame everything on inadequate spending and look right through the family issues in front of our noses. Gordon Brown's appeal in May 2024 to combat the increase in child poverty is another case in point. I used to spend a lot of time going to conferences on equality and social mobility; I don't recall the issue of family structure ever being raised as a factor.

Yet for much of the social policy establishment family is, in a sense, always the background problem. The ability of successful families to pass on their success is the main transmission belt of inequality in the UK. This means that much of the work of the social state is trying to compensate for conditions originally established by the family, and it tends to do that not by helping less successful families look like more successful ones but by trying to take on the compensation itself.

There are other reasons why family is a fraught topic. Modern liberal politics in its long campaign against real prejudice, particularly in relation to homosexuality, has often used the idea of the sanctity of the private realm to defend minorities. The idea that what happens behind closed doors is a sacred realm of freedom from the state has thus come to leave us disarmed in the face of family failure. But this is to confuse arguments about privacy with what are the proper boundaries of politics or of what society has a legitimate interest in.

It remains a fraught topic, too, because of an unhealthy political reflex identified by Sebastian Milbank as 'whataboutmeism'.[36] The reflex is triggered when praising something (such as the married, two-parent family) is seen as an attack on everything else, (such as single-parent families or cohabiters). Sometimes praise for something does imply an attack on something else; back in the 1990s, when a Conservative politician made a speech about the family, it might well have implied hostility to single mothers. Today it rarely does.*

Clearly it is possible to both reject the stigmatisation of single-parent families and welcome the fact that the state supports them economically, while also wanting to use the levers of power to promote two-parent families, knowing that, on average, they produce better outcomes for children, something that a majority of single parents themselves acknowledge.†

This tendency to occlude the family has long infuriated Nobel Prize-winning economist James Heckman. 'Nobody wants to talk about the family, and the family's the whole story,' he told an interviewer. 'And it's the whole story about a lot of social and economic issues.'[37]

The 'Heckman equation' shows how disadvantaged children benefit most from early childhood interventions. But, crucially for Heckman, programmes must involve the parents, and especially mothers. He is concerned about inequality and lack of social mobility, but is frustrated that progressive-minded people refuse to see the central role that family plays in these outcomes. 'What we have come to

---

* Gavin Williamson, the former Conservative education secretary associated with the right wing of the party, gave a rare speech by a senior politician on the family in May 2021, focusing on the importance of fathers, in which he said, 'Let me be clear, I am not saying that all families should be or need to be headed by two parents of the opposite sex. The stock image of Mum and Dad with 2.5 children is now far less relevant as a model.' Nevertheless, one of the people involved in drafting the speech told me that the pro-family sentiments were diluted by political advisers for fear of offending single parents.

† More than half of single parents says it is important for children to grow up with both parents. See 'Why Family Matters', Centre for Social Justice, 2019.

understand is that some of the major growth of inequality is not just to do… with hourly wage rates at the factory; it also has to do with the change in family structure in the larger society: more single-parent families,' he told the interviewer.

Heckman is also an advocate of the importance of 'soft skills' or non-cognitive skills – the importance of self-control, conscientious- ness, concentration and so on – and claims that IQ differences account for only 5–6% of differences in lifetime earnings, far less than the character differences instilled by good parenting.

A similar position on the overwhelming importance of family is taken by John Goldthorpe, an Oxford academic sometimes described as the doyen of social mobility research. In his 2018 book *Social Mobility and Education: Research, Politics and Policy*, written with Erzsébet Bukodi, he argues that home background, and particularly the time that parents dedicate to their children, is far more important than schooling in determining life chances and social mobility.

To want the best for your children is one of the strongest human instincts and, especially since educational qualifications became a central determinant of life chances, affluent parents have invested heavily in their children's cognitive development. Family is necessarily somewhat in tension with equality, something Goldthorpe ruefully acknowledges. 'Would we want to stop parents from reading bedtime stories or engaging in supper table debates? Of course not.'[38]

Education can change lives and sometimes promote upward mobil- ity, but the claims made for it, including by organisations focusing on preschool education, are often exaggerated. Such organisations are right that the early years are often crucial in establishing patterns of both cognitive and character development, and there has recently been official concern about the growing proportion of children not developmentally ready for school aged four or five – over half in some areas. But the reflex is too often to want to place children in formal nursery settings, for as long as possible, rather than help mothers and fathers develop better parenting skills. Most parents would prefer support that leans in to family life, as the opinion data confirms.

REGRETS? WE'VE HAD A FEW

Where does the public stand on these issues? That is simply stated: there has been wide and deep support for more equality between the sexes (see the next chapter for further detail), with little difference in attitude between men and women but much less support for the abolition, rather than reform, of the gender division of labour. The public, in other words, sides heavily with the balancers and against the egalitarians.

Norms can change fast. Consider the fact that as recently as 1987 nearly 50% of people agreed with the statement that a man's job is to earn money and a woman's job is to the look after the home and family. That figure, as already noted, is now less than 10%. There is little nostalgia for the 1950s. But there is a sense of the care and attention deficit casting a shadow over our lives, in many different ways, as the domestic realm has ceded ground to the labour market at every turn.

Not all the regrets are captured in polling data. But I believe there is widespread regret at the dwindling number of stable two-parent, multi-child families, and the consequent rise in insecurity experienced by so many children. There is a sense of loss for the children that couples would have liked but never had. And there is often a sense of guilt about the use of formal care for very young children and the failure to support older relatives who, with more intact families, might have been supported at home but are instead seeing out their lives in care homes. Most of the freedoms that have led to these regrets were happily embraced when taken individually, but the cumulative effect has often produced outcomes that hardly anyone would have chosen. And once policies and payment streams are established, it becomes difficult to reverse them.

The polling we do have suggests that the British public are less inhibited than the political class about expressing support for policies that might strengthen the family. According to polling by the Centre for Social Justice, 83% of adults say stronger families are important in addressing the UK's social problems, 67% of divorced parents agree that family breakdown is a serious problem and more should be done to prevent it (with 63% believing divorce is too easy), and 60% of single parents say it is important for children to grow up with both parents.[39]

On questions about domestic arrangements there has been some movement in an egalitarian direction, but with continuing strong support for a modified gender division of labour. The latest BSA survey, in 2023, found that only 12% of people now agree with the statement 'a job is all right but what most women really want is a home and children', down from around one third in 1989. Similarly, support for the idea that a preschool child is likely to suffer if their mother works has fallen from almost half in 1989 to 21% now. Nearly 40% believe that paid parental leave should be evenly split between mother and father. Most men and women think that with women doing so much more work outside the home men need to take a fairer share of the work inside the home, though 63% of women still think they do more than their fair share.[40]

On the other side of the coin, and maybe reflecting a certain cognitive dissonance at a time of flux in gender norms, only 7%

of the public believe that mothers with children under five should work full-time. And 36% of women still believe that being a stay-at-home parent is as fulfilling as working for pay, down from 45% in 1989.*

For balancing work and care, the most popular arrangement remains the so-called 'modified male breadwinner model', with women working part-time and men full-time when children are young: 33% support this arrangement, while 18% support the more traditional woman at home and man working full-time. Another 18% support both parents working part-time and 9% support both parents working full-time, even though this is now the case in about 35% of households with preschool children.†

The biggest gap between public opinion and public policy, where egalitarian priorities simply ignore majority balancer preferences, concerns what women want in the first few years of motherhood. The UK's Department for Education (DfE) produces an authoritative childcare survey each year which, among other things, asks mothers of young children what their ideal arrangements would be. This section of the survey, which is not publicised by the DfE, shows that large majorities of working mothers with preschool children would work fewer hours if they could afford it, and a substantial minority would give up work altogether.[41]

There are just under 3 million mothers with children aged four and under, of whom 72% are employed, split almost evenly between

---

* The same question was asked in the UK edition of the World Values Survey 2023, and it found a much larger proportion of women (65%) either agreeing or agreeing strongly.

† There is a big 'don't know' response (22%) to this question about the best way to manage work and care, perhaps reflecting some of that dissonance and/or how difficult it is to generalise about the increasingly complex reality of care.

part-time and full-time, with 20% classified as full-time mothers. Of the 2 million mothers who are employed or seeking work, around one third say they would prefer to stay at home if they could afford it and fully two thirds (almost 1.5 million) would work fewer hours if they could afford it. It is, however, also true that around half of those not working (about 450,000) would work if there was non-family childcare that was good quality, convenient, affordable and reliable (an unlikely eventuality at present in the UK). And of the 2 million working mothers, about 28% (600,000) would work *more* hours if such childcare existed.

But the great weight of preference for mothers of preschool children is for *more time at home*, and less time doing paid work, when children are of preschool age, especially if children are under two. If you take the number of current stay-at-home mothers who do not want paid work and add the one third of working mothers who would *like* to be full-time mothers, it comes to 1.2 million. That means nearly 40% of mothers of children aged four and under would prefer to be stay-at-home mothers, at least for those early years, almost double the number who are.

Recent opinion surveys by think tanks Onward and the Centre for Social Justice confirm the DFE's findings, with between 50% and 60% of parents agreeing that if finance was not an issue they would prefer it if they or their partner could be at home when children are of preschool age.

Employment rates rise for mothers of children aged between five and eleven, but there are still large minorities wanting to work less or not at all. And these numbers are not shifting much over time, with 60% of mothers with children under fourteen saying consistently between 2009 and 2022 that they would prefer to work fewer hours. Such sentiments are also reflected in BSA survey data, which finds that when asked who should provide childcare for preschool children nearly half say family members, with government agencies backed by 20% and private childcare providers backed by 14%.

The preschool years are a time of maximum developmental sensitivity for infants plus maximum stress and relationship pressure for new parents. The new patterns of life are a source of joy but also conflict between the sexes. You are suddenly responsible for a small human, needing 24-hour care, and you can no longer do all those enjoyable things that, perhaps, defined your pre-baby self and relationships. You are both having to make big sacrifices for another person, something that may be new to you. And you are both exhausted from lack of sleep. It is little surprise that so many relationships trip up in these early years of parenthood. Divorce peaks after between three and seven years of marriage, and where children are involved splits are most likely to happen in the first three years, particularly among unmarried couples.

This is the time when many parents, and their children, are in particular need of support from the surrounding society, whether via the welfare/health system or family or friends (or preferably all), to alleviate those often unexpected pressures. Too many find that the support is not there and find the loneliness, anxiety and, in Margaret Thatcher's word, 'drudge' work of motherhood unbearable, especially after the brief window of full-time support from the father.

Many women do want to return to work as soon as reasonably possible, to rediscover something of their pre-baby selves and the validation of their public realm existence, especially those with good careers, and they often do so with some combination of family/grandparent support and formal childcare. But there is a large minority, maybe a majority, of mothers who, whether struggling or not, do not want to be separated from their baby yet feel they *have* to return to work to help pay the bills. This important section of opinion is barely visible in the public debate about childcare. The shadow of the driven workaholic, Margaret Thatcher, hangs over our society in more ways than is normally appreciated.

In this context, the government's expansion of free hours of formal childcare to infants from nine months to three years, doubling spending to more than £9 billion, seems unbalanced. The Office for Budget Responsibility estimates that by 2027 this will mean an extra 60,000 part-time jobs and allow 1.5 million mothers to work longer hours (creating the equivalent of another 60,000 part-time jobs). But if £4 billion creates just 60,000 full-time jobs, that means a subsidy of around £67,000 per job, far more than the state will recoup in tax or than the jobs will pay.[42] The country needs decent, affordable childcare but why not use some of that £4 billion to subsidise a parent to stay at home to look after their own preschool child, as many would prefer to do, and promote growth in other, more cost-effective ways? No better example can be found of the disproportionate influence of care egalitarians in UK politics.

To conclude: there is a minority of younger and more highly educated people who increasingly embrace egalitarian assumptions, but there remains a large majority who stubbornly reject the complete transferability of men and women. Many of those balancers want more support for working mothers *and* stay-at-home mothers, want more support for family stability overall and would be attracted to a politics of moderate pro-natalism. They are the missing majority in the country's family debate, and they worry about the care and attention deficit in modern society. This includes women *and* men. A bigger role for fathers in combating the care and attention deficit is an important part of the story, and the next chapter turns to look at the role of men more generally in the post-1960s upheavals to the private sphere.

5

WHAT ABOUT MEN?

Masculinity is not a problem to be solved... but a way of being that needs to be channeled in directions that are both good for men themselves and for society.

Aaron Renn, Institute for Family Studies

The response of many women to the baby bust, motherhood workplace penalties and the recruitment crisis in traditionally female care jobs is simple: men must step up.

Public conversation focuses mainly on how they are failing to do so. On the one hand the care egalitarians, in academia and politics, complain about the persistence of aggregate pay inequalities and how little has changed in the home.[1] On the other hand, there is the minority of disaffected men who have lost the civilising responsibilities of the old husband/father provider role and have nothing obvious to replace it. A small section of these men have attached themselves to the anti-woman 'manosphere' on the internet.

There is, however, a much more positive story to tell about both the attitudes and the behaviour of most men in the past few decades. Well-educated, more affluent men, who have not suffered any significant disadvantage either from greater sex equality or from the shift to a knowledge/education based economy *are*, by and large, 'stepping up' and turning a motherhood penalty into more of a shared parenthood penalty.

FATHERHOOD AND THE DOMESTICATION OF MEN

It was only in the 1970s that it started to become the norm for fathers to attend the birth of their children. Today, international sports stars miss important fixtures to be there. When it came to my turn in the 1990s no constructive role had yet been found for us in the birthing room, beyond being a sympathetic onlooker (and occasional punch-bag) for our wives' and partners' suffering.

Nevertheless, in the years since 1964 fathers have, on average, become far less aloof, no longer simply the breadwinner and chief disciplinarian of tradition. In many cases fathers have not had much choice, thanks to the rise of dual-earner households. But each generation has become both more involved in the domestic sphere, and more competent too.

To borrow from sport again, the pugnacious England fast bowler Stuart Broad had this to say on his retirement aged 37: 'I wanted to commit more time to family, your kids aren't young forever. I just wanted to make sure I was there for them and experience as much of that upbringing as I possibly could.'[2] It is impossible to imagine the great England fast bowler Fred Trueman having said anything remotely similar when he retired in the 1960s.

Both my sons are better cooks than I am, and are likely to be more involved in the care of their children than I was (though the domestication gap between me and them is likely to be smaller than that between me and my father). My youngest son works in the overwhelmingly female primary school sector. This trend in my own family is largely supported by broader attitude surveys and by time use studies.

It is also now widely accepted that fatherhood is as instinctive as motherhood, and that men are as biologically primed to parent as women. According to anthropologist Anna Machin, all new fathers experience a permanent drop in testosterone after the birth, as much as one third in some cases. Machin also argues that fathers potentially build bonds with children that are as strong as maternal ones, but somewhat distinct. They are particularly involved with smoothing the child's entry into the world beyond the family. 'Regardless of culture, fathers are seen to push developmental boundaries and introduce their children to risk and challenge, which helps build their mental and physical resilience,' says Machin.[3] Rough-and-tumble play with infants is one way that takes place, and later in childhood it might include an introduction to physically challenging sport.

Within the home, the overall share of all unpaid work done by men has risen to around 40% in most high-income countries (with some regional variations), slightly higher in Nordic countries and lower in Southern Europe. None of the many surveys and time use studies cited in the next few paragraphs are wholly reliable, but they broadly align with observation: men are doing more domestic work, but not as much – and sometimes not nearly as much – as women.

The main category, *all domestic work*, in the time use studies includes core domestic work (cooking, cleaning and clothes care), childcare, and other domestic work like gardening, DIY and shopping. In the UK, from 1974 to 2015, men's share of all domestic work has increased from 27% to just under 40%, with minutes per day rising from 98 to 151 for men and falling from 271 to 245 for women (thanks to greater use of labour-saving appliances as well as the big increase in paid work). There is a particularly big increase in the least rewarding 'core' domestic work for men (albeit from a low base of 22 minutes in 1974 to 48 minutes in 2015), while the times for women fell sharply from 189 to 109.[4]

There is some evidence that the rebalancing of domestic and paid work stalled in the early 21st century. But the average amount of time that fathers spent on childcare almost doubled during the pandemic, from an overall average of 48 minutes in 2015 to 90 minutes during lockdown and then falling back to 56 minutes in 2022. The ratio of female-to-male time spent on childcare fell from 2.6 to 1.6 in the same period, and for housework more generally it fell from 1.8 to 1.4.

But time spent by women and men in *all* work, both domestic and paid, is almost the same, with women working only a few minutes more. Men in the UK still work on average more paid hours, with a roughly 65:35 paid/unpaid balance, while women now average 50:50.

It should also be noted when calculating the average time shares of both sexes that there remains a significant minority of stay-at-home parents, mainly mothers, albeit one which has declined from about 40% to 20% across the 1974–2015 period. Both the stay-at-home mothers and part-time working mothers will expect to do a higher proportion of domestic work than a working mother in a two-parent household, which boosts the female domestic contribution. It remains true, however, that in households where both the man and woman work full-time the woman still does more core housework.

In the 1990s, as we saw in earlier chapters, the idea of intensive parenting and more involved fathering spread widely, especially among the highly educated. Highly educated men and women tend to share domestic work more equally. And the highly educated of both sexes do more childcare than the less educated (though there is some evidence, according to the IFS Deaton Review, that the childcare gap with the less well educated is narrowing). The percentage of involved fathers, according to the admittedly undemanding official definition of fathers who complete at least one meaningful childcare task a day (changing a nappy, reading a story) rose from 31% to 64% between 1974 and 2015. But the *average* time involved fathers spent with children was already 74 minutes a day in the 1980s, rising to 109 minutes by 2015.

The most recent ONS time use survey comparing employed men and women in the UK suggests that the gap on all domestic work seems to be narrowing further. Men on average are spending 5 hours a day on paid work and just over 2 hours on domestic work of all kinds, while women are spending 4 hours 18 minutes on paid work and 2 hours 37 minutes on domestic work, a gap of just over 20% on domestic work.[5] The latest research on US fathers also shows a narrowing of the gap, with average hours on childcare rising by one hour a week in the past twenty years, to around eight hours, at a time when mothers' childcare time remains stable. The biggest increase has ben among college-educated, married fathers.[6]

Most of the academic research finds improved family well-being when fathers are more involved with childcare, especially for mothers.[7] A mother's postnatal depression is often linked to a poor relationship with the baby's father, while men who take solo charge of an infant for at least some of the time before the age of one are far less likely to split up with the mother. Involved fathers report higher general life satisfaction. But, as noted earlier, mothers also tend to report higher levels of anxiety when fathers take on more than 40% of childcare, suggesting a degree of ambivalence about fully relinquishing the dominant role.

There was some excitement among family and fatherhood charities when in 2022 the number of stay-at-home fathers in the UK briefly touched 141,000 – one in nine, or 15% of all stay-at-home parents, up from one in fourteen in 2019. More recently it has fallen back to around 120,000. There has also been a rise in the number of single-parent households led by fathers in the UK: now up to 16%. A recent University College London survey of 9,000 families in England found that the father was the primary carer in 7% of all families, compared to almost none twenty years ago. These numbers will grow in the coming years and men are likely to make up at least 20% of stay-at-home parents by the mid 2030s. According to one Pew survey, that 20% has almost been reached in the US.[8]

A new model of fatherhood does seem to be gradually emerging, though it is concentrated among the highly educated, often with both parents in full-time professional jobs. Elsewhere the story is more mixed. For a start a large number of UK fathers, as in the US, are simply absent. In about half of the homes where a mother is raising a child on her own, the father is seldom to be seen. There are an estimated 1 million children growing up without a full-time father in the UK, up from 800,000 in 2010, and many more growing up with a man who is not their biological father.

State support for fatherhood is minimal. There is a well-publicised complaint about the inadequacy of maternity leave and the cost of childcare, but in international comparison the UK does even worse in its support for paternity leave. Since 2003 fathers have been given two weeks' statutory paternity leave, now paid at £184 a week (less than a quarter of median male earnings). In the year to March 2021, only 25% of new fathers (170,000) took the full leave, and only 7% of employers offer to top up state provision. Shared parental leave was introduced in 2015, allowing the mother to transfer some of her 52 weeks of maternity leave (39 weeks paid) to the father, but it is a complex process and for most couples where the man is still the higher earner it is unaffordable. Only about 3% of eligible fathers used it last year.

It is harder for men to be more than a mother's helper and to shoulder more of the burden if they are at work. Care egalitarians complain that as women work less and earn less after motherhood, often for decades, the opposite happens with men. A more equal sharing of parental leave and a greater awareness of the importance of men in child development on the part of the state and employers should, over time, shave down those differences.

Something that is often forgotten, however, is that in a happy, equal partnership there is usually an *agreed* division of labour, with the partner or husband deliberately working more hours and doing more overtime in the early days of fatherhood to increase the family income at a time when the mother's income has usually declined and costs have suddenly risen. Harder work outside the home when building a family is also a form of care.

The egalitarian one-sided focus on the power imbalance between men and women, the reluctance to imagine an uncoerced division of labour in which men and women share paid and unpaid work *unevenly*, and the economistic assumption of the income-maximising, androgynous individual, leaves too much out of the picture. By insisting on a blank-slate view of male–female differences, it also overlooks the fact that there is generally much more of a physical-emotional tension for women returning to work after their child is born than there is for men. I recall feeling excited to return home after work when my first two children were babies – I was mainly working from home for the youngest two – but don't recall thinking about them much when I was at work. This is much less likely to be the case with mothers.

Of course, there are always exceptions. One friend, recalling her feelings as a young mother, puts it like this: 'It's probably true that women in general feel more of a wrench, but if a woman has good childcare and a job she loves, returning to it when a child is still small is not necessarily hard. You hear stories about babies left in cars because Daddy forgot to drop the child at the creche on the way to work, but I sometimes forgot to wave goodbye to my three-year-old in the kindergarten window because my thoughts were with my job the minute I left the building.'

There is some pushback by women's organisations in several European countries against the equal splitting of parental leave, with the not unreasonable argument that women need the leave more than men. In a survey of this resistance in *The Atlantic* magazine, Stephanie Murray concludes: 'The experience of the newborn period, like pregnancy or childbirth itself, is inherently unequal. Leaving the choice of how to split up parental leave to each couple and allowing for the possibility of a gender-unequal division, is in their view the equitable approach. If taking more time out of formal employment to care for children puts mothers at an economic disadvantage, then the government should focus on overhauling the economic system to better value and support caregiving.'[9] And even in egalitarian Sweden it has recently been discovered that women are taking a larger percentage of parental leave than had previously been thought, an average of 12 months to men's 3 months.[10]

Meanwhile, men are stepping up, even on their Zimmer frames. There are more than 5 million people in the UK, mainly in late middle age, who are providing informal unpaid care, usually to an elderly family member, and around 40% of these are men. Around the age of 75, the gender balance evens out, and then at the age of 80 the majority of those providing care become men.

THE WEAKER SEX?

The story of female advance is well known, but it is worth a brief reminder of the scale and speed of the change. Girls outperform boys at school, and increasingly in maths and science too. Many more young women now go to university – in the UK in 2021, this was 45% of 18-year-old women and just 32% of their male peers (and only 14% of white working-class boys, the most under-represented group). In 2021, for the first time, there were more female PhD students than male.[11]

The gender pay gap for people under 40 in full-time jobs is now low to non-existent, and for those over 40 – where it essentially becomes a motherhood pay gap – it has been in steady decline too. There are 9% fewer women in the highest-paying occupations, and more women in the lowest-paying jobs (25% women to 15% of men), such as care and cleaning work. There are, however, now marginally more women than men in the professional world of doctors, lawyers, teachers and managers, though fewer at the highest levels. It is there that the lingering pay gap is to be found, especially in the highest-paying fields like finance and consultancy: this is partly a function of the fact that the top of the ladder reflects the norms of an earlier, less equal era.

Some women do evidently still experience some pay and promotion penalties that are not purely the result of their choices to become a mother. But Claudia Goldin, the Nobel Prize-winning economist cited earlier, points to how the long-hour/high-commitment jobs – so-called 'greedy jobs', often dominated by men – can be made more mother-friendly (see Chapter 9 for more on this).

There has been a rapid increase in women's representation on company boards and in public appointments: in 2011 just 9.5% of those on the top FTSE 350 company boards were women, it is now 40% in two thirds of such companies. Of serving public appointees, 47% are women. Meanwhile, about half of academics in the UK are women; they make up about 30% of professors, and this figure is rising.

Areas of gender segregation persist, with most care-related jobs being 80%-plus female and STEM jobs in the UK being less than one third female, with engineering only 9% female and IT 21%. But around one third of STEM students in the UK are now women, promoted by the widely adopted Athena Swan gender equality charter in higher education. In the US more than half of STEM degrees are now awarded to women, and social psychologist Cory Clark says that job recruitment experiments in the US show that in recent years there has been a bias towards recruiting women into male stereotypical jobs, including STEM jobs.[12] Indeed, an academic paper looking at more than 360,000 job applications between the 1970s and today found that discrimination against women in male-majority sectors went into reverse in 2009, while there has been no change in discrimination against men in majority female jobs.[13]

These sectoral gender gaps are likely to narrow further over time, though the gender equality paradox – that women in the most gender-equal societies like Sweden have a *stronger* preference for jobs in health, care and welfare – is unlikely to disappear completely, much to the frustration of egalitarians. Moreover, the traffic so far is almost entirely one-way, with little movement of men into care jobs.

The overall effect of these changes is surprisingly under-analysed. The lower tolerance of risk and stronger impulse to avoid harm, which can be partly attributable to a greater female weight in politics and society, may have played a role in the dramatic lockdown response to the pandemic. It may also be there in the expanding web of regulation and safety nets in business – the human resources department has become overwhelmingly female.[14]

These rapid changes to the gender division of labour in the home, the workplace and the wider culture have obviously had a big impact on men too. The mundane truth seems to be that most men in rich, liberal societies have accepted gender equality. But many remain unsure of where that leaves them, and a minority feel an acute loss of status and opportunity.

Employment status is usually more strongly connected to well-being in men than women. The well-documented loss of skilled, well-paid jobs for low-educated men has thus hit some men hard in the past few decades. Some women have been moving up the escalator as some men have been moving down. A celebrated paper on the politics of social status found that over the past 25 years the subjective social status reported by women rose relative to men in 9 out of 12 rich countries.[15]

In the US, women are the main earner in 41% of households, and almost all the income gains in US households since the 1970s have been thanks to the rise in women's earnings. Some of these households are single mothers, but 30% of wives out-earn their husbands. In the UK it is also estimated that women in 30% of households earn as much or more than their partners.*

Perhaps unsurprisingly, research suggests that women have adapted to this shift more happily than men, especially where it arises from male unemployment. There is some evidence of higher divorce rates, more domestic abuse and less satisfactory sexual relations in households where women out-earn men. An optimistic reading would

---

* According to a US Census Bureau study, women tend to lie about earning more than their partners.

see this as part of the inevitable stresses and strains on the path to new, more egalitarian gender norms, though a pessimist might instead see a new rift between the interests of women and (at least some) men.

ADAPTATION AND RESENTMENT

Most men under 60 have grown up in a world in which sex equality is the prevailing assumption in most areas of life. Among some older men there persists an old-fashioned male chauvinist paternalism, which is very different to the self-consciously anti-woman rhetoric of the so-called manosphere (the section of the internet that focuses on men's rights and, in many cases, resentments).

My own unscientific estimate, perhaps betraying the influence of my current location in affluent, liberal North London, is that in relation to sex equality men can be divided into four broad groups: the enthusiastic (10%), the comfortable (65%), the uncomfortable (15%) and the hostile (5%).

My estimates are broadly supported by a recent BSA survey that found that just 9.8% of people (11.8% of men and 7.6% of women) agreed that 'attempts to give equal opportunities to women have gone too far or much too far', compared with 40% who think they are about right and 49% who think they have not gone far enough. More than three times more men thought that equality had not gone *nearly* far enough (11.7%) compared with 3.3% who thought it had gone *much* too far.[16]

A recent Understanding Society survey found only around 8% of British men under 60 agreeing that a husband should earn and a wife should stay at home (albeit with 25% saying 'don't know'). The same question when asked in 1991 had around 25% support.[17]

The 2022 World Values Survey for Great Britain on sexist attitudes, including attitudes to women in politics and business, had huge anti-sexist majorities, with men only slightly behind women. Both men and women – at 79% and 74% respectively – disagreed that it was a problem when a woman earns more than her husband.[18]

There is some evidence, though, that there is a plateauing of more equality-friendly attitudes among younger men. A recent Kings College London survey found that only 14% of the public think it's harder to be a man than a woman, but 25% of men under 60 believed this, compared with just 17% of men over 60. And 16% of young men aged 16–29 say feminism has done more harm than good, compared to 9% of women of the same age.[19]

What about those with less benign attitudes? The so-called manosphere on the internet is usually described as having four main groupings: Men's Rights Activists (MRAs), Men Going Their Own Way (MGTOW), Pick-Up Artists (PUAs), and Involuntary Celibates (Incels). There is a lot of misogynistic resentment and anger in all these zones.

It is hard to know how many men they engage. One study that did try to quantify the manosphere found around 130,000 regular users of the main forums but a larger group of 835,000 who took part in subreddit chat forums.[20] The numbers will, however, be inflated by the same person using multiple sites and seems reassuringly small considering there are more than 200 million adult males in the English-speaking world who are potential participants. A small number of people can still make a lot of noise.

And how significant is the phenomenon of Andrew Tate, the internet celebrity and former kick-boxer who promotes ultra-masculine and misogynist views and has 8.2 million followers on Twitter? It is hard to tell how much the noise around Tate reflects a real movement of disaffected, women-resenting young men or if it is just a tribute to his showmanship and his ability to tap into the desire to offend of teenage boys, particularly working-class boys. Recent polling finds that around 15% of young men approve of Tate. That might seem a shockingly high number, but some of those approvers will be attracted less to Tate's message of how to dominate and use women and more to his focus on physical fitness and business acumen – and most of them will, in any case, grow out of their current desire to transgress. And how does it compare with a few decades ago? Is the anti-equality movement now bigger than it was, say, 30 years ago, when it was men muttering in the corner of a pub, or is it in fact smaller but made to seem bigger by the megaphone of social media?

A lot of intellectual energy in the women's studies section of academia has gone into trying to locate a significant backlash against equality or in linking sexist attitudes to Brexit or the election of Donald Trump. As one would expect, there is some connection between chauvinistic attitudes towards equality and anti-immigration and hyper-nationalist sentiment, but a broader backlash against equality is notable by its absence.* It may be that so much focus on a relatively small number of real misogynists deflects attention from a larger group who are not anti-women but do feel they have lost out thanks to recent changes.

Over the last 50 years the female graduate has been one of the main winners, and the male skilled manual worker one of the main losers, from the rise of the knowledge economy. It would be a surprise if there was not a rump of men who felt hard done by and saw the shifting status between men and women in general, though not

---

* A Google Scholar search reveals 114,000 recent references to misogyny compared with just 2,300 references to misandry (hatred of men).

necessarily individual women, as part of their problem. The patriarchy does not benefit all men, they might reasonably conclude.

A minority of that minority are attracted to the noisy belligerence of the manosphere, but a larger group are left rudderless and demotivated. They see all around them a positive story for women who are largely maintaining their role in the domestic sphere while adding a new dimension in the workplace and the public realm. For some men, by contrast, it has felt like a *subtraction*, with a higher share of childcare failing to compensate for the loss of a meaningful traditional role as provider/protector.

Just like women, men have always had their own unique disadvantages: reduced life expectancy; much more likely to die at work or at war; many times more likely to be both victims and perpetrators of violence (globally, 90% of homicides are committed by men and 70% of victims are men); 95%-plus of prison populations; much higher suicide rates and school and college drop-out rates; much more likely to be excluded from school and have SEN; longer commutes; criminal justice biases in paternity, divorce and sentencing; domestic abuse against men that runs at half of female levels but is barely recognised; higher death rates from diseases ranging from cancer to Covid.[*]

In the US men are three times more likely than women to die before age 25, three times more likely to become addicted to drugs or alcohol, and 19 times more likely to end up in jail.[21] A recent analysis of mortality figures found the *average* age of death for the least fortunate US men to be 36, thanks to guns and opioids, compared to over 50 in Europe.[22]

---

* It is sometimes argued that male disadvantage stems from maleness itself whereas female disadvantage is mainly imposed by men.

Until 1990 the so-called 'deaths of despair' from drug/alcohol abuse in the US ran at below European levels, but they have doubled in recent decades, far outstripping Europe. Non-college-educated men in the US have suffered stagnant wages for several decades, have a suicide rate four times higher than women, and are much less likely to be married or attached to a church. Black American men still suffer many disadvantages, and high levels of incarceration, but non-college-educated white men have gone from having mortality rates 30% below Black American men in 1999 to 30% higher now.

In the UK these kinds of death are at a much lower level than in the US, but they are ticking up. Suicide rates are more than three times higher for men than women but have remained relatively stable since the early 2000s after a steady fall since the 1980s. But drug deaths of close to 5,000 in 2022, about 70% male, were nearly twice the number of 2012, and the 10,000 alcohol-related deaths in 2022, about two thirds male, were a 32% increase on 2019.[*]

It is sometimes argued that while womanhood is a biological given, manhood has to be *achieved*. As psychologist Roy Baumeister puts it, 'In many societies any girl who grows up automatically becomes a woman... Meanwhile, a boy does not automatically become a man, and instead is often required to prove himself by passing a stringent test or producing more than he consumes.'[23] This means, says Baumeister, that a man's well-being is more dependent on his standing in the status hierarchy.[†]

---

[*] There were 8.4 drug overdose deaths per 100,000 in England and Wales in 2022 (though twice that in Scotland), compared with 34 per 100,000 in the US.

[†] This may downplay the pressures on young women in the internet age over looks and body image.

Some of those things are, perhaps, permanent aspects of the male condition, but there are also aspects of modern life that are more troubling for boys and young men: boys struggle initially at school because their prefrontal cortex develops later, and they react less well to family breakdown and absent fathers, while men have far fewer friends than women and are less likely to ask for help if in trouble. Meanwhile, the post-industrial economy has favoured those with communication and 'soft skills', who are more likely to be women. Average pay in the UK adjusted for inflation has fallen 7% for men since 2008 and risen 2.2% for women, according to the ONS.[24]

Gender inequalities can cut both ways. That is the simple idea that mainstream men's rights organisations in the UK such as the Men and Boys Coalition (including organisations such as Lads Need Dads) want to promote. They campaign on issues of men's health, or men's access to their children after divorce/separation, or promoting positive ideas of fatherhood, and complain about the lack of political recognition for such issues.

Yet thanks to a lingering assumption of patriarchal domination there is a general tendency for mainstream opinion to take a woman's perspective. Martin Seager and John Barry, in their work on gamma bias, show how in news reporting there is a tendency when women do something positive, like saving someone from drowning, for the reporting to be sexed, and when women do something negative it is desexed, and vice versa for men.[25]

The pandemic was another recent example. There was a great deal of focus on claims about women suffering increased domestic abuse (though this has not been substantiated in the UK), women being more likely to lose their jobs, and a general reversal of equality (actually, the domestic labour balance improved). There was very little focus on the fact that the death rate among working-age men was twice as high as that among working-age women.

Some of the trends noted above are also having an impact on partnering and marriage. Increasingly, lower-earning, lower-status men are struggling to find partners, and there are fewer women who feel the need to settle for a suboptimal partner, even if they want children. Demographer Michaela Kreyenfeld found that 36% of German men without university degrees born in the early 1970s were childless in their early 40s, compared with 28% of men with degrees.[26] According to economist Marianne Bertrand, one third of the decline in marriage in the US in the past 30 years is down to the expectations of both men and women that the man will be the higher earner.[27] In the UK, 25% of men over 42 are childless, compared with less than 20% of women. A study from 2019 found that a man at the top of the earnings distribution has a more than 90% chance of obtaining a committed romantic partner.[28] In contrast, for men at the bottom, less than 40% find one.

British social scientist Geoff Dench argued that we ignore at our peril the old-fashioned idea that family obligations bring out the best in men. His own research, a couple of decades ago, found that low-qualified men with a wife or girlfriend, and therefore an incentive to take a job, however menial, had an 83% chance of being in work, while those without had just a 50% chance.[29]

Redundant men without responsibilities are a potential danger to themselves and to wider society. How many are there? In the US, the number of men in the 25–54 age group who are not working or looking for work – in other words *not* officially unemployed – is now 7 million, according to demographer Nick Eberstadt.[30] If you add in the 3 million-plus men in that age group who are unemployed it comes to around 10 million men, nearly 20% of men in prime working age.

That is a lot of men, most of whom appear not to be contributing to society or a family. And there are currently about 9.5 million job vacancies in the US.

In the UK the corresponding figure of those not working or unemployed is not as high as the US but is still around 2 million men, with the economic inactivity rate among men aged 16–64 at around 13% (excluding students), while about 15% of men aged 18–24 are NEETs (not in employment, education or training). There are 1 million men in the UK who are unmarried and without children and who are not in work or looking for work, with about 70% of these on some kind of sickness benefit. Some of these men will have experienced the pathologisation of ordinary boisterous, male behaviour in an increasingly female world. Indiscriminate use of the phrase 'toxic masculinity' after the election of Donald Trump and the #MeToo movement to refer to any male behaviour the user disapproves of, however trivial, can add to their sense of alienation.

Think of a young British boy growing up in a single-mother family – as around 20% of boys are – with a grandmother playing a big role in his life. He may see his father from time to time, but he is likely to be a shadowy and unpopular figure among the women who care for him. He may go to a nursery which is entirely staffed by young women and then on to a primary school where his form teacher and head are both women. If he has behavioural problems his therapist/counsellor and educational psychologist are all likely to be women, and if his problems get worse his social worker and probation officer will probably be women too.

A significant minority of young men are growing up with very few men around them, let alone positive male role models. Ed Clancy, one of Britain's greatest cyclists, was a lucky exception. He was born in a tough part of South Yorkshire, and experienced his parents' messy divorce as a young boy. He started going off the rails and could easily have ended up in prison. Then his mother met his stepfather, Kevin, who became his first mentor. 'Kevin showed me that I could have the good things in life by working for them,' Clancy told an interviewer. Even with that support, he said, it took him years more to come to terms with the emotional impact of paternal abandonment.[31]

Fathers are especially important for adolescents, girls as well as boys. In the US, fatherlessness is a better predictor than race of whether a man will spend time in prison. And the single most important determiner of the life chances of young black men in America is whether they grow up in a neighbourhood with a high proportion of two-parent families.[32]

American author Mary Eberstadt has pointed out how one of the dominant themes of rap music lyrics is anger towards absent fathers.[33] The buffoonish dad is a persistent figure in popular culture – Daddy in Peppa Pig, Homer Simpson, Peter Griffin. More generally it is men at the extremes of the masculinity spectrum who dominate the screen. In the popular British TV police drama *Happy Valley*, all the main adult male characters were either psychopaths or pushovers. Out in the real world the masculine culture that used to dominate the workplace (direct, piss-taking, crude, mock-aggressive) has been diluted and challenged to reflect the higher number of women, and the places after work where it used to flourish – above all the pub – are also in decline.

The rise of 'safetyism' and the reduction in risk and physical challenge from modern life seems to encourage some men to overcompensate by taking ridiculous risks, with extreme sports for rich men and inner-city gang wars for poor ones. And violent conflict-based video games offer a simulacrum of heroism for young men with no outlet in the real world for testing themselves.

One important outlet that does exist is sport, which may be one reason why it seems to take up a growing space in public culture. A friend who lives in south Manchester tells me that in the last ten years there has been a big expansion of local football teams for boys and girls. And there is a small army of mainly male coaches who are teaching life skills as well as football and often act as surrogate fathers to boys with few men in their lives.

Young people are now experiencing a longer adolescence, as Jean Twenge has established.* And, thanks in part to social media, they are socialising with each other less and having less sex. Dating and romance have become more complicated for both young women and young men in the post #MeToo world. When there are advertisements on the London Underground warning men that 'intrusive staring… is sexual harassment and is not tolerated,' it is not surprising that many men say they are afraid to make a first move for fear of seeming predatory. Meanwhile, the majority of women still expect the man to make that first move.

Easy access to online pornography, and especially violent porn, is often cited as another corrosive influence on relationships and well-being. But according to an academic literature review of the subject, the evidence on its malign effects is limited.[34] There seems to be no evidence to support the connection between violent porn and violence against women, though that is partly because of the difficulty of establishing credible experimental conditions. Men with a disposition towards such violence are likely to seek out such porn,

---

* Twenge's book *Generations* shows how in the US people are spending longer in all four stages of life: dependent child, young adult, mature adult and dependent old age (*Generations: The Real Differences Between Gen Z, Millennials, Gen X, Boomers, and Silents – and What They Mean for the Future* (Atria Books, 2023)).

though actual sexual offenders report little exposure to porn.* There is some evidence that excessive use of porn by men can lead to reliance on it to maintain sexual arousal. The common complaint that young women are pressurised into violent or extreme sex acts that their partners have seen online is hard to quantify, as is the counterclaim from men that the desire to push the boundaries often comes from women.†

Men have to negotiate this new world of relationships and of shifting norms around masculinity, and what is expected of men, with one distinct disadvantage compared to women – they are much less good at friendship. The Understanding Society survey mentioned earlier in this chapter found in 2021 that nearly 10% of British men said they had no close friends at all.

As with much of the 'left-behind men' story, the situation in the US appears to be worse. A reliable survey in the US by the American Enterprise Institute found that in 1990 55% of men said they had six close friends, while today it is only 27%. And 15% of respondents say they have no close friends.[35] The US TV show *Saturday Night Live* did a comedy sketch about women taking their friendless boyfriends to a 'Man Park' where they were encouraged, like dogs, to get to know other men. It was one of the most-watched sketches in the show's history.

---

* So far, France has gone further than other countries in trying to enforce age controls on access to online pornography, with a digital certification system requiring people to show they are over 18 before visiting a site. It is not clear how effective the reform has been, though: Neil Thurman, 'Lessons from France on the Regulation of Internet Pornography' [blog], City University of London (5 Apr. 2022).

† The website Everyone's Invited, set up by Soma Sara in 2020, has attracted tens of thousands of accounts of sexual assault from young women and a lot of publicity, partly because it focuses on elite schools and universities.

I do not need to be taken to such a Man Park, but I have always invested less in friendship than the women I know well. One reason sometimes given for lower levels of friendship for men is that male relationships tend to be more overtly competitive than female friendships. My brother-in-law, George, suffered a serious injury in a riding accident ten years ago and ever since has been a quadriplegic, paralysed from the neck down and needing 24-hour care. He says that in his new condition he has found friendship much easier, including with his own sons, because the element of competition has been largely removed.

The traditional masculine virtues of self-reliance and stoicism also discourage men from investing time in friendship beyond functional and activity-based companionship. If these virtues, along with the old provider/protector role itself, have become redundant or even destructive, then men, it is sometimes asserted, need to swap them for traits more adapted to a feminised world. But traits shaped over millennia cannot be simply traded in for a new set, and most men are happy being men. Masculinity, as Aaron Renn put it at the start of this chapter, is not a problem to be solved, but for some men it needs to be channelled in better directions. It has always had a degree of adaptability and, after all, takes significantly different forms in different times and places.*

Educated, middle-class men, as we saw above, are duly adapting to a more equal world by taking responsibility for more domestic labour and becoming competent in traditionally female domains. Many lower-status men are finding it harder to adapt and some are taking

---

* Young women who move from a poor country dominated by a traditional gender culture to a liberal, Western country usually report with relief the ability to walk down the street without being harassed.

refuge in a politicisation of masculinity, especially in America, where nearly half of men say that traditional masculinity is under threat.[36] Trumpism is sometimes explicitly linked to a defence of traditional masculinity. Senator Josh Hawley, a leading Trump supporter, has said that 'the attack on men has been the tip of the spear of the Left's broader attack on America itself.'

Another concerning trend is the recent divergence in political attitudes between young women and men. Women used to lean more to the right than men, but that has reversed in recent decades. In the US the switch came in 1980. At the 2016 US presidential election there was a 13-point gender gap, with 52% of men and 39% of women voting for Trump, though the gap narrowed at the 2020 election, partly thanks to a 5-point increase in the female vote for Trump.

In the UK 2019 general election 47% of men voted Conservative and 29% Labour, while 42% of women voted Conservative and 37% Labour. In the 2022 Swedish election more men voted for the hard-right Sweden Democrats (26%) than for the traditional ruling party and pro-feminist Social Democrats (25.9%). Meanwhile, only 14.9% of women voted for the Sweden Democrats, compared with 34.9% who backed the Social Democrats. The main divide is among younger Gen Z women and men. In the US, women aged 18–30 are now 30 percentage points more liberal than their male counterparts, the same as in Germany, with the UK at 25 points. This has happened in the past few years and is mainly about women moving left and men staying still.

The general factors that tend to push people to the left – affluence, higher education, identity politics – are evidently having a bigger impact on younger women. Academic Alice Evans, who is writing a book on the new gender divide, also points to social media and the rise of distinct 'female echo chambers'. There may be a more prosaic explanation, too – professional women are overwhelmingly employed in either the left-leaning creative industries (broadly defined) or the public sector, with the latter dependent on the high taxes and high public spending favoured by the left. In the Nordic countries there are signs that men, who are mainly employed in the private sector, are coming to resent the high tax bills that are mainly flowing to a large, female-dominated public sector.*

Some men are resisting further liberalisation in protest against the persistent assumption that society is fairer to men than women, which feels strongly at odds with their own experience. Yet, despite a loud voice for this male resentment in the US, the broad movement towards sex equality is still overwhelmingly accepted there too. In 2012 only 18% of Americans, male and female, agreed with the statement that 'women should return to their traditional roles in society', and I suspect the number is lower today.

Moreover, when Pew asked young adults (18–32) who didn't yet have children whether they anticipated that becoming a parent would make it harder or easier for them to advance in their career, young men were as likely as young women to say that children would likely slow down their advancement (roughly 60% in each group). This suggests that Millennial men are entering their careers with a more egalitarian set of expectations about balancing family life and work.[37]

---

* The retreat of young men and women into somewhat separate spheres is symbolised by the fact that the two most popular US podcasts on Spotify are *The Joe Rogan Experience* followed by *Call Her Daddy*. The first is popular among young men and, although libertarian rather than chauvinistic in its political outlook, often focuses on masculine concerns. Similarly, Alex Cooper, who presents *Call Her Daddy*, is listened to by millions of young women whom she encourages to maximise autonomy, avoid commitment, and enjoy casual sex without emotional attachment (or at least she did until she herself got married).

A NEW MALE MODEL?

It is men at the extremes of the distribution for competitiveness and for violence who somewhat blur the otherwise largely positive picture of male adaptation. Similarly, a relatively small number of men continue to dominate the highest, winner-takes-all earning positions in business, the professions and sport, contributing to the lingering pay gap. And a small minority of very violent men were responsible for most of the nearly 700 UK murders in 2022, including those of around 200 women (about 80 of whom were killed by partners or ex-partners), as well as most of the lower-level domestic abuse that casts a shadow over the lives of too many women.*

Psychologist David Buss says that violence against women, often sexual violence, is the most widespread human rights problem in the world, though he also stresses what a small proportion of men are perpetrators. When I was young it was still common to see women in the street with black eyes, the police seldom intervened in 'domestics', and until the women's refuge movement took off in the 1970s women often had nowhere to go. That has changed beyond all recognition, and I suspect that violence against women in the UK and similar countries has declined, maybe substantially, but it is hard to be certain as it is only recently that the relevant data has been collected.† A woman friend who has been a regular on the clubbing scene for 25 years in London and New York says it is now much more common

---

* About 2.1 million people reported being victims of domestic abuse in England and Wales in 2022/2023. This figure was made up of 1.4 million women and 751,000 men.

† In his book *The Better Angels of Our Nature: Why Violence Has Declined* (Viking, 2011), Stephen Pinker has compiled data on p. 412 that suggests a sharp decline in domestic violence by men in both the US and the UK in recent decades.

to see a man calling out another man for bad behaviour towards a woman.

Overall, judging by opinion data and observation, the sense of male entitlement and dominance has not yet disappeared, but it has been in steady decline throughout my adult life. A new norm is now well established in most high-income countries that domestic labour should be more fairly shared to reflect women's much bigger role in the public economy. It will not always be exactly 50:50, though, and most women are likely to continue carrying a somewhat heavier 'mental load' when it comes to the family, partly out of choice. Nevertheless, the more egalitarian highly educated couples are setting a standard that does seem to be trickling down. Though few in the UK can yet match my Swedish friend Simon, who took six months' paternity leave for his first child and seven months for his second, at close to full pay (something British men might look on with envy). The result is, he says, that he is just as much the 'go-to' parent as his wife when one of the children needs help.

Meanwhile, a small but growing number of left-behind men are either opting out of economic contribution and long-term partnership or failing to achieve them. As economist Melissa Kearney argues in *The Two-Parent Privilege*, this is at root an economic problem, and it requires enabling these demotivated men to hold down jobs that pay enough to make them long-term partner material.[38]

Many of the policy prescriptions are those that apply in general to raising up post-industrial areas. But there are a few approaches that could be particularly helpful to left-behind men. One is to recognise that a subset of young men are never going to perform well in the classroom but can still achieve in other ways. The phasing out of woodwork and metalwork from the school curriculum in the UK in recent decades in the name of raising everybody to a higher academic level should be reconsidered. Many more boys than girls find sitting still and absorbing abstract ideas challenging, but they can learn useful skills in other ways.

Paul Corby, a retired trade union leader, described to me his own experience: 'Like most working-class children in the 1950s and 1960s I failed my eleven-plus and ended up at a lousy school that taught me very little, and I was completely unable to grasp algebra and geometry. Many of us were dismissed as thick, but most of us weren't. We often flourished in the world of work. I left school at 15 and did a five-year construction apprenticeship. And I was soon using Pythagoras's theorem to work out my angles; soon after finishing my apprenticeship, I was laying the foundations of multimillion-pound buildings using Pythagoras.'[39]

A revised school curriculum would, ideally, be linked to a renewal of post-school vocational qualifications as a valued alternative to academic degrees, especially in the UK and the US, where vocational institutions have been neglected since the 1970s. There has been some movement in this direction in the UK recently, but much of the focus has been on higher-end degree apprenticeships.

Similarly, the military has historically provided structure and training for otherwise potentially lost young men, in a predominantly masculine setting, and still does so on a large scale in the US. In the UK, however, the combined armed forces have shrunk to around 130,000 and provide fewer opportunities.[*] As recently as 1990 the armed forces employed twice as many people as today.[†] General Sir

---

[*] The armed forces are still missing their recruitment targets, but that is partly because their selection criteria have got tougher and they are no longer so much in the business of providing growing-up classes for directionless young men.

[†] About 135,000 young people are involved in school cadet groups, which are usually oversubscribed and, according to a University of Northampton report, produce strongly positive outcomes. Neil O'Brien MP has called for a doubling of cadet capacity.

Patrick Sanders, chief of the general staff, recently proposed a gap year military boot camp to bolster the reserves, and national service was floated by the Conservatives at the 2024 election.

If a new 'citizen army' does not find favour with the Labour government, it should consider instead establishing a multipurpose emergency responder service with intensive military-type training for backing up the military and the emergency services. The training might focus on dealing with the fallout from the rising number of extreme weather events expected in the coming decades, a task the already stretched military would happily relinquish. The role could be equivalent to the police community support officers backing up the official police force.

Such an all-purpose emergency support service could offer a mix of full-time and part-time work, once training was complete, and would be aimed primarily at men and women aged 18–30. A force of, say, 40–50,000 young people would not come cheap but could provide life-changing skills, a driving licence, and character development that might also save on the cost of social failure.

Another possible initiative is about making it harder for left-behind men to harm themselves with addictive behaviours. And that also requires knowing more about what such men are doing all day. Podcaster Chris Williamson expresses surprise that this army of young men are not being more socially disruptive and speculates that they are sedating themselves with video games, pornography and weed.[40] We need our social scientists, researchers and reporters to find out more about the nature and scale of this problem. It might then be possible to devise ways to intervene in drug or alcohol markets in appropriate ways, including with video game designers.

The video game industry has in recent years become bigger than the film industry, and gaming has become an important part of the lives of many young men. One of my sons went through a period of being semi-addicted as a teenager. I was talking to him about it recently and telling him what a pain in the neck he had been. But he unrepentantly embraced his earlier addiction, saying 'Dad, you have to understand, they were the happiest times of my life!'

Mainstream games like *World of Warcraft* or *Call of Duty* are impressive products and are capable of taking up large parts of someone's life. And for men who are not working or contributing, the games, which are relatively cheap and omnipresent, can offer an easy – but potentially damaging – escape, albeit one that usually involves friends.

There is one other big potential opportunity for policy to shift behaviour in a way that would benefit both lower-income men and the gender balance: incentivising more men to work in majority female sectors such as social care and nursing. There are, as a share of the profession, twice as many women flying US military planes as there are men teaching in US kindergartens.[41] This illustrates the trend in most high-income countries for women to be making big inroads into majority male fields while men are making almost no headway into majority female sectors.

In the UK, just 11% of NHS nurses are men, 13% of primary school teachers (and 35% of secondary school teachers), 3% of nursery/early years staff, and about 19% of people working in social care. One UK survey found that 85% of men would not consider a career in social care, and in *A World Without Work*, author Daniel Susskind reports that most US men displaced from manufacturing jobs prefer not to work at all rather than take up 'pink-collar' work.[42]

There are understandable reasons for this reluctance. Majority-female jobs often involve face-to-face interaction with others, one of the reasons they are better protected from automation, but men who struggle at school and are in danger of dropping out often lack the social skills to perform this kind of job well. Such jobs are often low-paid and low-status, and even if men do overcome a reluctance to consider 'women's work', they are sometimes not welcome in jobs requiring physical intimacy with very old, very young or disabled people.

Many domiciliary care providers in the UK offer the option of female-only care, and the NHS is being urged to follow suit. One disabled female acquaintance who receives home care told me that she had considered complaining when a young man was sent for the first time. 'But I got used to it quickly and just came to accept that I am not physically attractive any more. I'm just a body, and he was a good carer,' she reported wistfully.

Men who do enter female-majority sectors, such as nursing, often rise rapidly up the 'glass escalator'. And there are niches such as mental health nursing, where men have always been strongly present. Technology tends to attract men, and as more technology is employed in social care, it is likely to increase the male quota. But as with women entering male-majority fields, it takes role models and time and public policy effort, and to date there has been little of the latter in the UK compared with the effort to get women into male-majority jobs. And there is more incentive for women to move into male-majority sectors because they are mainly better rewarded and higher status, whereas it is the other way round for men moving into female-majority sectors.

Oonagh Smyth, whose organisation Skills for Care has launched the project New Demographics into Care, pointed out to me in an interview that the roughly 300,000 men working in social care in the UK is more than twice the number of men in the armed forces. She told me it is a bit easier to recruit older men, who may have been more exposed to care through looking after relatives. She also points to the example of Norway, where nearly 25% of the health and social care workforce is now male thanks to targeted recruitment drives over many years. Norway has even managed to treble the proportion of men working in childcare, which now stands at 10%.

A gradual increase in the male share is inevitable, but it is unlikely to match the movement the other way and will still require more Norwegian-style effort. As American sociologist Janette Dill told the *New York Times*: 'More men will go into care because they don't have a choice, but they're going to carve out spaces for themselves that feel less like women's work.'[43]

In summary, the process of domesticating men, albeit in a masculine manner, has made big strides. Western men, particularly the highly educated, have been willingly assisting in the dismantling of the patriarchy. The process still has some way to go and needs to accommodate lower-income men who feel the loss of economic status and the provider role in the family more acutely.

But a relatively small number of angry men shouting at each other in one fetid corner of the internet does not amount to a backlash. And if the family and domestic realm are to be renewed, and more men can be viable partners to more women, both sexes will win. Narrowing some of the gender gaps that have been opening up in recent years in women's favour and directing more men into activities that make them good partner material is also one of the keys to reversing the baby bust. This is the subject of the next chapter.

6

SLEEPWALKING INTO LOW FERTILITY

Never has the case for having children been more urgent, or more
difficult to make.

Paul Morland, *No One Left*

In most societies, having children was a cornerstone of adulthood.
Now it's something you have if you already have everything else. It
becomes the capstone.

Anna Rotkirch, *Financial Times*

I used to live close to a children's playground. Having been surrounded by children for most of my life, I liked the sound of them
playing and shouting and could easily shut it out if I needed to. But
one of my childless neighbours was always complaining about the
noise and frowning at the little ones as they ran past. As fertility levels
have fallen and children have become rarer and more noticeable, such
intolerance towards children has grown. I notice the sentiment in
myself, something I'm sure I didn't feel 20 years ago.

Demographer Paul Morland compares it to the decline of smoking.
When smoking in homes and public places was much more common,

most of us took it for granted and barely noticed the smoke or smell. Now it is rarer, we are much more likely to notice the smell in a room or on our clothes.

Children do not damage your health and, contrary to some claims, parenting is generally good for your mental and physical health. Yet increasingly in rich countries we often think about children, if not quite as a disease then at least as an obstacle to other equally (or more) desirable things, like freedom and wealth and a smaller carbon footprint.

There is a debate among demographers about whether the desire to have children is an instinct or a muscle that may atrophy and even disappear completely if not used. But maybe it is best described as a habit that humans are increasingly losing because, especially in rich countries, there is no *need* to have a child, or even an intimate relationship, and millions of people are, perfectly rationally, placing their individual freedom and choices first. And the surrounding culture, whether in the form of religious teachings or the expectations of parents, grandparents and peers, is no longer reinforcing the baby habit.

When lots of your peers are having babies it reduces the opportunity cost of having one yourself: there are fewer people available for a casual cinema trip and, simultaneously, more people who want to do child-friendly things. And more members of the group get to see and hold a baby, something many young adults have never done. There is a ripple effect.

Like a growing number of people, I believe that the disappearance of this ripple will have enormous costs – economic, psychological, even civilisational – but they do not weigh heavily on the scales here and now, when a couple or a single young woman is deciding to postpone or abandon parenthood. It is a private, not a society decision, and those who want the UK government to incentivise higher fertility are often seen as not simply old-fashioned but authoritarian. The result is that a new, childless habit is forming with little resistance, especially among Gen Zers in their 20s.

While writing this chapter, I came across an eminently reasonable account of how this new childless habit has evolved. Charlie Gowans-Eglinton, a 35-year-old freelance writer, says that at 28, and earlier, she definitely wanted a child, but she kept pushing back the age when she thought she would finally take the plunge: 'The longer I wait, the more I face having to give up... At 35 I love spending time alone in my rented flat, where I've nested, painting bannisters and reupholstering armchairs, but with only myself in mind. I can afford a few holidays a year with friends, since I can avoid the pricier school holidays. I spent a fortnight in Greece and another in Italy with friends this summer, writing on-the-day freelance commissions in cafes beside the beach. I never have to turn down a job opportunity or a spontaneous holiday to accommodate someone else's schedule.'

Gowans-Eglinton says she does still want a baby, but not at any cost, and this reflects two other commonly cited reasons for the baby bust. The first is the greater fragility of relationships, the so-called crisis of intimacy, and a world of both higher expectations of partners, particularly by women, and acceptable alternatives if one fails to show up. 'A good partner would make raising a child not just easier, but happier – but not all partners do... If I met someone who I thought would pull their weight – not just financially but as true partners – and we could afford all that together... then, yes, I would try to have a baby.'

The second is the expense of parenthood: 'I would have a child if I could afford it... I'm freelance, so I'd have to cover my own maternity leave past the statutory pittance... and I'd need to be able to afford to buy a flat, or be able to swallow sudden rent increases or surprise evictions. But for the money, I'd do it alone now.'[1]

A host of surveys tell us that many people in the UK today are delaying having children, or having fewer than they want, or not having children at all, because of the cost. A poll commissioned by the Pregnant then Screwed lobby group in 2022 found 63% of people saying they were delaying parenthood or not having a second child because of the high cost, with the cost of housing and the cost of childcare the two most frequently cited items.[2]

In earlier decades couples often waited until they could afford their own home before planning a family, but fewer are now in that position, with the average house costing almost nine times the average salary. Between the beginning of 2004 and the end of 2014, home-ownership fell from 60% to 35% among 25–34-year-olds. *Financial Times* columnist John Burn-Murdoch reported that in 1980 almost half of 18- to 34-year-olds in the UK lived in their own property with children of their own; today that is true of just 20%.[3] In the UK, 28% of 20- to 34-year-olds are living with their parents (33% of men, 22% of women).

A recent study showed that fertility tends to be lowest in areas where house prices and rental costs are highest. This certainly applies to London, which has the lowest fertility rate in the country.[4] Housing of all kinds is not only more expensive, but you also get less space for your money, which means that to afford enough space for two or three children you need two full-time salaries and so are exposed to high childcare costs. A family with two full-time workers on the average wage with two children will spend around 30% of their after-tax income on childcare (with the percentage higher in London).

But reducing the cost of childcare and housing is only one part of a much bigger picture, cultural as well as economic, to return to parenting some of its lost allure. There are, after all, many countries where the cost of both housing and childcare is much lower than the UK yet fertility rates are even lower. And some of the poorest people in the UK, those of South Asian Muslim background, have the highest fertility rates in the country.

This does not mean that people are fibbing when they say they cannot afford to have more children because of housing or childcare costs. But whatever the obstacles, they are now no longer trumped by the forces of religion, culture, habit and expectation that used to prevail. My older brother, who has only one child, did consider having a second with his wife, and he thinks that 'loss aversion did play a big role' in sticking to one. They had accommodated one child easily enough and retained a comfortable, relatively low-stress routine, and did not want to risk disturbing that.

Gowans-Eglinton did not mention climate change or general anxiety about the future as a reason not for bringing a new life into the world. But many young people do say such things. A recent poll among British 18- to 34-year-olds (Generation Z and Millennials) found that only 55% planned to have children, with another 20% undecided.[5] Of the 25% who said they did not want children, 38% cited the state of the world and 35% climate change. Similarly, a 2021 global poll published in the *Lancet* medical journal found that 39% of young people were 'hesitant to have children'.[6]

Some of this is fashionable pessimism that people will grow out of. It is seen as smart to be critical and pessimistic, qualities more likely to be found among graduates, who also tend to postpone parenthood longer than non-graduates. As radical US Congresswoman Alexandria Ocasio-Cortez told her 1.5 million Instagram followers: 'Basically, there's a scientific consensus that the lives of children are going to be very difficult. And it does lead young people to have a legitimate question: Is it OK still to have children?'

There is no such scientific consensus. Yet having a child is an act of faith in the future and birth rates tend to rise after periods of threat or disruption. The end of the Second World War and optimism about the future has usually been the main explanation for the 1940s/1950s baby boom, which briefly defied the 200-year trend that rising incomes mean fewer babies. A recent paper has, however, challenged this idea, arguing that not only did the baby boom start before the end of the war, across a broad range of countries, but it was driven not so much by either optimism or returning soldiers but rather by practical things such as medical improvements that made giving birth safer, domestic technologies from electrification to refrigeration that made everyday life easier for mothers, and plentiful housing.[7] Something similar could, therefore, in principle happen again even without a return to high levels of economic growth and a new, more optimistic outlook. Perhaps a drug that makes childbirth completely painless or safely regularises babies' sleep patterns.

Nevertheless, it is hard not to feel that the fog of gloom that has hung over most rich countries since the 2008 financial crash followed by the pandemic and the Ukraine and Israel-Hamas wars – with the UK adding in the austerity period and Brexit rupture – is acting as a low-level, background, contraceptive hum.

The possibility that she might live to regret not having a child was, candidly, not ruled out by Gowans-Eglinton. And there is quite a lot of regret. Indeed, if opinion polls on such a sensitive subject are to be trusted, the regret leans heavily one way. According to a YouGov poll, there are almost four times as many people wishing for more children as wanting fewer or none.[*] Even allowing for some social

---

[*] In a 24 June 2021 YouGov poll of 1,249 British parents, 4% of parents admitted to wishing they had not had children at all and another 4% that they had had fewer children, whereas 29% wished they had had more children, rising to 32% among 25- to 49-year-old parents.

desirability bias in the answers – it is a hard thing to admit, even in an anonymous survey, that you regret having a child – that is a big vote for children.

HOW BAD IS IT?

2023 was the 50th anniversary of the UK falling below replacement fertility levels of 2.1 live births per woman (the 0.1, now often calculated at 0.08, takes account of the fact that not all newborns make it to reproductive age, even in rich countries). It is only in the past few years that this has attracted public attention, partly because we have been insulated from the effect by high immigration. Less well known is the fact that the decline has accelerated in the past few years, with the idea that the pandemic might trigger a mini baby boom turning out to be the opposite case. The number of puppies sold during the pandemic, however, went up 12%.

The 2022 figure for England and Wales of 605,479 births (around 620,00 for the whole UK) implies a fertility rate of 1.49, down from 1.55 in 2021. And with roughly 577,000 deaths in 2022, it won't be long before the population, excluding immigration, will start shrinking. This shrinking has already begun in Scotland. Among mothers born in the UK, the number of births has fallen by 22% *in a single decade*. And if the fertility rate was calculated only among UK-born mothers, it would be bumping along with southern European countries like Spain and Italy (on 1.3), or Japan (also on 1.3, and where the population is now falling), though not as low as South Korea's 0.72. (Sardinia is now the South Korea of Europe, with a rate of 0.95.)

Rapidly falling birth rates are now a global phenomenon, and the process is happening even faster than most experts predicted a few years ago.* Back in 1950 the average woman on the planet had 5 children; today she has about 2.3, and nearly three quarters of countries in the world are now at or below the replacement level. India is down to 2, Iran 1.7, Brazil 1.6, and China 1.2. About the only places above a 2.1 fertility rate are in sub-Saharan Africa (and even there it is down from 6.8 children per women in the 1970s to 4.5 today) and a few Muslim countries such as Afghanistan and Pakistan. Once the baby habit is broken, most countries seem to keep heading downwards, with a few exceptions – notably Israel, Georgia, Sri Lanka and Indonesia – which have paused, at least for now, at between 2 and 3.

Secularism clearly contributes to plummeting fertility, at least in high-income countries. In the UK, observant Catholics have on average half a child more and observant Protestants one third of a child more than secular families. It is unclear whether this is down to religious doctrine itself, the more traditional gender roles of believers, or the fact that they tend to have stronger family and support groups.†

In the UK, the story has been one of consistent decline since about 1870, with the single big exception of the baby boom spike from the late 1940s to the early 1960s, when briefly the fertility rate almost touched three. This suggests that there is something more fundamental at work than the more contemporary factors that are usually cited, such as the cost of housing or childcare.

That fundamental thing is, surely, the human desire for the kind

---

* The global population grew from 1.6 billion to 6 billion in the 20th century and is expected to peak at just over 10 billion in the 2080s.

† In the US, adults who attend a religious service at least once a week have 2.1 children, compared to 1.3 for those who don't.

of freedom and choice that only a childless life provides.* And life has got far richer for a childless person in a high-income country in recent years. There is a much greater range of stimulating experiences available – travel, entertainment, food, connectivity, the opportunity for professional or artistic creativity – than a few decades ago, especially for women, and even for people on modest incomes.

Meanwhile, the experience of being a parent has not really changed and may even have got harder, especially since the arrival of intensive parenting in the late 20th century. We invest so much more in children that a large family is now unthinkable for most people, and even a second child is challenging. 'We are pro-child but anti-natal,' as American commentator Ezra Klein puts it.[8]

'Societies progress up the hierarchy of needs from physical survival to emotional self-actualization, and as they do so, rearing children gets short shrift because people pursue other, more individualist aims. People find other ways to find meaning in life,' according to demographer Wolfgang Lutz.[9]

The enjoyment of freedom and self-actualisation also rubs up against the hard constraint of female fertility, which medical technology has only extended to a small extent in recent decades. This is also one of the explanations for the fertility gap – the gap between the number of children people want and the number they have. Many women leave it too late to have any children at all, or more than one, because of the time taken in education, establishing a career and finding a partner.

But the outlook is not completely bleak for those who hope for a fertility bounce. Even in the UK there has been some wobbling

---

* This is less of a factor in more collectivist Asian societies, where the work-based culture plus the high investment required in children's education is the bigger constraint.

around, with the fertility rate rising briefly to almost 2 in 2012, for reasons nobody seems to understand. And those countries that have deliberate pronatalism policies, such as France (1.68) or Hungary (1.5, but up from 1.2 a decade earlier), or generous parental leave and heavily subsidised childcare like Sweden (1.5), can buck the rich country trend to a small extent, though Finland and Norway, with similar incentives, both have fertility rates below the UK.

There are other counter-trends, such as men undertaking more domestic labour, that appear to have had a mildly positive impact on fertility, at least helping to slow the decline.[10] The recent decline in Nordic fertility has cast some doubt on the equality = high fertility claims, yet the lowest fertility rates in high-income countries are still those with more traditional gender roles. Swedes have one third of a child more per woman than Italians. And pronatalists might take heart from the sad fact that something like 80% of women who end up childless did not intend to.

It is also possible that both governments and society more broadly will start to be genuinely alarmed at the economic implications of the fact that in 2022 in the UK nearly 950,000 people celebrated their 56th birthday and just 620,000 babies were born. The famous dependency ratio pyramid – a relatively small number of retired people at the pinnacle, with a large base of the working population – will not be inverted, but it will start to look increasingly rectangular, with big implications for taxes and public services.

THE FERTILITY GAP, CHILDLESSNESS AND HYPERGAMY

The idea of sleepwalking into low fertility implies that it is an avoidable fate. The overall number of children that women want, like the number they have, has been falling in recent decades, but almost all surveys suggest that there is still such a gap worldwide, and the biggest part of it derives from women who remain *unintentionally childless*.

Most surveys compare women's stated fertility intentions in their early 20s with the same cohort's actual completed fertility 25 years later. An obvious problem with this is that it doesn't take account of the fact that fertility intentions can change over time. As author Jill Filipovic put it in an article celebrating women in the US having *fewer* children: 'The 24-year-old who says she wants children someday but is focusing on her career can easily turn into the 30-year-old who says she wants children but with the right partner. Later, she can easily become the 45-year-old who has a meaningful career, a community of people she feels connected to and a life rich in pleasure and novelty that she doesn't want to surrender. Likewise, a mother sold in theory on three children might discover that her family is complete with two, or one. Is that a woman who had fewer children than she intended? Or is she someone whose intentions were largely abstract in the first place, and they shifted as she did?'[11]

Nevertheless, an often-cited 2019 paper looking at 19 European countries concluded that in all countries women had fewer children than they had intended in their early 20s, with the highest gaps among the highly educated.[12] Overall, intentions averaged slightly above replacement level at 2.1, compared with average actual fertility for those countries at around 1.6. Spain, Greece and Italy had the biggest gaps between intention and outcome, at around 0.7; France had the lowest gap, at 0.1, with the UK somewhere in the middle, at 0.3. The figures are more dramatic for childlessness, with intended childlessness chosen by 5% or fewer women in most of the countries and actual childlessness turning out at around 18% in the UK, 20% in Austria, Spain and Greece, and 22% in Italy and Germany (32% in Hamburg).

A Eurobarometer survey of 2011 found that UK women wanted 2.32 children at a time when the fertility rate was around 1.8, so a gap of just over 0.5.[13] A paper using the UK's General Household Survey found a lower fertility gap for those born in 1975 of just 0.2.[14] A more recent 2023 survey of young British women by the New Social Covenant Unit found a much bigger fertility gap of around 0.7, with women aged between 18 and 24 wanting 2.25 and those aged between 25 and 35 wanting 2.41, though a surprisingly high number wanted to remain childless – 13% for the younger group and 12% for the older group.[15]

The UK fertility gap is therefore likely to lie somewhere between 0.2 and 0.7, with the midpoint enough to bring the fertility rate back up to close to replacement. But many analysts predict that rising childlessness on its own will confound any attempt to close the gap. They point to Japan, where childlessness has shot up from 11% for women born in 1953 to 27% for women born in 1970.

Historically, a high number of women have never married or had children. The image of women in earlier centuries struggling with large families is not inaccurate, but it coexisted with a large number (10–15%), who either never married or married too late for children or who were medically unable to have them. Childless women often had a special role in society, in the Church or in caring professions and teaching. 'It is poverty only which makes celibacy contemptible,' says the protagonist of Jane Austen's *Emma*. The 'maiden aunt' has long been a familiar figure in popular culture, sometimes fierce, sometimes pitied. My mother's sister, Aunt Ursula, never married, and lived with and partly cared for her own mother. She had a successful career as a literary agent – Wilbur Smith was for a period one of her authors – but an unsatisfactory private life and a drink problem.

Childlessness has followed a U-shaped pattern in the 20th century across most of Europe. The century started with around 20%

childlessness, dipping to half that mid century and then rising again to around 20% at the end of the century, though with regional variations. There seems to be no link between childlessness and overall fertility: in central and eastern Europe, for example, childlessness is rare but overall fertility is low.

The UK has followed this broad European pattern. For the 1960s cohort, education was a key divider, with 22% of graduate women remaining childless compared with 12% of those with no more than secondary education (though this gap has shrunk and in some high-income countries is now reversing).*

Yet according to one of the biggest recent studies of childlessness in the UK, the common assumption that much childlessness is driven by the tension between a professional career and motherhood is not the case. The reasons for childlessness given in the British Cohort Study for those born in 1970 are many and varied, but easily the biggest single reason at 31% is 'not wanted children' (presumably having changed their minds along the way), followed by 'never met the right person', cited by 19%. 'Career' was cited by a mere 2% of women.

Beyond a few online 'crazy cat lady' jokes, there is no great stigma attached to chosen childlessness. Childless women are no longer looked down upon as lonely, barren spinsters. Indeed, there is now a well-established 'childless by choice' identity group, with national organisations in the UK like Gateway Women, a visible media presence, and several books celebrating childlessness, such as Ruby Warrington's *Women Without Kids: The Revolutionary Rise of an Unsung*

---

* The highest rate of childlessness is found among women who study non-vocational degrees. Researchers at Stockholm University found that 33% of Swedish women born in the late 1950s who studied the social sciences did not have children, compared with 10% of primary school teachers and 6% of midwives.

Sisterhood, published in 2023. As with many identity movements there is an attempt, at least at the more radical end, to change thinking by policing language and insisting on *child-free* rather than *childless*. Some maintain that eschewing motherhood is the ultimate expression of feminist pride. In the US, Melanie Notkin of SavvyAuntie.com and inventor of the acronym PANK (Professional Aunt No Kids) points out that childless women are more likely to start businesses, volunteer, and both donate to and run charities.

Yet intentional childlessness remains the choice of a small minority, albeit a growing one. According to an analysis of data from the Netherlands and the US by Renske Keizer of Rotterdam University, 10% of childless women are childless by choice, 10% childless for medical reasons and 80% by circumstance.[16] So why is the proportion of actual childless women in the UK heading towards 25%, according to some estimates, over the next decade?

Childlessness is not, it seems, the result of an active decision not to become a mother or father but the cumulative effect of other choices: prioritising education and then career into the mid 30s, then not finding the right person, or experiencing a relationship breakdown at a key time, or focusing on other life projects, what researcher Ann Berrington has called 'perpetual postponers' (such as Charlie Gowans-Eglinton).[17]

Some commentators argue that almost all of the decline in fertility in high-income countries is the result of increased childlessness.[18] If this is the case, then it makes sense for pronatalism policy initiatives to focus on encouraging those who have children to have more, as the move from childlessness to having one child is a bigger step than that between one child and two. It would also mean fewer one-child families, which would be preferable given the acknowledged benefits of siblinghood, something I will touch on later in this chapter.

When modernity gives people more freedom from social obligation, and more space in which to design their own lives, they do not
always make the right choices. Freedom has costs and unintended
consequences, and unintended childlessness is one of the biggest,
as feminist writer Germaine Greer and many other less influential
women would confirm. Greer, having inspired a generation of women
to reject motherhood and domesticity, came to mourn her unborn
babies. And motherhood, she argued in *The Whole Woman*, can be a
fulfilling career: 'In *The Female Eunuch* I argued that motherhood
should not be treated as a substitute career; now I would argue
that motherhood should be regarded as a genuine career option...
Meaning that every woman who decides to have a child would be
paid enough to raise that child in decent circumstances.'[19]

Regret applies to men as well as women. Around 25% of UK men
over 42 are childless, many of them unintentionally, and as many as
40% of Finnish men, and about half of those UK men are unhappy
about this, according to research by Dr Robin Hadley.[20] Feminist
Ruby Warrington and others complain that there is far less attention
on male childlessness and that all the responsibility for preventing a
population collapse is placed on women. But this is hardly surprising
when it is women who bear children and are usually the key decision
makers on the issue in a couple. Moreover, men are less defined by
reproduction and do not have the same pressure of the sharp fertility
decline in their late 30s, though men too become less fertile as they
get older and are more likely to father children with autism and
Down syndrome.[*]

---

[*] It is also argued that environmental factors related to plastics are contributing to
male infertility. See for example Jessica Freeborn, 'Microplastics in Testicles May
Play a Role in Male Infertility, Study Suggests', *Medical News Today* (24 May 2024).

Men's diminishing status in relation to women is another contributing factor summed up in the term *hypergamy* – meaning that women tend to prefer partners of higher status and earnings potential than themselves ('marrying up', in common parlance). But what happens when women heavily outnumber men in higher education, and increasingly in well-paid professional jobs, in most Western countries? If there is a smaller pool of higher-status men for the new wave of high-status women to partner, could this be contributing to higher childlessness? The common cultural meme on the dating scene, among both younger women and middle-aged women returning after divorce, of 'where have all the decent men gone?' may in part be a reflection of the hypergamy problem.

But is hypergamy real? Evolutionary psychologist David Buss's work on partner preferences has shown that there are differences in the traits preferred by men and women.[21] Women place more value than men do on partners being educated, a proxy for having high earning potential and the ability to provide comfort and protection, while men place more value than women do on partners being physically attractive; the fact that we see this across cultures suggests there may be at least an element that is hardwired.

These differences should not be exaggerated. Men and women are in the main remarkably similar in their preferences. The sex difference traits are far from the top of the list for both sexes, and below traits like kindness and dependability. Nevertheless, there is plenty of evidence from simple observation and social science data that hypergamy has been a real factor in patterns of partnering, at least until recently. It was a perfectly rational strategy for women living in societies where, on average, their earning capacity was lower than men's. If your future standard of living and that of your children depends primarily on your male partner, it makes sense to seek someone with higher earnings potential than yourself.*

We are probably in a transition phase out of hypergamy. It persists for now and, thanks to the declining proportion of highly educated males, is therefore contributing to lower fertility. American anthropologist Marcia Inhorn, author of *Motherhood on Ice: The Mating Gap and Why Women Freeze Their Eggs*, puts it bluntly: 'There is a massive undersupply of educated, equal male partners for highly educated American women.'[22] The situation is even worse in very status-conscious societies with high proportions of female graduates, like Japan and South Korea – one reason for their plummeting fertility.

Yet women and men do seem to be adapting, with women now increasingly likely to marry down, at least in educational terms. In fact, according to one influential paper, among those born in the 1970s, women are now more likely than men to be the more educated partner in a relationship in all but a handful of high-income countries (Slovakia, Austria, Germany, Switzerland, Romania and Luxembourg).[23] It is impossible to say for certain whether this is because men's and women's ideas about desirable partner traits have shifted as a result of greater sex equality, or whether it is because of a more limited supply of highly educated men.

Science writer Ellen Pasternack sums it up like this: 'Perhaps an analogy could be drawn to preferences in height. A majority of women find it unattractive for men to be shorter than them. But if the average height of women went up by 6 inches over the next half

---

* A survey conducted on the Tinder dating app found a strong tendency for women to favour highly educated males, even to the extent of preferring those with master's degrees over those with merely bachelor's degrees.

century, and men stayed the same, I don't think we would expect all these tall women to remain unmarried.'[24]

Some American demographers are arguing that income but not education hypergamy is persisting in some 'red state' areas of the US. Say a man working in a traditional blue-collar skilled job (e.g. welder, plumber) without a degree marries a woman who went to the local state university and now works as a librarian or in a mid-ranking white-collar job. Who has the higher status here? It feels like a convenient match of a man bringing in income and a woman performing high-status but modestly paid work that could be scaled back to part-time when children arrive, without much damage to family income. A similar alliance higher up the social status ladder could be a male banker who marries an artist or charity worker.

But even if hypergamy is abating, it is part of a cluster of issues relating to partnering and intimacy that have nibbled away at the assumptions that once led to the habits of long-term marriage and parenthood. Moreover, parenting itself is viewed in a different light – not as an adventure or a blessing, but as something highly demanding that, to do well, requires considerable psychological and financial resources. This is a positive development in some respects, but it may mean that many people of below average incomes will, increasingly, feel more inhibited about parenthood. Indeed, the tendency for highly educated and more affluent women to have fewer children than the less well educated is now reversing in places like Finland: the fertility rate there has declined from 1.9 to 1.4 in the last 10 years, partly thanks to lower-status women and men remaining childless.

Relationship uncertainty is a growing factor in falling fertility. A world of greater freedom and autonomy is one in which relationship contracts are easier to break, largely without stigma. And they are being broken as never before, making people warier about making the sort of long-term commitments that having children should imply. Meanwhile, people wait for something better to turn up, a tendency that is probably encouraged by the endless possibilities presented by 'relationship shopping' on dating apps. This is true for men too, especially high-status men, who can be spoilt for choice.

Men and women end up childless for partly different reasons. Women are usually childless by circumstance and leave things too late. Many men, too, can leave it too late to settle down, remaining passive or complacent about commitment. But plenty of others don't become fathers because they are not viewed as good enough partner material by women. And some of those who do settle down are uncomfortable about their wives or partners being more economically successful than them. As noted, such relationships tend to be less happy, less permanent and also less fertile.

People are still adjusting to the changes in relationship norms of the past few decades, and it is possible that a new age of solidarity between the sexes will eventually emerge. But for now, we live in an age of relationship insecurity, and people born in the 1980s and 1990s simply seem a lot less interested in having children than people born in the 1960s and 1970s, perhaps also because they were the first generation that experienced the big increase in family breakdown.*

The next generation, born early this century, looks set to be even less interested in parenthood as they settle into extended adolescences,

---

* Even some of those who do have children are advising against it. An influential TikTok account a few years ago called 'The Girl with the List' consisted of women recounting their negative experiences of motherhood.

often still living at home in their late 20s.* And an increasingly large minority of them are opting out of heterosexual identification – 25% of people aged 18–21 in the UK identify as gay, lesbian or bisexual according to one recent poll (and a much smaller but highly publicised minority are experimenting with a trans identity).† An increasing number of gay and lesbian people are getting married and a growing minority are having children together, but the rate lags far behind heterosexual couples: about 1.7% of all couple families are same-sex, but only 24% of female same-sex couples have children and 7% of male ones.

Cultural trends can change swiftly, and none of these patterns are set in stone. But what cannot change much is women's fertility. A friend who gave a talk recently at a London think tank to a group of mainly young women in their 20s asked them what they wanted from the state that they were not currently getting. Their unanimous answer was more support with IVF treatments. Some of these highly educated young women were already planning to freeze their eggs on the assumption that they might not want to consider motherhood until past the fertility 'cliff' of 37. IVF treatments, about three quarters of which take place in the private sector, are also very expensive, costing about £6,000 to £12,000 for a single cycle. It is recommended that the NHS offers three cycles, but most health trusts offer either one or none (usually three in Scotland). It is understandable why the

---

* Jean Twenge, in the US, has found a sharp fall among 17- and 18-year-olds who say they 'ever go out on dates' over the past 40 years, from 85% to 60%, see iGen, (Atria Books, Sept 2017). A survey of British 18-year-olds by the Higher Education Policy Institute found just 16% excited at the prospect of having sex as a student.

† Though the more official ONS statistics for those aged 16–24 in the UK find that 10.6% of women and 7.9% of men identify as gay, lesbian or bisexual.

young women were keen to get more taxpayer support, but the success rate for the process is, currently, relatively low.

About 55,000 women in the UK underwent fertility treatment in 2021. The technology has improved a lot since the 1990s, but the IVF success rate for women over 40 using their own eggs is only around 10% (compared with around 30% for women in their mid 30s). The newer technology of using eggs frozen when a woman was younger, or using donor eggs, now works in about 20% of cases for those 40 and over, but experts say the success rate is unlikely to rise much above 30%. Yet there remains much ignorance and wishful thinking about fertility treatment: the New Social Covenant Unit survey referred to earlier in this chapter found that 61% of young women believe that scientific advances mean women can have a baby at almost any point up to the menopause.

THE PSYCHOLOGICAL COST

Men and women find happiness and validation in many ways, both with children and without. Before the modern era, the issue of whether children make you happy would not have been a relevant one. Children were unavoidable and necessary: an economic asset and an old-age pension.

Children are now costly consumer goods and a lifestyle choice. Families are smaller, and in an age of brainwork, so-called intensive parenting is thought by most parents to be necessary to help children into the safety of a well-paid job. This is stressful, time-consuming, and sometimes boring.

It is often said that modernity, with its promise of individual freedom and self-realisation, is in direct conflict with something as unavoidably self-sacrificing as having and rearing children. Is it nevertheless worth it in the long run because on average you will end up happier than those without children? The answer seems to be: not necessarily, but for most people probably yes.

An influential US paper on the subject, led by professor Jennifer Glass, says that surveys first started picking up greater *unhappiness* among parents compared with non-parents in the 1970s at a time of the breakdown of conventional family arrangements along with 'the decline in men's earnings, the increase in women's employment, and the rise of both dual-earner and single-parent families'.[25]

Work–family conflict became a more common feature of life in high-income countries and seemed to swing the happiness balance towards non-parents. The Glass paper, which looks at the story in 22 countries, finds non-parents to be happier in 14 and parents to be happier in 8 – Russia, France, Finland, Sweden, Norway, Spain, Hungary and Poland. The paper argues that parental unhappiness can be mitigated by state investment in family-friendly policies, as happens in most of the 8 'happier parent' countries. The US scores least well on parental happiness, with the UK not doing much better but just ahead of Ireland and Greece. Having a large proportion of single parents in the lowest income bracket probably acts as a drag on happiness figures in both the UK and US.

There are many other papers that show no significant difference or positive life satisfaction from parenting. Outcomes seem to depend on the country in question, the research design, questions asked and the point in the parental experience that the question is asked.

A distinction should probably be drawn between *having* children and *caring* for them. The latter, when children are young, is hard work, expensive and often damaging to relationships. As noted, a high number of marriages, and even more cohabitations, break down in the first few years of parenthood. Life satisfaction and happiness levels are likely to sag under the strain, but looked at over the whole life course it is often a different story. And the latest figures for the happiness of both mothers and fathers in the US from the General Social Survey 2022 find that those married with children are happier than the childless and the unmarried.

Parenthood aligns with many of the things that are known to contribute to a meaningful life and mental health: having a role and an external focus to your life, mattering to other people and being responsible for them, having connections both to your offspring and the people you meet through them. As sociologist Viviana Zelizer rather dramatically puts it, the modern child is 'economically useless but emotionally priceless'.[26]

The issue of meaning can cut the other way too. Jill Filipovic again: 'At the heart of declining birthrates in the world's most prosperous countries might be the matter of meaning. Historically, men dominated the realms of paid work, politics, economics and world affairs, while motherhood was the clearest and most acceptable path to adulthood, community respect and purpose for women. As more women either find jobs that bring in a pay cheque and the attendant power of independence, or maybe even a sense of satisfaction and purpose, fewer women use motherhood as a conduit to respect and adulthood.'[27]

States as subjective and elusive as happiness and meaning are hard to be scientific about, but there are other, more objective, ways to measure the impact of parenting, such as health outcomes and longevity, both of which favour parents.[28]

If parenthood is good for you, so is having siblings, and the gradual disappearance of siblings as more people have just one child will have unpredictable consequences for society. I am of course biased, being one of seven children and having four of my own, but there are many, obvious, reasons why the disappearance of siblings could be damaging. Some of them are spelt out in Colin Brazier's *Sticking up for Siblings.*[29]

Brazier lists the following advantages of siblings, many of them backed up by authoritative research: they create economies of scale for families; they help to socialise each other, are good for social skills and make people less selfish; they are a constant reference point in a transient world and hold us to account; they can make you healthier and reduce the risk of obesity; they can mitigate the impact of over-parenting and help in divorce; when children are small they mean higher levels of play, now recognised as important for emotional and cognitive development; they seem to be good for marriages; they reduce the burden of care for older parents.

Siblings can often 'see' you in a way that ordinary friends cannot. As one friend put it: 'Something I really value about my siblings is they are the only other two people in the world who know what it was like to grow up in my family, which means in many ways they are better placed to understand me than anyone else, and vice versa. Like parents, siblings know us from before we formed our adult selves that we now show the world – which can be very humbling – but unlike parents, they are our peers and will hopefully remain with us the whole length of our lives.'

Brazier also points out that in a world of more polarised opinion and confirmation bias you have to learn the skills of conflict resolution with siblings, because they don't go away. After a squabble at bedtime, a sibling will wake up with their brother or sister still there at the breakfast table the next day, and for years to come.

I have several friends who are happy and well-adjusted only children, but in my informal polling of friends and acquaintances I discovered that a large proportion do believe that the most narcissistic people they know – 'my two worst flat-sharers by a mile' – are only children. As the proportion of only children in high-income countries has risen, is it a coincidence that a narcissistic sense of entitlement seems to be becoming more common in recent generations?*

Older generations have been saying this about younger generations since ancient Athens. But psychologists Jean Twenge and W. Keith Campbell claimed in their 2009 book *The Narcissism Epidemic* to have hard evidence of narcissistic personality traits among US college students rising sharply from the 1980s into the 2000s, though they seem to have stabilised since. And the Chinese one-child policy, not officially stopped until 2016, has, according to a 2013 study by Australian researchers, created a legacy of single children who are more selfish, pessimistic and risk-averse than children with siblings.

There is an even more obvious consequence of a low-fertility society, and that is loneliness. Already about 30% of households in the UK are single-person ones. That amounts to 8.3 million people, a 16% increase in 20 years. And 7% of UK adults report being lonely often or always. It seems to follow a U-shaped curve, with high levels among those aged 16–29, dipping in middle age, and then rising again as people age. According to the Understanding Society survey mentioned in the previous chapter, about 20% of British people say they have only two close friends or fewer, and, as also reported in the last chapter, nearly 10% of British men say they have no close friends.[30]

Some people thrive on their own. But for the majority who do not, loneliness, according to some recent research, rivals smoking and excessive drinking in damaging health and shortening lives.

---

* US political scientist Robert Putnam reports that in 1950 just 12% of survey respondents agreed with the statement 'I am a very important person', compared to 80% in 1990. R. D. Putnam, *The Upswing: How America Came Together a Century Ago and How We Can Do It Again* (Simon & Schuster, 2020).

This is thanks, mainly, to raised levels of the stress hormone cortisol. And unlike mental health problems, which have been substantially destigmatised, there is still inhibition about admitting that you feel loveless or friendless.

The importance of good relationships to physical health is strongly reinforced by the celebrated Harvard Study of Adult Development, the longest in-depth longitudinal study on human life, that began in 1938 with some Harvard undergraduates, later including some boys from disadvantaged homes in Boston, and now looks at all their spouses and descendants. The participants are interviewed regularly about their lives and their physical and mental health.

Robert Waldinger, current study director, says this: 'The Study has brought us to a simple and profound conclusion: good relationships lead to health and happiness.' The trick, he adds, is that those relationships must be nurtured. And one part of the explanation as to why relationships matter so much for health takes us back to those highly stressed babies in institutional childcare. 'What we find,' says Waldinger, 'is that people who are… lonely, don't have those stress regulators that we get from good relationships and they stay in chronic flight or fight mode, so that their bodies have this chronic stress, chronic levels of inflammation and stress hormones.'[31]

The proliferation of cheap and easy means of long-range communication can be a countervailing factor that sustains family relationships and friendships. And unchosen families can be supplemented by chosen friendship groups and communities of many kinds. But there is little evidence that the latter are fully replacing families.*

---

*   It is plausibly argued that community still flourishes just in less localized and formal settings, such as online; see for example Jon Lawrence, 'Individualism and Community in Historical Perspective', in Shana Cohen et al. (eds), *Austerity, Community Action, and the Future of Citizenship in Europe* (Policy Press, 2017), 239–54.

THE ECONOMIC COST

The death of birth is already having a big impact on economies. And things are set to get much, much worse. People are becoming more aware of the problem, but potential solutions involve difficult trade-offs.

Darrell Bricker and John Ibbitson, authors of *Empty Planet*, neatly capture the future advantages and disadvantages: 'Population decline isn't a good thing or a bad thing. But it is a big thing. A child born today will reach middle age in a world in which conditions and expectations are very different from our own. She will find the planet more urbanised, with less crime, environmentally healthier but with many more old people. She won't have trouble finding a job, but she may struggle to make ends meet, as taxes to pay for health care and pensions for all those seniors eat into her salary.'[32]

We want rising incomes and functioning public services, and therefore a sufficient number of young people to achieve that, without sacrificing sex equality or having to work into our mid 70s or throwing open the door to even more unprecedented levels of immigration. Paul Morland has called it the 'three Es' trilemma: an *economy* that is thriving, a degree of *ethnic* continuity (modest levels of immigration), and lifestyles of *egotism/equality*. This means that neither women nor men must sacrifice too much for the sake of their children. It is simple enough to have any two of these three, but much harder to have all three.[33] 'That leaves the depressing prospect of economic stagnation via low fertility and low immigration, like we see in Japan, or endless populist nativist backlashes via low fertility and high immigration, like we see in Europe and North America,' writes blogger Peter Hurst.[34]

There are several ways that the baby bust will act as a drag on the economy. The best understood is the shrinking workforce having to support a growing number of older people living for longer, which makes pay-as-you-go public pension systems unviable. In 1950 there were more than 5 people of working age in the UK to every one person over 65: in 2000 there were 4, and there are now just over 3 working people per retiree. By 2060 it will be closer to 2. In 2026 the number of over-65s is expected to overtake the number of people under 18. The pressures on the public purse thanks to an ageing population are already severe. Moreover, there is the danger of a vicious cycle emerging in which governments have to keep raising tax levels on the shrinking number of younger citizens to pay for the growing army of the old, making having children even less affordable.

Immigration-driven population growth of 9.5 million between 2021 and 2046 is expected by the ONS, more than matching the 8.9 million growth of 1996–2021, with population rising from today's 68 million to 76 million. But even with net immigration at the unprecedented level of around 300,000 a year, that will still only *slow* the deteriorating dependency rate and those rising bills for pensions and health. And, on current fertility and immigration assumptions, the Office for Budget Responsibility is projecting government debt rising to around 300% of GDP by 2070 without drastic action on tax or public spending.

The fact that those OBR projections are not implausible can be understood by noting that Japan's debt-to-GDP ratio is 225% and rising. As the Social Market Foundation has put it: 'In terms of its impact on the public finances, the UK's long-term demographic challenges look set to eclipse the impact of the world wars, the global financial crisis and the coronavirus pandemic. And, unlike these events, it is set to be a persistent financial challenge rather than a temporary blip.'[35]

Other factors will exacerbate the fiscal challenge, such as falling demand both from fewer people earning an income from work and the fact that people will be saving more for retirement, fearing a decline in state provision. And as families shrink, they are likely to hand over more care of older people to the state.

There is also the invisible force of demographic 'momentum'. Remember that the UK fell below replacement fertility more than 50 years ago but it is only now that, despite high immigration, the dependency rate is starting to play havoc with public finances. We have been sustained by historic fertility levels. But, more alarmingly, momentum works in reverse too. Even if, by some miracle, we return to replacement fertility in the next few years, we will remain top-heavy with old people for many, many decades to come.

Then there is the loss of dynamism, risk and innovation in societies with fewer younger people. We already have a Nimbyism problem in the UK of older people objecting to changes that could benefit younger people, especially in housebuilding. According to the *Economist*, 'Younger people have more of what psychologists call "fluid intelligence", meaning the ability to solve new problems and engage with new ideas. Older people have more "crystallised intelligence" – a stock of knowledge about how things work built up over time.'[36]

Researchers have, indeed, found that most of those filing patents for new inventions or techniques tend to be under 40, and younger still for the most disruptive inventions. Again, Japan may be showing us our future. In 2010, Japanese inventors produced the most patents in 35 global industries. By 2021 they were ahead in just three.[37]

There is a long list of countervailing benefits of a falling population, such as spending less on education and other parts of the public infrastructure, and a list, too, of potential remedies – robots, AI, immigration – some of which I will consider in Chapter 9. And one obvious way to adapt to the coming economic crunch is to push back the age that people qualify for their pension, increasing to 70 and beyond from today's 66 in the UK (rising to 67 in 2027). Around half of men and two thirds of women in the UK currently stop work before pension age, something that will not be sustainable on current projections. (Across the EU only 6% of those over 65 are working compared with 25% in Japan.[38]) Pushing back retirement will not be popular, however, and may not work with the happily propertied baby boom generation, now entering retirement, because they will have little financial incentive to work longer.

My baby boom generation is contributing to the low fertility problem by not sufficiently sharing the proceeds of our good fortune. The tax cuts and sale of public assets of the Thatcher era were only possible thanks to the UK's then demography of a fast-expanding workforce that heavily outnumbered the old and retired. Now those boomers are pensioners it seems there is nothing but tax rises for the following generations. A demographic tailwind has turned into a headwind.[39]

The property boom of the past few decades has ensured a big windfall to the propertied baby boomers, especially in the south of England, and when it is transferred it will go to a smaller number of children than in previous generations, further concentrating wealth. Almost three quarters of retired households in the UK now own their home outright, compared with 20% where the main earner is an employee. Around 25% of pensioner households have assets of more than £1 million – some of which should be channelled into paying for elder care – and the wealthiest fifth of people paying inheritance tax are passing on an average of £400,000 per child. Someone born in 1956, my year of birth, will on average pay £940,000 in tax while receiving state benefits of around £1.2 million, but someone born in 1996 will enjoy less than half of that figure.[40]

No wonder young people are becoming disillusioned – and we are only in the foothills of the low fertility/ageing society. According to academic Ben Ansell, only 20% of people under 40 agree that a person's position in society is mostly the result of their own efforts, against about half of people over 70.[41] And even if there is an upturn in optimism and economic growth, it will not necessarily be translated into more babies. The New Social Covenant Unit survey, mentioned earlier in this chapter, reported a strong desire for a higher fertility rate among the young women polled, but they were markedly hostile to any state intervention to encourage it, beyond better education about fertility. Most agreed with the statement that 'lower numbers of children being born in the UK would either not matter or lead to mostly positive consequences for society.'

Pronatalists have a mountain to climb, and I will consider some of the routes up that mountain in Chapter 9. But in the final third of the book it is time to shift – from the care and attention deficit in a shrinking, looser family to the related undervaluing of care work in the public economy, and what lies behind the apparently permanent recruitment crisis in social care.

7

BIGGER, NOT BETTER: WHY THE CARE ECONOMY IS STRUGGLING

When my gran was in her eighties she had a home help from the council, who did her shopping, did her cleaning, got her pension ... and gave her a hot meal a couple of times a week. The district nurse helped her with bathing and dressing her legs. There was a lot more help in those days and a lot more time for older people.

Cathie Williams, Association of Directors of Adult Social Services

Many women today are less socialised into caring roles, and some women have just given up on care, but men have not, in general, taken up the slack.

Madeleine Bunting

If you add together all the functions relating to people's health, welfare and physical and mental well-being – all healthcare and adult social care, welfare benefits and state pension, social services, mental health and therapy services, nursery care and children's services – these care functions account for around half of all public spending. Add in the private sector, and the care sector, broadly defined, probably accounts for more than one third of the whole economy.

This is a huge transformation, and it is on an unstoppable upward trajectory. In the mid 1950s, the UK defence budget was one and a half times that of NHS *and* education spending combined. Today it is less than one sixth. We have moved from a warfare to a welfare society. This is wholly unsurprising: as individuals and societies all over the world get richer, they spend more on making life more comfortable and, if possible, longer.

Indeed, once both feet are firmly planted on the care economy escalator, we are compelled to spend an ever rising proportion of public and private budgets on care. This is driven by three factors: longevity, technology and expectations.

Back in 1950, in the UK the average number of years that a man was likely to live in retirement was seven (14 for a woman), and in 1967 one third of men were still dying before reaching retirement age. Today only 18% of men don't reach retirement and, and on average, men live an extra 16 years and women an extra 19. And the longer we live into old age, the more demands we make on the pension, care and health systems. The OBR predicts that over the next 50 years, public spending on people over 65 will rise from 10% of GDP to 21%.

Rising life expectancy means a big increase in the incidence of expensive chronic illnesses. The so-called Four Horsemen of the medical apocalypse – heart disease, cancer, obesity and dementia – account for about 80% of deaths in people over 50 who do not smoke. But thanks to advances in medicine most people now live for many years, even decades, with one (or more) of the Four Horsemen. In the case of dementia, the rising incidence is itself a result of people living long enough to suffer from it. There are close to 900,000 cases now in the UK, and it is responsible for 11% of all deaths. Back in 1950, when dementia was classified as senility, this figure was about 3%.

Meanwhile, the behemoth of the NHS responds by sucking up ever more spending and people. After the NHS workforce plan was published in 2023, it was calculated that expanding the workforce from the current 1.5 million to the planned 2.3 million by the mid 2030s would mean it employed half of the entire public sector workforce, and nearly one in ten of all workers in England. UK annual spending on public healthcare has doubled in the past 20 years to almost £200 billion, and is projected to rise to around £300 billion in another ten years, a third of all public spending.

And our expectations will continue to rise too. As Oonagh Smyth, head of the Skills for Care organisation, said to me: 'We have a very different idea of what we think a civilised society is. Until recently younger disabled people, for example, would not have been expected to be economic contributors, but now they often expect to have jobs and to live independently. But to have this quality of life they often need support, support that isn't always there if we cannot find enough people to work in social care.'*

Even when targets are met by governments, such as the pledge to increase GP appointments by 50 million compared with 2019, it is barely noticed, because demand is growing insatiably.[1] It is not only NHS spending that has multiplied but welfare and support services of many other kinds too, services that in the past were provided in the family, or in hospital geriatric wards, mental institutions and orphanages largely removed from public view, or not at all.

Social care is an inherently vague concept but is defined by one analyst as 'supporting people of all ages with certain physical, cognitive or age-related conditions in carrying out personal care or domestic

---

* The rise of disability activism in the 1980s played an important role in reshaping attitudes to care.

routines. The support can be in their own home or in a residential setting.'[2] About 300,000 of the 850,000 people in receipt of long-term care are younger people with often severe impairments and learning disabilities, accounting for half the annual social care budget. And, partly because of continuing improvements in medical technology, that cost trajectory is ever upward. As IFS director Paul Johnson wrote, 'There are not just more older people, but also a continuing rise in the number of young adults in need of care: one consequence of a health care system that keeps more children alive into adulthood, but with severe needs.'[3]

Not only are more babies with serious impairments like cerebral palsy kept alive, we also have more sensitive diagnoses of disabilities such as autism and ADHD. As noted, 17% (1.5 million) of UK children are classified as having SEN, while 4.3% attract extra spending with a care plan – an increase of 64% since 2016, driven by autism diagnoses. About 8% of all 16-year-olds claim some kind of disability support, or about two pupils in every class.[4]

Alongside the cost consequence of technological advances and new diagnoses, consider the enormous difficulty governments of all parties have had in merely slowing the rise in disability spending in recent decades. Notwithstanding regular headlines declaring official tightening of the eligibility criteria, more billions are spent every year. The number of *working-age* people in the UK self-reporting a disability that restricts their daily activities was 10.2 million in 2023 (24% of the 42 million people of working age), up from 6.6 million in 2012/13. There is probably an element of so-called social contagion, and definitional shift, in this number, and not all of the 10.2 million qualify for a benefit – but 2.7 million working-age people are economically inactive because of disability, up from 2.1 million before the pandemic and 600,000 in 1992/93. According to the IFS, the state paid around £78 billion in all health- and disability-related benefits in 2023 (mainly, but not all, to working-age people), nearly 7% of public spending (and 3% of GDP), which is projected to rise to £100 billion in 2028–9.*

One might have expected the number of disabled people of working age to be *falling* rather than rising, as back in the early 1990s there were still many millions of people working in physically demanding jobs in manufacturing or mining, where physical injury was commonplace. The recent increase in disability benefit recipients has several causes: effects of long-term Covid; longer NHS waiting lists; the fact that some disability benefits are more generous and with fewer demands on the recipient than unemployment benefit; the switch to a new system of Personal Independence Payments in 2012; the loss of a culture of 'tough love' from GPs, who now sign off 94% of those who ask, with many slipping into long-term sickness with minimal reviews; and a real increase in stress- and mental health-related problems, especially among younger people. Mental health now accounts for more than a quarter of all people not working because of a disability, and more than half of all new claimants.[5] There are now more people aged 18–24 that are signed off sick – mainly with mental health issues – than people in their early 40s.[6] This system as it stands cannot continue indefinitely.

---

* There are many kinds of disability benefits, the main ones being Employment Support Allowance and health-related Universal Credit, which is needs- and means-tested for those who cannot work, and Personal Independence Payments, which are needs- but not means-tested for people both in and out of work. The official OBR figure for disability payments in 2023–4 was just under £40 billion (which doesn't include all health-related benefits, hence the higher IFS estimate).

THE FLIGHT FROM CARE

There is a fourth factor that is driving all that state spending, along with longevity, technology and expectations. It is the smaller, less stable and more dispersed family.* Many lifestyle diseases, including obesity and moderate depression, are triggered by loneliness and unhappiness that are themselves often related to unstable family life. And a weaker and smaller family means a bigger state, as the state now often does expensively, inefficiently and sometimes uncaringly what the family – historically meaning mainly women at home – used to do for free for those they knew and loved.

In recent years the dissonance between our sentimental, quasi-religious attitude to the NHS in the abstract and our daily experience of substandard care has loomed ever larger. As in any other sector there are some very good doctors, nurses and carers, a majority of average ones and a few poor ones. Why else do we read constant stories of neglect and even abuse in NHS hospitals and in care homes? There are devils as well as angels. An extraordinary two thirds of maternity units in England are deemed 'not safe enough' by the Care Quality Commission (CQC) and, astonishingly, the NHS pays out more than twice as much in maternity-related compensation payments (£8 billion) a year as it spends on maternity care itself (£3 billion).†

---

* According to Understanding Society data, more than 40% of UK-born people over 21 live more than 30 minutes from their mother, and 20% live more than two hours away.

† This is partly because medical mistakes at the start of life attract high compensation. But every year around 4% of women who give birth are so traumatised by the experience that they meet the criteria for post-traumatic stress disorder. See Hannah Barnes, 'The Trauma Ward', *New Statesman* (12 Apr. 2024).

Public satisfaction with health and care services is at record lows, despite record funding for the health service. A YouGov poll in October 2023 found 86% of people agreeing that the NHS was in a bad state.[7] Such surveys tend not to distinguish between complaints about overall funding directed at government and complaints about the nature of care provided by today's health workers. The latter, especially if they work for the NHS, tend to be protected by the collective sentimentality towards the NHS and the fact that it is easy to deflect blame upwards or onto 'cuts', despite the fact that the NHS was largely protected from austerity. More than 60% of NHS staff themselves say they cannot provide an adequate level of care, and almost one third say they have thought about leaving in the past year.

Similarly, in social care, the 2019 BSA survey found that only 38% of adult social care users were satisfied with the care they received. I have spoken to dozens of residential home carers and former carers in the past year, and many of them have said they would think twice before putting their own parents or grandparents in the home they worked in. One young woman, who now works for my disabled brother-in-law, estimated that the proportion of her fellow workers who cared to those who didn't was about two thirds to one third. 'After what I've seen, I would never want to put my nan in a home,' she said.

Rising state spending on health and social care is not keeping pace with either rising demand or expectations. Care delivered by strangers through the state or the market, particularly to old people, can rarely replicate care delivered by a close relative. But this previous model of care often placed an intolerable burden on women, and as people have grown richer one of the first things they have chosen to do is live separately from older relatives and, in many cases, pay others to care for them. Back in the 1950s and 1960s between half and one third of older people lived in a household containing one of their children, but by the 1990s that had fallen to below 15%.[8]

Although the family is not about to step up on a significant scale, it has also never gone away. The ONS estimates that there are around 5 million people, mainly in late middle age (55–64), who are providing informal care for a family member or friend – generally an older person, though sometimes a younger person with a serious impairment – for at least a few hours a week, though one third care for at least 50 hours. Those providing care for 35 hours or more can claim a Carer's Allowance of £81.90 a week or, in some cases, the slightly more generous Attendance Allowance; in total, about 3 million people are in receipt of these allowances.

The number of informal carers in England has fallen from a recent peak of 5.6 million in 2012, and the smaller size of the family, the rise in childlessness, and fewer intact families, is likely to mean even more people relying on the state or market in the coming decades. Bucking this trend will be family-friendly ethnic minorities, particularly those from South Asia. According to one survey, 44% of older people from ethnic minority backgrounds receive care from a child living in the same household, compared with 18% from majority backgrounds.[*]

That same survey finds that just under half of parents aged 70 and over currently receive help from a child not living with them (and give financial and other support in return). Younger generations, the

---

[*] The survey is the English Longitudinal Study of Ageing (https://www.elsa-project.ac.uk/). Rishi Sunak himself pointed out in a think tank report that just 7% of Asian households consist solely of retirees, compared with 25% for the population as a whole. (Rishi Sunak and Saratha Rajeswaran, 'A Portrait of Modern Britain', Policy Exchange, 2014).

survey implies, are no less willing to provide care, but other decisions and priorities, and more family breakdowns, mean that they are often simply less available to provide support.*

British individualism, if not selfishness, probably does provide some insight into why our elder care system seems under even more pressure than many comparable countries. According to the World Values Survey, British people are among the least likely to support the statement 'adult children have the duty to provide long-term care for their parents'. Out of a list of 24 countries, only Japan (26%) and Sweden (30%) had fewer people agreeing than the UK (31%). The US number was 40%, Germany 48%, France 73%, Nigeria 94% and China 98%.

But many people *prefer* being looked after by a friendly stranger than their own child, or even a partner, especially if they are suffering from incontinence or other undignified conditions. And there are many conditions where family care becomes impossible beyond a certain stage. Milder forms of dementia are usually managed by partners or within families, but that is impossible when symptoms become more severe. And in the next decade nearly half of all 75- to 85-year-olds and a full three quarters of those over 85 are expected to suffer from dementia in some form.

Notwithstanding this caveat, building the family into the public care system and preventing further decline of family support ought to be a priority of any government. And there are several ways this can be incentivised that I will consider in Chapter 9.

---

* The survey points out that 72% of the 1940s/1950s cohort of old people said they could rely on their children 'a lot', compared with 52% of the 1960s cohort. That may be a function of the greater neediness of the older cohort, though another factor is the higher divorce rates and greater geographical mobility among the children of the younger cohort.

But are there enough British people who *want* to work in the public care economy at all levels? By and large, recruitment into care *professions* – half of all NHS jobs – is not a problem, though retention has been. Where there are shortages it is because the state has been reluctant to foot the bill for the expensive training of doctors and others, preferring to rely on immigration and the false economy of agency staff instead. There are in fact 10% more nurses and consultants today than in 2019, and 16% more junior doctors. Moreover, the NHS workforce plan aims to train hundreds of thousands more doctors and nurses in the next 12 years, at a cost of £50 billion. It is hard to imagine there ever being a shortage of doctors as it is such a high-status and well-paid career and now attracts more women than men; there are still at least four applicants for every one accepted onto a medical degree course.

For nursing, though, the future is less clear. The NHS currently employs 370,000 nurses, projected to rise to 530,000 by 2036–7. There was a welcome upward spike in applications for degree courses during and just after the pandemic, but numbers have now dropped back, with applications for nursing degrees in the UK returning to around the 2019 level. More than half of all applicants now get onto a nursing degree course, with some courses now struggling to fill places.

Those who try to attract young people onto nursing courses will emphasise the huge variety of roles it opens up apart from that of an NHS nurse or midwife, from health visitor to senior hospital manager. And once inside the NHS, you can move up to become an advanced care practitioner, requiring many of the skills of a qualified doctor.

But there appears to be something about what is required of the modern nurse, particularly in the NHS, that appeals less to young British women (who still provide the large majority of the workforce).

They have more options than previous generations: many women who are training to be doctors today would have been training to be nurses in the 1980s. And maybe the Christian values of service and self-sacrifice that inspired some among previous generations of nurses to put up with the stress and exhaustion of a long shift are less evident today.

More prosaically, a graduate nurse typically starts work with a £50,000 graduate debt burden, which means that her marginal tax rate is the same as an investment banker, on a salary not much more than the national average. Forgiving some of that student debt for those that stay for more than five years, and wiping it out entirely for those who stay more than ten, seems an obvious step.[*]

Two other more recent factors are also relevant. First, nursing, like teaching, is not a job you can do from home in the way that you can with many other professional jobs. One of my daughters is a teacher and has found it particularly exasperating that many of her friends are enjoying the post-pandemic working from home perk and she is not. Second, the gradual decline of the idea of the job for life may be particularly tricky for traditional vocational professions with long training periods, which is what nursing has long aspired to be.

Even among those nurses who do qualify there is a high drop-out rate: one in eight leave during training and another one in five leave the NHS within two years. There are currently more than 800,000 registered nurses and midwives in the UK (160,000 non-UK-born), but only 370,000 work in the NHS. There are probably another 50,000 in social care and a similar number in the private sector. That still leaves at least 300,000 who appear not to be working as nurses.

---

[*] Such debt forgiveness was one of the proposals of *The Times*'s Health Commission that reported in Feb. 2024.

It seems that they often leave the profession to have a family or take another job and then don't return.

The system is partly propped up by international recruitment: around 50,000 nurses arrived from abroad over the two-year period 2022–3, and about 30% of NHS nurses are non-UK born. But there are still at least 30,000 unfilled nursing positions – a vacancy rate of 7.5%, more than twice the national average. Notwithstanding the cultural shifts that have made nursing a less attractive career for many young women, there must be ways of structuring and rewarding nursing-type work that could broaden its appeal. The status of nursing has been raised somewhat by making it an overwhelmingly graduate-entry profession, but that has created the problem of excluding many capable young people who may have struggled with exams. Maintaining a well-trodden path to registered nurse for those who enter at lower levels is essential.

The 2023 nurses' strike shone a light on pay. As one nurse observed during the industrial action, the median salary in her profession is around £40,000, for a job that involves the most gruelling encounters with trauma and suffering, whereas 'a train driver is rarely called upon to deal with any kind of emergency, sits peacefully in a cab and has a median salary of £59,000.'[9]

There is a broader *comparative* issue here. Most jobs, certainly white-collar ones, have got more pleasant in recent decades. Nursing has got harder. There are several reasons: there is more pressure on beds, quicker throughput of patients and more administrative work, reducing the opportunity to establish rewarding relationships with patients; there is more responsibility as nurses have taken on more quasi-doctor roles, and complex technology to handle; patients are more demanding and less deferential. On top of that, a typical young woman today will have had less prior experience of caring for a family member, as families are smaller and grandparents usually live further away.

A nurse's median salary is comfortably above the average and, with ten years' experience, a nurse could be earning around £45,000 plus a decent pension and a high degree of job security, which compares favourably with the average for many graduate jobs (although less so in London). But considering how much responsibility and challenge comes with a typical nurse's day, it is evidently not enough, as the vacancy levels make clear.

Recruitment for the less qualified, more hands-on end of the care labour market is even more of a challenge than nursing. The job of aiding frail older people, the disabled and those with dementia – helping them to dress, bathe, eat, go to the toilet, walk, read and so on – is neither glamorous nor well paid. Yet doing the job properly requires qualities that not everyone has: empathy, patience, the ability to communicate. As Camilla Cavendish wrote in her book *Extra Time*: 'The demand for carers will increase sharply as populations age, and the skills most needed will be the ones that... robots cannot provide: emotional resilience, intuition and empathy. Yet people who do caring jobs are often looked down on, or described as unskilled, by health professionals, because they have talents which are not academic.'[10]

Given such attitudes and the relatively poor pay that such jobs attract, there is already a recruitment crisis for many of these basic care positions. The NHS says it has an overall shortfall of 130,000 jobs. The social care sector talks about an even bigger shortfall: out of 1.6 million workers (or 1.2 million full-time equivalent jobs) it claims to have 150,000 vacancies, and a vacancy rate of just below 8% even after the surge of international recruitment in 2022–3.

Some of these figures should be taken with a pinch of salt, and in part reflect the sector's perpetual lobbying for more public money and a relaxation of immigration restrictions. But the demand for care jobs, particularly at the less qualified end, is only going to grow. Skills for Care calculates that the number of people over 65 will rise from the current 10.5 million to 13.8 million by 2035. On the basis that one social care worker is needed for every six people over 65, they estimate that the social care sector will need an *extra* 480,000 staff by then.[*]

Meanwhile, the supply of people competent and ready to work in hands-on care roles for the minimum wage or close to it is shrinking. This is partly because 81% of social care workers are women, and as the average woman moves up the occupational hierarchy there are fewer left who are ready and willing to fill the less prestigious care vacancies. The 18–24-year-olds of Gen Z make up only 8% of the social care workforce and have lower retention rates than older generations.[11] The number of social care apprentices has more than halved since 2016; although apprenticeships in general have declined, social care has taken an above-average hit. There are also 50,000 fewer baby girls born each year to British mothers than in 1990.

Society as a whole has benefited from the upward mobility of women, but many parts of the care economy, as well as teaching, have lost out. In the first decades after the Second World War some of the most capable women in rich countries, still constrained by glass ceilings and family responsibilities, were working as ward sisters or primary school heads. Public services benefited from this discrimination, but their daughters are now free to be lawyers, management consultants or, indeed, medical consultants, and are less willing to put up with low paid/low status care work.. As Madeleine Bunting, author of *Labours of Love*, said to me: 'Many women today are less

---

[*] It is a very labour-intensive sector. A senior manager at one medium-sized care home chain told me he had 7,000 staff for 5,000 beds.

socialised into caring roles, and some women have just given up on care, but men have not, in general, taken up the slack."*

Immigration is the answer favoured by many: since 2021, around 150,000 mainly non-EU social care staff have arrived, as well around 100,000 NHS professionals, including nurses and doctors, together accounting for around two thirds of all UK work visas in 2022–3. As I will argue later, I do not think this is a sustainable solution and it tends to reinforce the idea that care is not a decent job for a British-born person.

WOMEN'S WORK?

Is this hands-on care work undervalued? Yes. But this is a more complex story than it seems. And one of the standard explanations – that it is poorly paid because it is mainly done by women – seems to be only partly true.

Care in the non-market, private domain of the family is by definition not rewarded financially. Instead, it is usually based on some sort of implicit mutual support deal reflecting a division of labour in which one partner, usually the man, earns money to support a mother and child. Today, some sort of mixed arrangement is now the norm, with both parents earning.

For paid care work in the public economy, by contrast, we have the labour market. And how it determines the value of different jobs is a many-layered and mysterious thing. Behind the normal working of supply and demand, and returns to skills and education, lie social

---

* Emily Kenway's book *Who Cares: The Hidden Crisis of Caregiving, and How We Solve It* (Wildfire, 2023) illustrates the shock of a young professional woman not raised to expect a caring role suddenly having to look after her sick mother.

biases and preferences (and the fact that some people's preferences carry more weight because they have more money). Many factors conspire to confound the notion of a fair reward for labour. There is bargaining power, the custom and practice that used to reward office jobs a premium over shop floor jobs, the market distortions that still grant many finance jobs a premium over equivalent professional occupations, the gender norms that used to mean women were often paid less than men for doing the same or similar work (until that was made illegal), and the fact that for many low-paid care jobs the government is the main buyer and sets a low price in order to contain public spending.

Most people in the UK probably regard many financial professionals as overpaid and most care workers as underpaid. The way that is corrected is essentially through politics intervening in market outcomes, with special taxes (or occasionally pay caps) for those who are regarded as overpaid, and public subsidies, tax credits or high minimum wages for the underpaid. The latter usually requires the public to pay more through higher prices or taxes.

Labelling certain jobs as undervalued is a common refrain in public debate, but undervaluation is a vague and contested idea and people often have very different values and very different ideas about the economic worth of different activities. Interventions require a political justification based on the idea that markets are not providing the outcomes that most people want. But I believe there is such a case to be made for many hands-on care-related jobs.

Most *professional* care work needs no such intervention. Indeed, the median annual pay of a medical consultant has declined relatively in recent years but still stands at £126,000. There are many senior managers in hospitals, social services departments and even social care organisations, who enjoy six-figure salaries. Many of these senior managers are women. Care professionals in general – nurses, doctors, managers, therapists of many kinds – suffer a care pay penalty only in relation to even higher-paid professionals in finance and law. But what of the claim that domiciliary care workers, residential care home workers, nursery staff, childminders and NHS care assistants, all of whom are doing work that usually involves handling the feelings and sometimes the bodily fluids of others, are in some way systematically underpaid?

Most people would expect these jobs to be in the bottom half of the income spectrum as they are classified as low-skill – meaning they require little by way of formal qualification. But should they be as low as the bottom 20%? And how do they compare with similarly low-skill majority male jobs in transport, construction, manufacturing and so on?

The standard academic explanation for low pay in the hands-on care sector is that it is because in most rich countries the sector is 80% to 90% female. A 2009 paper by US academics found that as women enter an occupation its wages fall, and that as more men enter an occupation its wages rise.[12] Yet how can this apparent discrimination be compatible with the 'equal pay for work of equal value' legislation in operation since 1975 that has been bearing down on the gender pay gap? The argument is summed up by American academic Nancy Folbre: 'Debates over the causes of gender differences in pay have polarised into two camps: those who argue that women face opposition to efforts to improve their economic well-being, such as discrimination in the labour market, and those who argue that women simply prefer jobs with lower pay... either because they derive intrinsic satisfaction from these jobs or because they prioritize the needs of their own family.'[13]

Women are both more likely to work part-time (often for family reasons) and are less likely to be represented at the top of the highest-paying sectors like finance and IT. But if much of the persisting pay gap comes from the top end of the professional hierarchy, then it is not very helpful in explaining the pay differences between ordinary jobs towards the *bottom* of the income spectrum. And it turns out that notwithstanding the fact that a London bus driver (male-majority profession) of five years' experience is paid close to double an elder care worker (female-majority profession) of five years' experience, the gender pay gap in most lower-paid, everyday jobs *is almost non-existent* – there are simply more women doing them.

When I first started looking into the pay data, I expected to find jobs such as refuse collector, forklift driver, hospital porter – unionised, traditionally male-majority jobs – to be considerably better paid than those female-majority care jobs. This turned out not to be the case. An ONS hourly pay list of 30 ordinary jobs in 2022, ranging from train driver and registered nurse at the top (earning respectively £30.54 and £19.90 per median hour) to nursery nurse and kitchen porter at the bottom (earning respectively £10.74 and £9.75 per median hour) found the most typical care jobs, such as childminders and NHS care assistants, mainly in the bottom 20% of the list. Yet they shared that bottom quintile with plenty of typically male jobs, such as delivery driver. Moreover, if you look at how relative pay has shifted in the past 25 years, female-majority care jobs have been somewhat *upgraded* relative to low-skill male jobs. Registered nurse was third from the top, with a 75% increase in hourly pay, while NHS care assistants and childminders were in the middle, with 28% increases each. The three bottom jobs were forklift truck driver, refuse collector and fisherman, all majority male, with increases of 12%, 0% and -4%.

This change is probably less to do with equal pay legislation than with the disappearance of the premium for those male-majority, unionised manual jobs, thanks to weaker unions, the export of many male manual tasks and immigration bidding down the price of those positions that remain. A relatively high minimum wage – it rose to £11.44 an hour in April 2024 – has also helped to narrow the differential between some of the most basic care jobs and typically male jobs like chef, builder and driver.

The 2023 data from the Annual Survey of Hours and Earnings found care workers on a median hourly rate of £11.82, 2p *above* the £11.80 of a refuse collector. NHS care assistants were somewhat better paid (on a median rate of £12.72), childminders and childcare assistants in nurseries somewhat less well (£11.64 and £11.45 respectively).* But the hourly rate is only part of the story. The Skills for Care organisation points out that many care workers get no overtime or antisocial hours pay, have ungenerous pensions and related benefits (if any), and limited pay progression. Moreover, domiciliary care workers who visit people in their homes are often not paid for their travel time, which means they can, in effect, be paid below the minimum wage.

Employers in the social care sector also complain that increases in the minimum wage have nearly doubled their staff costs in recent years and forced them to erode the small care premium that used to exist over jobs such as supermarket cashier, and so made recruitment even harder. The Migration Advisory Committee (MAC) calculates that in 2011 the average care worker's hourly pay was 5% higher than other low-paid jobs, but by 2021 that differential had fallen to 1%. The MAC has noted that such care workers tend to be poorly paid in all rich countries, but the situation is somewhat worse in the UK.

---

* This is well below the median hourly rate for all employees in 2023 of £15.88, or for skilled trades of £14.51 or for administrative and secretarial jobs of £13.43. But it is above the median rate for elementary occupations, such as cleaner or security guard, of £11.11.

Across the EU those working in residential long-term care were paid 79% of average earnings, compared with 71% in the UK.

The 1.6 million people who work in adult social care make it one of the largest employment sectors in the economy, with around 5% of all workers – more than the transport and construction sectors. Of the total of 1.2 million full-time equivalent jobs, around 860,000 are front-line basic care workers – so-called first-rung workers – with most of the rest being managerial and professional roles of various kinds. Annual staff turnover (28%) is almost double the national rate, though most remain in the sector and turnover is lower than hospitality (37%) and retail (33%). One fifth of care homes, though, have turnover of less than 10%. But high turnover rates mean that about one third of front-line carers have less than three years' experience, far from ideal when dealing with the needs of older people who want a familiar face and voice and someone who knows their likes and dislikes.

Adult social care does seem to be a particularly hard case of poor remuneration in the UK, sitting slightly above nursery carers and cleaners but below other low-paid jobs in offices, call centres and transport. Indeed, given how stressful it is working in an adult or elder care home, or working as a home visitor dealing with people who are often weak and ill and confused, it is remarkable in some ways that the vacancy and turnover rates are not even higher. As one care manager said to me, 'It is a miracle sitting on top of a disgrace.'

One reason for this is that people derive considerable satisfaction from working in social care. Though everything must be carefully recorded, they enjoy a high degree of autonomy and responsibility. In fact, looking at the most authoritative surveys on job satisfaction and the sense of achievement from work, it is almost the reverse of the pay tables. Care jobs, including NHS care assistants, home carers, nursery nurses and midwives, all cluster in the top 10–15% of people saying they are very satisfied with their work.[14] Working with people, and seeing a visible and generally positive impact on their lives, produces a human reward that the jobs clustered at the bottom, such as civil service executive officer, chartered surveyor or pension and insurance clerk cannot emulate.[*]

The lack of progression and training opportunities is sometimes given as an explanation for the sector's recruitment difficulties, and this can be an issue for some current and potential staff. Staff with five years or more experience, some of whom take on the extra responsibility of a senior carer, are paid only a few pence more than someone with less than a year's experience. The next step up would be into a management role that would require a higher care qualification, and more than half of social care staff currently have no (or only basic) qualifications, such as an NVQ level 2.

But several care home managers have told me that most of their staff are not looking to progress and are attracted to the job for other reasons. One reason it is valued is that it is part-time-friendly – almost half of all front-line care jobs are part-time, meaning less than 31.5 hours per week – and in a sector with little technological innovation it is also the case that caring skills tend not to erode as fast as in some other sectors.

One of my cousins has MS and has lost the use of both legs and one arm and so needs three home care visits a day from two carers.

---

* One report (Nye Cominetti, 'Who Cares?', Resolution Foundation, Jan. 2023) found that 88% of care workers reported satisfaction with the job, compared to 83% in other low-paid roles. As a rising minimum wage has improved pay at the bottom of the labour market it has, however, in many sectors been accompanied by a *reduction* in job satisfaction thanks to greater intensification of work. This does not seem to apply to the social care sector.

One of her regular carers, Nancy, who has become a friend, says she adores the job and wishes she had done it straight from school. It is also convenient for her as a mother of school-aged children. Nancy usually does an early shift from 9 a.m. to 2 p.m. so she can pick up her children from school in the afternoon. She has a husband earning a decent income and can put up with the low pay.

The job is attractive to women like Nancy with family caring responsibilities, and it is a job that can be returned to after several years' break with little danger of losing your competence or confidence. The sector also scores highly on job security and geographical convenience. There are, however, fewer Nancys than there used to be, and without some step change to pay levels, and a more intangible sense of status, there will soon be even fewer.

WHY EMOTIONAL LABOUR IS UNDERVALUED

Is the relatively poor pay in the Cinderella care services like adult social care and nursery care a function of basic economics? Is it no different to low pay in, say, retail or hospitality, other sectors where jobs require no (or only basic) qualifications and where high staff turnover is expected? Much of the low pay can indeed be seen as part of a wider problem of sectors with relatively low productivity and tight margins. But there is also a confluence of factors, especially affecting face-to-face care work, that explains why relative pay has not risen much despite the increasing demand for care workers and the apparent lack of supply.

The first and most obvious point is that care workers of the kind we have been discussing tend to have *very limited bargaining power*. When care workers are gathered in large units like a hospital they can, and do, sometimes withdraw their labour, as we saw with the recent nurses' strike. But this is relatively rare and, in some countries, restricted by law.

In any case, most care work takes place in smaller units, whether in smaller nursing homes; care homes for adults and older people or in nurseries for young children. The adult social care sector in the UK is highly fragmented, with around 5,500 mainly private organisations operating from 17,000 separate homes (including 11,000 residential homes and 5,300 nursing homes). More than 30% have fewer than five employees, though there are some bigger chains that together employ almost half of the workforce. Unionisation is low, at around 15%, and concentrated in the larger organisations.

The fact that a disproportionate number of workers in basic care jobs are part-time women, like Nancy, with their own family responsibilities, reinforces the difficulty with bargaining power. It is also weakened by the commitment of the carer to the cared for, what is sometimes called the 'prisoner of love' syndrome.[15]

A second explanation is *the problem of measuring and pricing emotional labour*. As Albert Einstein is reputed to have said, 'Not everything that can be counted counts and not everything that counts can be counted.' It is easy to see how much a financial market trader has earned for their firm at the end of a given period.[*] But how do you measure or price the contribution of a conscientious parent, a long-suffering dementia nurse or an inspiring primary school teacher?

Or, to be more specific, consider an excellent hospital nurse, popular with all the patients, finishing a ten-hour shift on a geriatric ward, who has just made the lives of 25 older people that little bit

---

[*] Rewarding individual performance is more complex than it seems, as many high-flyers are over-rewarded because the teamwork, support staff and infrastructure that lie behind the top trader or fund manager are not sufficiently factored in.

better. What if the nurse who follows her (or him) is not as good, treats the patients brusquely and handles them roughly? How can one reward these different contributions in the way that they would be remunerated in some other walks of life?

Care work is too often seen as a kind of undifferentiated lump of labour. But there is an ability hierarchy in care as in all other areas of life, yet the first-class carer who all the residents of the home adore and who brightens everyone's day is paid the same as everyone else. One of the questions this raises is whether it would be desirable to introduce more merit pay into care jobs, and how this could be done in a way that would be seen as fair and that would help to raise the overall status of such jobs. Individual merit-based or performance pay tends to be unpopular in workplaces, but there are other ways to reward performance through, for example, creating more rungs on the workplace ladder, with promotion opportunities reserved for the best performers. In many freelance jobs, including in the private care job market, there is an implicit merit system based on whether you get the call back.*

The standard economist's explanation for why work in care is so poorly paid is that almost anybody can do it. What they mean is that the work is mainly learnt on the job and requires few, if any, qualifications

---

* My brother-in-law, George, who, as mentioned in Chapter 6, damaged his spinal cord in a riding accident and has been quadriplegic ever since, requires two carers, twenty-four hours a day. He receives a Personal Health Budget from the NHS, which means he employs freelance carers direct from a website (he uses one called PA Pool) and can therefore pay them more than he would if he went through a normal domiciliary care agency. He has kept a core of carers in recent years with whom he has a close relationship. But sometimes he needs to recruit someone new for a few shifts. If that new person doesn't perform well or is unsatisfactory in some other way, he or she does not get called back. If they do well, they potentially join his core group of carers if they wish to.

of a cognitive kind. Most nurses in rich countries do now have university degrees, reflecting the more medically technical aspects of the work. But what is often most significant in the care aspect of nursing, and social care work, is implicit and embodied and hard to capture in an exam. Emotional intelligence is not the written, articulated kind.

Another factor in keeping pay depressed is the so-called Baumol effect, named after economist William Baumol, who argued that as productivity increases in the more automated economic sectors the displaced workers end up in *sectors where productivity is inherently low.* Adult social care is one such sector and productivity has, indeed, been declining in recent years, partly because it is mainly delivered by small, family-owned companies who are wary of innovation. Some of the bigger chains, by contrast, are highly leveraged, private equity-owned entities expert at extracting cash – generally in affluent retirement areas – so even if productivity improves, it is unlikely to provide a route to higher staff rewards.

There is a final, more fundamental, factor behind the undervaluing of public care work, which is that most of the poorly paid care sectors, in both adult/elder care and nursery care, are *directly or indirectly dependent on public spending.* Local authorities oversee commissioning and pay for most forms of ongoing non-NHS care for disabled children and working-age adults as well as old people, for which they receive a central government grant to pay the mainly private providers of that care. Central government used to pay directly for some social care through the housing benefit system, but that stopped after the 1988 report by Sir Roy Griffiths.*

---

* For an overview of the changes, see https://en.wikipedia.org/wiki/Care_in_the_ Community. The transfer of responsibility to local authorities is one reason why there was a sharp fall in planning permission for residential care homes after the 1990s; local authorities knew they would have to pay for all of the care.

And unlike politically sensitive spending on the NHS, the Treasury is able to squeeze the social care budget – as it did by 8% in real terms between 2010 and 2017, despite rising demand. While the NHS serves the whole population, long-term care for older people and younger adults at any time directly serves less than 1 million. For most people under 50, it does not seem a pressing issue. The 300,000 working-age recipients of care are divided between about 50,000 in care homes and 250,000 at home, while the 550,000 older people are split between about 250,000 receiving care at home and over 300,000 receiving residential or nursing home care (split about 60:40 between state and self-funders).[16]

Public spending on social care has picked up in recent years. It now stands at £27 billion a year, with another £9 billion paid by private funders. Yet many local authorities (for whom social care often represents *more than half* of their total budget) have been forced to tighten their criteria for who gets care and use their power as the main bulk purchaser of places in homes to drive down unit costs to well below the cost of provision.

The average weekly cost of an older person in a care home is around £800. Local authorities only cover about 80% of the cost to the care home, and the difference is made up in many cases by the self-funders, who therefore pay more than £1,000 a week. The result is that profit margins are tight and many homes go out of business every year, which in turn means there are fewer long-term residential places for older people than in 2015. The Nuffield Trust says that fewer than half of the nearly 2 million annual requests for support, for adult and elder care, result in a service being provided.[17]

This system has been recognised as dysfunctional almost since its inception, with what often seems like an arbitrary distinction between tax-funded NHS cancer care and self-funded dementia social care, and now a knock-on effect on a bed-starved NHS when older patients cannot be released because of the bureaucratic complexity in arranging a suitable care package. (There is actually spare bed capacity in the care system, usually around 30,000. It is not the lack of care home beds that stops people being discharged from hospital sooner, but rather the time it takes to establish an agreed care package.)

Most private funders are not rich, as they include anyone with assets of £23,000, including the value of a house (for home care, the house is not included in means testing). Several reports, including the Dilnot Commission report of 2010, have recommended big increases in investment in the sector as well as caps on the high costs faced by a small number of self-funders. A substantial minority will face costs of over £50,000 and one in seven over £100,000, so some have to sell their home as a result. Politicians of both main parties have repeatedly postponed major reform, and at the July 2024 election both parties were, again, promising a cap on costs and more investment in the workforce.

The system has been able to limp on thanks to the relatively small number of people who are adversely affected at any given time. This reduces the sector's bargaining power, exacerbated by the fact that, unlike the NHS, it has no single voice. Meanwhile, a rising minimum wage and, recently, higher immigration has prevented an even bigger recruitment crisis. The sector was quietly hopeful that the new government elected in July 2024 would make a difference, at least when it comes to pay and recruitment with Labour's proposed Fair Pay Agreement (see Chapter 9).

In a typical consumer services market, with sharply rising demand and a shrinking labour supply, wages would rise and new providers would enter the market competing on innovation and quality. If that did not happen it would be regarded as a market failure and a case for political intervention. But social care is already a quasi-market overseen by the state. This is, therefore, a case of *political* failure, indeed one of the biggest in the UK in the past generation, and one that raises questions both about the country's ability to plan and invest over longer time horizons and about its flattering self-image as a benevolent and caring place.

It also provides a classic case of the structural problem facing so many of the low-paid hands-on care jobs in rich country economies. As academic Amy Wax points out, those jobs, when done well, produce benefits for society and the recipients of care that are not captured in the rewards to caregivers. We recoil from the idea that being able to enter the home of an elderly stranger and help them to take a shower with dignity and humour is *unskilled*. Yet that is what the pay packet says.

What seems to be happening now is this: there is a silent, unco-ordinated withdrawal of labour by many hundreds of thousands, maybe millions, of women who are no longer prepared to provide that demanding, intensive emotional labour for the minimum wage. They are no longer prepared to be prisoners of love. And through the invisible decisions of many women choosing *not* to become care assistants in the NHS or domiciliary care workers in the social care sector, instead taking a less stressful clerical or retail job, a recruitment crisis has arisen.

It is a silent revolt of everyday women, who are often more family than career-orientated. But, like their graduate sisters, they have other options too, and will take them if care jobs (which many of them, like Nancy, would *like* to do) are not made more attractive. It is noticeable how weak their public voice has been. Addressing the concerns of these women could help to alleviate two of the country's separate long-term problems: the recruitment crisis in social care and the plunging fertility rate. But there is no cross-party group of MPs lobbying for either a higher minimum wage in social care nor to make motherhood less stressful by making it affordable for one parent to stay at home for a couple of years after giving birth.

Most women's organisations, most women MPs and bodies like the Women's Budget Group do support more investment and higher pay in the hands-on care sector. But that cause has not had the galvanising power, or the media impetus, of the #MeToo movement or the lobby to increase childcare subsidies. As Madeleine Bunting puts it: "I wish a fraction of the energy and profile of the #MeToo movement could find its counterpart exposing the care deficit."[18]

The concerns of professional women, who have most to lose from the motherhood career penalty, tend to dominate public policy on these issues. And the Treasury, with its concern to maximise employment and GDP, is on their side. The result is that in spring 2023 it was announced that an extra £4 billion or more a year would be spent on childcare for children as young as nine months, more than twice what would be needed to pay social care staff an extra £1 above the national minimum wage.

The majority of women, including those in public life – and most men too – would support *both* improved childcare and better pay for women in Cinderella caring jobs. But when there are limited resources, the squeaky wheel gets the oil. And the cause of raising the pay and status of jobs in female-majority care sectors seems to speak to women's past, trapped in stereotypically female work, not to women's future, as free as men *not* to do care work.

To care egalitarians, that future is achieved by a well-funded system of formal childcare, at least for those who still want children, freeing up women to do more rewarding work at their office desks. But this new arm of the welfare state has had a difficult birth, which helps to explain why it leaves so many feeling dissatisfied.

WHAT'S GONE WRONG WITH CHILDCARE?

The UK's childcare system, uniquely among rich countries, is both relatively highly subsidised by the taxpayer yet still among the most expensive to parents, especially for infants under three years of age.[*] It is currently undergoing a big expansion of state support for those younger infants, which is likely to be given further impetus by the Labour government which is proposing to open another 3,000 nurseries in primary schools. But its development over the past 25 years illustrates some of the themes of this book: the prioritisation of recorded GDP over well-being; a distrust of conventional family life and a desire to 'save' young children from family, especially those from disadvantaged homes; bypassing family and extended family-based care in favour of the formal nursery care favoured by egalitarians and the professional parent lobbies.

What is less well known is that the bureaucratic, top-down childcare framework that has grown up over this period also illustrates the pitfalls of allowing legislation to be influenced by lobby groups in response to tragic events. The tragic event in this case was the death of eight-year-old Victoria Climbie, who was tortured and murdered by her great-aunt and great-aunt's boyfriend in London in 2000. Although she was known to various state agencies and made repeated visits to A & E, nobody in authority joined the dots or interviewed her on her own.

In the shadow of her death, the Labour government produced a Green Paper, Every Child Matters (2003), that informed the Sexual Offences Act (2003), the Childcare Act (2006) and the Early Years

---

[*] According to the OECD, between 2004 and 2021 the UK has come top, or second to the US, in costs of childcare to parents.

Foundation Stage (EYFS, 2008), the statutory framework which governs all education for under-fives (and some years later the Working Together to Safeguard Children regulations). Much of this legislation was influenced by the 'Big Five' children's charities: Save the Children, The Children's Society, the NSPCC, Barnardo's and Action for Children (formerly National Children's Home).

Obviously, the care and safety of children is a proper goal of government, and the focus on childhood vulnerability chimed with broader New Labour goals to reduce child poverty and inequality. This was embodied in the Sure Start centres for infants and parents that began to be opened in 1998. The backdrop to Every Child Matters also, however, helped to build in an excessive bias towards regulatory safeguarding, established the most stringent carer-to-infant ratios in formal care settings in the rich world, and helped to undermine the traditional childminder sector by including them in the same regulatory framework as nurseries. It is a good example of the 'ratchet' problem in welfare states: there is always political pressure for more protection and regulation, and much less to scrap or even revisit measures.

The original Every Child Matters Green Paper was anodyne enough, mainly focusing on reshuffling the social services bureaucracy to avoid another Victoria Climbie case and unveiling a Children's Commissioner and a Minister for Children. It had little to say about real families and their problems: single-parent families were scarcely mentioned, there was nothing on help with parenting or couple relationship trouble when children are young, and, most important in the Climbie case, nothing on the informal fostering arrangements among some diaspora communities that caused her to fall into such unsuitable hands.

There was, however, a pervading sense that the state must step in to protect children from their parents, with 3–4 million children, out of a total of 11 million, described as 'vulnerable'. There was also an academicisation of the early years, with an assumption that two- and three-year-olds should already be learning, not just playing, and that this learning should be monitored and recorded. This was underlined by a simplified graph from a 2003 academic paper by Leon Feinstein, now an Oxford professor, that showed bright but poor two-year-olds being overtaken educationally by less bright but affluent two-year-olds by the age of seven.[19] The graph helped to give moral impetus to New Labour early years policy, though it turned out to be based on a misreading of the data.

The initial focus on education and school preparation for disadvantaged children has faded somewhat in recent years, but free childcare hours have been lapped up by middle- and higher-income dual-earner households.* These free hours, for parents who work more than 16 hours a week and earn less than £100,000, plus tax breaks and support through Universal Credit, currently cost the taxpayer more than £4 billion a year, but that figure is set to rise to over £9 billion following the big expansion to 30 hours per week for 38 weeks for all children from nine months by the end of 2025.

Professional couples who have been using formal childcare intensively for infants under three, with no subsidy, have been hit with high costs in recent years. The costs have been so high thanks both to the high level of regulation that the Childcare Register and EYFS have imposed on private nurseries and childminders and the fact that the

---

* A reminder: subsidised childcare began in earnest in 2001, with 12.5 hours of nursery for 33 weeks of the year for 4-year-olds, extended to 3-year-olds in 2005. In 2010 the coalition government extended the free hours for 3- and 4-year-olds to 15 per week for 38 weeks a year, and later included 2-year-olds from disadvantaged homes. In 2017 the entitlement for 3- and 4-year-olds was raised to 30 hours a week, but only where *both* parents work.

state subsidy for free hours has not fully covered actual nursery costs, requiring nurseries to cross-subsidise from families who need extra hours. A family with two full time workers on the average wage, with two children, has been spending an average of 30% of their after-tax income on childcare. A colleague of mine who lives in Leeds, where she and her partner work full-time, pays £1,200 a month for nursery care for their 2-year-old plus £400 a month for an after-school club for a 5-year-old. Their combined care bill is more than their monthly mortgage payment. The bill would be significantly higher in London. The lobbying power of this group partly explains the big subsidy expansion of 2024 and 2025 to much younger children.

The EYFS is an outlier among high-income countries in setting out a curriculum and detailed learning and development targets for children from birth to five. Ofsted, the school inspectorate, then ensures that all nurseries, playgroups and childminders on the Childcare Register are pursuing them appropriately. The register lays down demanding carer-to-child ratios of 1:3 for children of 2 years and under. For infants of 2 years and over the number rises to 1:5, and for those aged 3 years and over it is 1:8. The number of infants per carer is significantly higher in most comparable countries. In France, for example, the ratio for children aged 2 and under is 1:5, and for over-2s it is 1:8.

And once strict ratios have been established, it is difficult to undo them. When England recently followed Scotland, switching from one carer per four children for two-year-olds to one carer per five, it attracted vocal resistance. A more radical deregulation proposed by Liz Truss in her brief premiership was seen off by the lobbying of Mumsnet and the Early Years Alliance. These restrictions have kept the cost of providing formal childcare high and discouraged new entrants, so the total number of childcare places in the UK has remained around 1.5 million for ten years (around 1 million nursery based places, 350,000 school-based and 150,000 childminder places).

What about the workforce and the quality of childcare? As with other areas of low-paid care work, many nurseries struggle to recruit and retain the staff they want. Like care of older people in the UK, nursery care is delivered by a large number of mainly small, private organisations – around 56,000 providers in all (including childminders) – though some consolidation is starting to take place in the sector. The private nursery workforce is about 350,000 strong, with most non-managerial nursery staff paid around the minimum wage. Low pay levels contribute to an annual turnover rate of around 15%, with some nurseries hitting 25%. A 15% turnover is around the national average, but in a job that requires strong attachment between an infant and a key carer, especially below the age of three, it is suboptimal. Infants can create secure attachment relations with nursery carers, but not if they are changing every few months.

The UK has opted for a high-regulation/low-qualification childcare model. It is possible to get a job in a UK nursery with no (or only basic) qualifications. A majority of staff in most nurseries will have a level 3 NVQ in childcare and education, the vocational equivalent of an A level, and about 20% have degree-level qualifications.

This top-down system of paying subsidies direct to childcare companies to provide a preschool curriculum does not fit well with the hugely varied wishes of parents with young children. But the regulations have been an even bigger problem for the traditionally more informal and flexible childminding sector. Childminders have to adopt an EYFS 'school-readiness' curriculum, register with Ofsted, and take various safeguarding, paediatric and food hygiene courses. Unsurprisingly, the number of childminders has more than halved since 2008, from almost 70,000 to around 25,000, though that is also partly because nobody is promoting recruitment to the sector since local authorities handed over inspection to Ofsted.

Some parents would prefer an old-fashioned childminder, for a few hours a week, who may have little book learning but loves children and has plenty of experience with them, including having some of their own. Others will want a more full-time, demanding preschool experience. And there are, indeed, some disadvantaged children from homes that are either neglectful or incompetent, or where they are not spoken to in English, who are better served in formal childcare even before the age of three for both educational and socio-emotional reasons.

But it is not clear that the big taxpayer subsidy has had a positive effect, so far, on either children's school readiness – which has deteriorated since the pandemic – or more maternal employment. The IFS has found that the free entitlement has had an 'underwhelming' impact on both.[20] Christine Farquharson of the IFS predicts that the 2024/25 expansion will provide little benefit for the poorest 30%, partly because of the condition that both parents must work at least 16 hours a week. The main beneficiaries, she says, are expected to be two full-time worker households in London and the south-east with no grandparent care available.[21]

For most infants under the age of three the formal preschool aspects of the EYFS seem excessive, as it is socio-emotional development that matters more than education at that age. A 2014 longitudinal study by researchers at the London School of Economics concluded: 'The most important childhood predictor of adult life satisfaction is the child's emotional health, followed by the child's conduct. The least powerful predictor is the child's intellectual development.'[22]

The childcare story is an example of overly statist support for families that cuts against the grain of family affections and makes support dependent on both parents working. Support that cuts *with* the grain and channels public subsidy direct to families should be the guiding light for reform. The next two chapters look at some of the ways in which that can be achieved and how the status of nurture and care work, in both the domestic sphere and the public economy, can be placed on a new footing.

8

BRINGING IT ALL BACK HOME

Now women are in a stronger bargaining position with their fertility than at any point in history. But the private incentives to have children are in decline. If we want fertility to increase we will have to offer better incentives than we currently do.

Ellen Pasternack, *Works in Progress.*

Feminist ideology has never dealt honestly with the role of the mother in human life.

Camille Paglia, *Free Women, Free Men*

I do not worry that my two daughters might fail to achieve their professional goals because of sex discrimination. I do, however, worry that they may leave settling down and having children too late to have the number they want, or any at all. It is a worry shared by others in my circle of parents. It has many causes, of course, but flows in part from the deeply embedded downgrading of the domestic realm.

Consider this: The official Department for Education guidance that seeks to attract people to work in childcare says that 'no job is more important than working with children in the early years.' On the other hand, mothers who leave the labour market to do this same job, unpaid, are implicitly being told by the government, and explicitly by countless think tank and academic reports, that they are wasting their potential and must return to work to regain status as contributing members of society.

What if aspiring to become a parent was welcomed as much as aspiring to have a career, and nobody felt they had to choose between the two? It would not require revolutionary change, but our streets, companies and public institutions would certainly look different.

Raising the status of the domestic sphere should be seen as the *culmination* of what Claudia Goldin calls the 'grand gender convergence', not its reversal.[1] This should mean not only that women are free to pursue careers, with men pulling their weight at home to make that easier, but that stay-at-home mothers and increasingly fathers – and their work of raising children and contributing to neighbourhood life – would be regarded as equally important.

Goldin's economic work on how 'greedy jobs' (those jobs at the top of the professional tree that demand your life and soul) can be made compatible with family life helped to win her the Nobel prize for economics. But the work of being an attentive, conscientious parent is also a greedy job, at least when children are very young. And, with some planning, it can be shared between two parents and other primary carers to reduce the motherload.

It is not a job that requires forgoing advances in sex equality. Historian Erika Bachiochi puts it like this: 'For those of us who grew up with the anti-discrimination gains of the 1970s securely in place, there is no question that women are as capable of educational and professional achievement as men. The questions have now become why the essential work of caring for dependents – still

undertaken disproportionately by women – is not valued and supported as it should be, and why poor women, especially, continue
to be bereft of the paternal support they and their children so
heartily need.'[2]

Neither is it a job that requires disappearing into a stay-at-home
bunker. As Ruth Kelly, the former Labour education secretary, says,
'These debates tend to be framed as "mother at home in nuclear
family" versus "state liberating women from drudgery of homemaking", but there is a big space in-between with, for example, parents
coming together to organise and run things.'[3]

Anne Fennell, the chair of Mothers at Home Matter, says that part
of the problem lies in the very phrase 'stay-at-home mother'. She told
me: 'Not much of my time is actually spent at home, let alone at the
kitchen sink. Home is base. I have developed interests often around
what my children were doing: helping to run toddler groups, chair of
the PTA, and so on. Affording not to go out to work has been hard
at times, but when we needed the money, I did some paid work. Life
doesn't stop when you have children – on the contrary, it can open
up. We just don't tell that story. It doesn't appeal to everyone, but so
long as one is in a positive relationship there can be more freedom
than being tied to working hours and office structures.'

Not all stay-at-home mothers have the drive or accomplishment
for a life like Fennell's. But her perspective is not often heard in public
conversation, which overwhelmingly frames freedom for women in
terms of the freedom to participate in the labour market on equal
terms with men. And why do we rarely hear from women or men
who want the domestic realm to receive its due?

A stay-at-home-mother friend, Caroline Ffiske, puts it pithily:
'I'll tell you why. Women at home are too busy actually doing what
they do – caring, loving, building a home, running the PTA, etc,

to raise their profile in the public domain. By contrast, women in the workplace are in the position to argue the case for closing the gender pay gap, more women in the boardroom, and so on. Moreover, actual face-to-face caring is not scalable. So, a woman who spends her entire life looking after her disabled son is not going to get an OBE, but a woman in the workplace who campaigns for recognition for women looking after their disabled children will get the OBE. By definition, it's those in the workplace who can participate in the national conversation, while those at home quietly get on and do what they do.'

This is not an either/or. Family-focused women are, in my experience, almost always fully supportive of their sisters pursuing careers. Care balancers and reasonable care egalitarians should be able to agree on a cluster of moderate reforms that address three overlapping goals. First, the old equality goal of making it easier to combine motherhood and work, including at the highest level. Second, strengthening the family and supporting family-focused parents to remain at home when children are young. Third, the pronatalist goal of attempting to stop, or at least slow, the plunge in fertility. The rest of this chapter looks at how to achieve those goals.

TRANSCENDING THE HOME V WORK DIVIDE

State and employer support in the UK both for the family in general and for better enabling the combination of parenthood and work is still patchy, and far less good than in many other high-income countries. The fact that such support is less generous than elsewhere must be one factor behind the UK's depressing status as the family breakdown champion of Europe. It is also a factor behind the shockingly high level of abortions in England and Wales, 251,377 in 2022, representing around one third of all conceptions, again the highest in Europe, with rates twice as high in low-income regions. Even in the area where there has been a strong elite consensus and considerable policy action – subsidising formal nursery care and promoting flexible arrangements for mothers wanting to return to work – the UK lags behind many comparable countries.

So, to recap, what does the parental support deal look like? In the UK maternity leave lasts a year but is only paid for 39 weeks, and for only 6 weeks at a decent rate (90% of previous average salary). Most Organisation for Economic Co-operation and Development (OECD) countries pay mothers more than 50% of their previous earnings for most of the leave period, and 17 countries, led by the Nordics, pay between 80% and 100%. And paternity leave is much more generous in several European countries, with three months now becoming the norm, rather than the two weeks that the UK gives, with simpler sharing arrangements between parents. A mother's pension contributions and holiday entitlement continue while on maternity leave and employers must keep her job open, though any employment lawyer will tell you that companies are adept at escaping this obligation if, for whatever reason, she is not wanted back.

After birth a mother, at home, will receive some support from a midwife and then health visitors and should receive a full health visitor assessment for mother and infant at two weeks and eight weeks, and then again when the infant is aged one and two. The mother will also start receiving child benefit at £106 a month for a first child and £70 for subsequent children, usually stopping at the age of 20, though the benefit is reduced and then withdrawn for high earners.[*]

---

[*] The 2024 budget reduced the clawback somewhat for higher earners.

For poorer parents there are other benefits.*(Though, thanks to welfare cuts since 2010, including the benefit cap and the two-child limit, parents with children who were on benefits have lost an average of £1,900 a year, single parents £2,600 and families with three or more children £4,600.)[4]

When returning to work there are 30 hours of free childcare now starting at age two, though falling to nine months in 2025. There is also the right to request flexible working from day one in a job. But for a mother who plans to stay at home for a few years while children are of preschool age there is no support at all, apart from the fact that pension contributions continue so long as you are claiming child benefit (until the child is 12). And, as already noted, there is only very limited recognition of family responsibilities in the individualised tax system, so there is a big bias against single-earner households. Plus there is the welfare system's so-called 'couple penalty' that withdraws benefits abruptly when a non-earner forms a household with an earner.

This is not a generous package for most people and might be looked at with some trepidation by a young woman without a well-paid partner, and if British politics does become serious about dealing with the baby bust, then almost every aspect of it will need to be improved.

The political class is somewhat insulated from how stingy the package is by the fact that better-paid people in professional employment, or those employed in blue chip companies and parts of the civil service often receive much more generous parental leave and support.

---

* Benefits include support for housing and child support through Universal Credit (which has absorbed Child Tax Credit), plus a £500 Sure Start maternity benefit, support from local Sure Start centres or Family Hubs (if there is one in your area), and free school meals when a child starts school. For single mothers, there should also be child maintenance payments from the father (though these are unpredictable and nearly half of mothers receive nothing).

It is not unusual for higher-paid professionals to receive close to full pay for a year or more while on maternity leave and for paternity leave, too, to be much longer and more generously supported. The daughter of an acquaintance of mine got a top job at a well-known entertainment company on a salary of £160,000 a year, and no sooner had she been offered the job than she discovered she was pregnant. She offered not to take up the post but the company, perhaps aware of their legal obligations, insisted that she still join them. She worked for the company for a few months then took a year's maternity leave on full pay; she then returned for a year and then became pregnant again and repeated the process.

For women doing ordinary non-professional jobs for whom promotion is not an important issue, the UK is a decent provider of part-time jobs (23%), more than most high-income countries. And nearly 40% of women work part-time compared to 14% of men, in most cases because of domestic caring responsibilities. As discussed, this is one of the reasons for both the continuing motherhood pay gap and poorer pension provision for mothers, along with the fact that the sectors where women predominate are not the high-paying ones. Nearly half of all women in the UK are employed in just three sectors: health/social care, retail and education.

Women are still rarer at the top of professional and corporate hierarchies, and less well paid when they do get there – at the 90th percentile, women's hourly pay is only about 80% of men's. That is partly because of missed promotions thanks to motherhood breaks and also the fact that at the pinnacle those very highly paid so-called greedy jobs predominate, requiring the kind of 24/7 commitment that is not easily compatible with family responsibilities. In addition, the UK's female labour market participation rate used to be one of the highest in Europe but has recently slipped behind Germany and the

Netherlands, both of which have more generous parental leave and childcare provision.

Yet there are several grounds for optimism on the motherhood/career balance, and the UK does at least as well, and often better, than comparable countries. For a start, reducing the motherhood penalty has been a central concern of human resources departments and women's professional and business lobby groups for three decades or more, with the emphasis on flexibility and family-friendly employment (for men too) at all levels in an organisation. Pronatalists, as well as anyone concerned with fairness between the sexes, should be cheering them on.

Employers have had to adjust to many kinds of maternal returners. There is the professional high-flyer who is back at work within a few months, perhaps expressing and storing breast milk, and wants no interruption to her career progress despite having, say, a couple of children. Assuming she is a valued member of staff, most large organisations will strive to eliminate any kind of motherhood penalty. The motherload pressures are, nevertheless, likely to be more intense than the equivalent for a young father in the same organisation. Who goes to pick up the child when the school rings to say there has been an accident? These issues will be played out differently in different families, with men increasingly becoming an equally go-to parent. And office norms are also changing. A Swedish friend tells me that no important staff meetings are ever scheduled after 3 p.m. at her university now because fathers as well as mothers are responsible for the school pickup.

Another kind of returner will be back soon after maternity leave but has lost some of her career focus because of motherhood and actively wants to join the 'mummy track'. In jobs where it is possible, such returners might prefer a mother-shaped job starting early and finishing at 2.30 for the school pickup, or a four-day week, or a job with lower intensity in the school holidays.

A third kind of returner is a mother who has taken a bigger chunk of time out to have a couple of children and is returning five years later with, possibly, professional confidence dented and skills rusty. Employers clearly require a degree of patience with such returners but, anecdotally, they will often amply repay the investment.

There is no escaping the fact that the flexibilities required by all three kinds of returner cost organisations, especially smaller ones that find it harder to adapt. Two recent pandemic-led developments – the normalisation of working from home and videoconferencing technology – help reduce the cost of that flexibility, for fathers too. These developments can not only ease the transition back to work for all women, at least for those doing office jobs, but can also help mitigate Claudia Goldin's 'greedy jobs' problem at the top for people with family responsibilities. There will remain some jobs that will always be 24/7 and demand the unsubstitutable person: CEOs, some barristers, merger and acquisition bankers, actors and sports stars, permanent secretaries, leading politicians. But just one rung down the ladder, technology and job design can do its work.

Goldin cites the example of pharmacist, an occupation which used to be dominated by men, often owning their own business and working very long hours. In recent years in the US many pharmacies have been incorporated into big chains and pharmacists have become better substitutes for each other with the standardisation of procedures and drugs. Computer systems, too, mean that the needs of a customer can be called up on a screen and do not require personal knowledge.

Pharmacy is a high-income profession in the US and is now one increasingly dominated by women, with a minimal part-time penalty and the lowest gender earning gaps among high-earning jobs. Such reforms are not possible in all professions, but Goldin thinks that working from home and videoconferencing technologies could be a 'game changer', providing the biggest boost to equality in professional careers since the arrival of the contraceptive pill.

And it is not only professional mothers who can benefit from this blurring of the line between home and work. For women without career ambitions who prefer to stay at home when children are of preschool age but want or need to continue working, the technology-enabled gig economy allows for bite-size working that can be fitted in around childcare. In the US, many young mothers drive Ubers or work in a call centre for a few hours when they have childcare help. My primary school teacher son has recently given up his job at a London school and is living in Cornwall for a few months. Every morning at 7 a.m. he can check whether there is supply work for him nearby or whether the surf is looking too good to miss. A parent can similarly indulge in such just-in-time working when childcare opportunities arise in ways that technology has only recently made possible.

One of the most important trends of the next couple of decades could be the return of the pre-industrial cottage industry, so long as regulation doesn't strangle it. A former science teacher friend gave up work when she had her second child, and a couple of years later started to feel a bit restless. She didn't want to go back to work full-time, so she started doing online GCSE science tutoring instead. There are many other jobs that lend themselves, wholly or substantially, to working from home: marketing and public relations, tutoring, therapy and counselling, journalism, researcher, childminder, designer of many kinds, personal trainer. Those are mainly middle-class graduate jobs, but thanks to the internet it is also now possible to run a small business from home, including something like a beauty parlour or nail bar. Shopify and other e-commerce internet platforms are also helping hundreds of thousands of home-based small businesses to flourish.

Before the great home–work schism caused by industrialisation, the household, in the words of Erika Bachiochi, was society's 'grandest sphere'.[5] (It's true it didn't have much competition, as for most people it was society's *only* sphere.) Then, for the next 200 years, the male-dominated world of paid work outside the home and the public realm of politics, media and collective action sucked up most of the prestige and status, and framed sex equality primarily around work outside the home. Women had to detach themselves from the domestic realm, and the fields of traditional female pre-eminence, to achieve status.

There is now an opportunity to partly heal that schism by providing women, and some men too, with a more genuine choice between two valued activities, in the domestic and public realms, and thereby give parenthood more room to breathe. That will only happen if we significantly improve on the current package that young parents contemplating a child can expect.

A BETTER DEAL FOR PARENTS

The UK offering on parental leave, child benefit, childcare support and family-related tax breaks and benefit payments currently represents a little over half of what is spent in the Nordic countries and about two thirds of that in France and Germany. The UK is now close to the OECD average on childcare subsidies and general family support (at 2.5% of GDP), but still has ungenerous maternity and paternity support, and little tax allowance for family life, so rounds out at around 3%.*

---

* These comparisons are notoriously difficult to calculate accurately, as different countries often differ in their categorisations. The OECD has lower % estimates but with a similar range. See their Family Database at https://stats.oecd.org/index. aspx?queryid=68251 to compare countries.

The Nordic countries, as well as France, Germany, Belgium, Poland, Hungary, Estonia and a few others, are all in the 3.5–5%-plus of GDP range. UK public spending is already at historically high levels, so we will not be able to match those countries, at least in the short term. Yet merely rearranging the current spending, and bolstering it in one or two places where we are outliers in our meanness, could relieve the pressure on young families, reward marriage, reduce the cost of formal childcare, and make it easier for one parent to remain mainly home-based in the preschool years.

There is a lot of anxiety around the whole process of childbirth at present in the UK, not helped by the current problems in NHS maternity care as well as a shortage of midwives and health visitors.[6] We have fewer antenatal appointments with a midwife in the UK than almost any other European country. Only a minority of parents attend antenatal classes, and the National Childbirth Trust has lost its once-dominant position.

A return to lying-in for any length of time after birth is not feasible for the NHS, but more intense support in the first few weeks would often be welcomed by first-time mothers, especially given that nearly 30% of new babies are now delivered by caesarean section, leaving the mother even more incapacitated. The Netherlands has an enviable system called *kraamzorg* (maternity care), paid by the Dutch health insurance system, under which a midwife comes to a new mother's house for several hours a day for the first eight to ten days after birth and guides her on health issues, breastfeeding and child development, and generally looks after her and the baby's well-being.

If we want more British babies, someone in the NHS should be working out how to create a home-grown *kraamzorg* system that mothers and fathers can opt into, especially if they lack extended family support. It might also be a way of increasing the supply of midwives who are currently leaving the NHS faster than they can be trained – thanks, it is said, to impossible, hierarchical working conditions. The relative autonomy of the *kraamversorgsters* (maternity nurses) themselves, rather like the admired Buurtzorg model for care of older people in the Netherlands, makes it an attractive professional career.

A friend of mine who recently gave birth in South London had six visits from five different midwives in the first few weeks after birth, all of whom gave somewhat different advice on baby feeding regimes. In an era when maternal wisdom is less likely to be handed down the generations, continuity of care and advice becomes more important. Regular face-to-face meetings with other mothers with new babies, preferably under the guidance of a knowledgeable individual, would relieve some of the anxiety. One of my sisters had one of her babies in New York, where her health insurance covered a weekly new mothers' group run by her paediatrician. She says it contributed to making her post-birth experience far better than in the UK. Another highly educated, highly capable friend said she had felt inhibited about joining a parenting group because she felt she shouldn't need the support, but was so relieved that she did. Without the multigenerational support that was once routine, most mothers can benefit from such support.

Labour's manifesto at the 2024 election promised to review the current system of parental leave, and one inexpensive improvement to the existing offer would be to extend statutory *paternity* leave from the current two weeks to closer to what is becoming the rich country norm of around three months. The BSA survey finds that almost 40% of people support an equal sharing of parental leave, and yet only about 25% of British men currently use all of the two weeks paid at £184 a week. Only 5% of men (about 10,000) take advantage of the current shared parental leave arrangements. The shared leave system is unnecessarily complex but even taking the two weeks' paternity leave would cost a man on average about £1,000 of lost earnings at a time when household costs have sharply increased with the arrival of a new baby. To make it easier for more men to take extended paternal leave, the first month should be paid at close to average earnings, along with doubling the higher-paid period of maternity leave from six weeks to at least three months.

This would cost the taxpayer and employers, but providing time for fathers to properly bond with their babies would give another shove to the popular idea (among most men as well as women) of a more equal share of domestic and childcare work, and thereby contribute to family stability. It would also help to adjust the expectations of people working in maternity care who often ignore the father's role, despite the growing understanding in the academic literature of his importance.[*]

Like paternal care, care by grandparents cuts with the grain of family life and, where feasible, is far more popular (and cheaper) than formal childcare. According to the Understanding Society household panel mentioned earlier, half of mothers returning to work after maternity leave rely to some extent on grandparents. But only around one quarter of grandparents are doing more than ten hours a week, so for those mothers who are working more than very part-time it is probably supplementing rather than replacing other forms of childcare.

Despite the fact that families in general are becoming smaller and more dispersed, in many places the extended family is still alive

---

[*] Marvyn Harrison, founder of Dope Black Dads, a support group for Black fathers, complains about having his presence 'erased' when wanting to help with his newborn.

in the UK. Around 60% of adults still live within 20 miles of where they lived when they were 14 and more than half, according to Understanding Society, live less than 30 minutes from their mother.

My own parents-in-law lived ten minutes' walk away when my children were young, and played an important role in their upbringing. Because they have no childcare training, the quality of grandparent care gets mixed reviews in the academic literature, but it is popular with parents and children themselves and is also good for the health and longevity of grandparents. It is especially important for single parents, and many people raised in single-parent households often talk about the special role that one or both of their grandparents played in their upbringing.

Not all grandparents can or want to care for grandchildren, but the extended family should be recognised and promoted by the state more than it is as a vital resource for both childcare and care of older family members. The charity Age UK estimates that there are 5 million grandparents over 50 who are providing regular childcare support, and some have stopped work or reduced their hours to do so. They ought to attract a Carer's Allowance in the same way that the 1.4 million people providing more than 35 hours per week of informal care to older people do. The broad principle is, in fact, already acknowledged in the fact that a grandparent under retirement age can claim National Insurance credits for childcare work.

Supporting young mothers, and the family and extended family more generally, with more generous maternity/paternity leave and formalising grandparent involvement, would be two small but useful steps. A much bigger step would be giving families the financial support to make it easier for one parent to stay at home, especially in the vital and stressful preschool years which so many partnerships don't survive.

This would be both popular and affordable. As noted in Chapter 4, nearly two thirds of the 2 million working mothers with children under five over the past 15 years said that they would work fewer hours if they could afford it, and one third would not work at all. It is true that some mothers currently at home would move the other way if they had convenient and affordable childcare, but the net result is still that the proportion of stay-at-home mothers with preschool children would be closer to 40% than the current 20% (23% with children aged 2 and under, and 15% with children aged 3 to 4).

The world is not ideal, because mortgage/rent and bills need to be paid, incomes have been stagnant in recent years, and children are expensive, so many mothers regretfully trail back to work. The state could, however, save many of them from having to do that merely by rearranging some of current spending on the early years into a Home Care Allowance (HCA) of nearly £10,000 a year for a first child and higher with subsequent children, for the parents to spend as they want.

There would be three elements to this package. First, instead of the state subsidising formal childcare through complex tax arrangements and paying nursery providers for free hours, the annual spend, which is heading beyond £9 billion a year, should simply be handed to all parents with preschool children to spend as they wish on themselves, on friends/grandparents or on formal childcare. This would work out at roughly £3,000 per preschool child a year.

Second, child benefit is worth about £20,500 for one child up the age of 16 (though it is often paid up to age 20). If it was 'front-loaded', with half being paid in the first three years of parenthood, it would give parents more than £3,000 a year. There is potential for abuse, for squandering the money on drink or drugs – as with almost any cash benefit – but the money is certainly more useful to most responsible parents when children are very young. The Child Poverty Action Group calculates that the weekly cost of a one-year-old child is double the cost of the same child aged ten and treble that of a sixteen-year-old.

The third part of the package, and the only one that would require significant extra funding, would be providing an extra tax allowance of around £5,000 each for couples bringing up children together (£2,000 for each additional child) and making it fully transferable between couples.[7] In the case of single-earner couples it would mean allowing the main earner to use all of their spouse's unused tax allowance, rather than the roughly one tenth that is currently permitted. As is widely recognised, the UK tax system is an international outlier in its unfairness towards families because it focuses on individual incomes and does not recognise households. An individual earning the average wage pays less in tax than their equivalent in France or Germany and less than the OECD average. By contrast, a single-earner married couple in the UK will pay considerably more than in either of those countries and well above the OECD average. A French person earning around £45,000 who is married with three children pays no income tax at all, while in the UK they would pay about £9,000 in tax and National Insurance.

This lack of a tax allowance for child-rearing not only disadvantages those who want or have to take on home-based caring responsibilities, it also reinforces the couple penalty in the benefit system by removing a potential incentive for a single mother to form a recognised new relationship. A tax allowance covering only parents with children under 18 would cost less than £4 billion, thanks to savings in benefits to poorer families. Restricting the allowance to couples with children below school age would cost just over £2 billion. This is not a large sum, and far lower than France's *quotient familial,* which takes account of family size, or Germany's income-splitting system.

The £2,800 average benefit of the tax allowance would take the annual value of the HCA to around £9,000 (and closer to £14,000 with a second child, with the additional child benefit and childcare support), something that would allow many households to support a mainly non-working parent when children are of preschool age. And this potentially game-changing reform would, if the tax allowance was restricted to couples with preschool children, cost about half of what the government proposes to spend on just the *increase* to free childcare hours planned for 2024 and 2025.[8]

Many people will sympathise with the case for supporting one parent staying at home when children are preschool but believe such support should cease once the primary school gates swing open. Why should mothers, or sometimes fathers, be helped to stay at home even when young children are at school?

But while it is the stressful preschool years that most deserve support, there is no reason why the HCA, in the longer run, should not apply to families with school-age children too. When a child is in primary school there are not many hours in the day once drop-off/pickup is factored in — certainly not enough time for a full-time job without the use of after-school clubs. Most stay-at-home parents who do want to work favour part-time work and should be allowed to keep the HCA, at a lower rate, for any earnings below £10,000 a year.

Some households with two full-time working parents survive happily enough, often with the help of nannies or au pairs for those who can afford them. Other two full-time worker households feel overstretched, with little time for cooking, household management and attentive childcare. When this is pushed to the sidelines it can make everyone more anxious, and contributes to those breakdown figures. If your job is not something you care about that much, it makes good sense for the individual to stay at home and it has clear, though hard to quantify, benefits for wider society.

National well-being should trump the small increments to GDP that might arise from persuading even more people, usually mothers, to swap parenting for paid work outside the home. Economic policy should be about maximising wealth, but in ways that are compatible with social cohesion, satisfying work and home and family life. Politicians have lately been worried about a post-Covid decline to the employment rate and an increase in economic inactivity levels. But the employment rate (at 75%) is already high by international standards and the economic inactivity rate (at 22%) is still below its average of the past 50 years. There are far better ways to improve growth rates than at the expense of family-focused parents. And should the 'economically inactive' category include stay-at-home parents at all? What is more economically useful in the long run than raising a well-balanced, productive citizen?*

Making it economically possible for twice as many households with preschool children to support a stay-at-home parent would represent a significant shift in the tempo of British life. Of course, parenting does not stop at the age of five, and were the HCA retained beyond the preschool years it would further incentivise worker-hungry employers to design parent-friendly jobs that take account of the school day and holidays. Family stress levels would also be reduced by making the UK's childcare offer more attractive.

* This is proposed by think tank Civitas in 'Back to Basics: What Is Childcare Policy For?', published in April 2024. The economic inactivity rate is also inflated by including the growing number of foreign students.

REFORMING CHILDCARE

Most of the countries that have the most generous parental leave, such as the Nordics, also have cheap, universal childcare, usually starting when the infant is 18 months or 2 years old. They cater both for the domestic-focused mothers and those wanting to combine motherhood with careers or jobs. This should be the long-term goal in the UK, too, though the public subsidy for childcare should be focused on children of two and older, mindful of the evidence suggesting that the emotional costs can outweigh the cognitive benefits for children in long periods of formal care under the age of two.

Many people working in nurseries are wary of the new initiative to subsidise formal childcare from nine months. One director of a nursery said to me: 'Of course, a child under the age of two who is put into long hours of formal childcare is going to suffer anxiety, not only because of the separation from their parent, but the fact that even the best nurseries cannot give them the one-to-one treatment, nor the warmth of cuddling, nor proper one-to-one eye contact so vital for their communication and language development. And then the anxiety levels of two parents working full-time is going to be absorbed by the child when they do get home.' Childcare has always had the double function of aiding child development and enabling both parents to work, and the two can be in tension when the ideal time in formal care for the child is less than the time needed by a parent to hold down a good job.

About 70% of parents with children under four use some form of formal childcare – nursery, playgroup, childminder – though for significantly varying time periods, and only around a third of parents were using formal care in the first two years before the 2024/2025 expansion. To repeat: the average childcare costs for such heavy users consumes on average 30% of parents' joint income, roughly three times higher than the OECD average of 9%, even though the UK government spend on childcare is above the OECD average despite 40% of parents not using their full entitlement.[*]

And even after the new subsidies fully take effect they will cover only a proportion of the costs of childcare for a double full-time working family with two children, as the free hours are only for 30 hours a week, for 38 weeks a year. That might be sufficient for the development goals of childcare, but not for its employment-enabling function. The combination of Childcare Register staffing ratios and EYFS detailed learning and development targets for under-fives, plus inspection of nurseries and childminders by Ofsted, has contributed to the high regulation-driven costs.

The EYFS learning and development targets cover communication and language; physical development; personal, social and emotional development; literacy; mathematics; understanding the world; and expressive arts and design. Most nursery care professionals say there is plenty of good sense in these targets, which mostly represent what an imaginative, conscientious parent might be doing at home. However, they are also highly prescriptive, and staff have to provide written records of progress in all these areas for inspection as well as feedback to parents. There is a strong sense among the early years advocates, who helped design much of the original legislation and continue to

---

[*] The lobby group Pregnant then Screwed claims that one in four mothers spend more than 75% of their pay on childcare. The cost of childcare is a real issue, but can be exaggerated. Most families use formal childcare only sparingly when children are under three, especially outside London and the south-east. Despite rising costs and stagnant incomes, fewer than a quarter of families found it difficult or very difficult to meet their childcare costs in 2022, rising to nearly a third for the more full-time children aged four and under: 'Childcare and Early Years Survey of Parents', Department for Education, Jul. 2023.

have the ear of government, that experts are better at raising children than parents, and that childcare providers themselves need onerous levels of oversight, and stringent staff-to-infant ratios, to make sure they are doing the job properly.

What childcare providers seem to want, however, judging by the nursery managers I have spoken to, is for Child Register ratios and regulations and the EYFS to be applied more flexibly. And they want the free hours subsidy to properly cover their costs – the 2024/25 expansion is, indeed, being generously funded – so they can afford to hire capable staff who will not leave after six months.*

The longer-term answer on staffing is to gradually raise the pay of senior nursery care staff to roughly the same starting salary as a junior teacher and to raise qualification levels, but not by simply trying to attract more graduates. Currently, every nursery must have someone with a first aid qualification and nursery managers must have at least an A-level equivalent qualification, though many managers do have degree-equivalent training. Nurseries that do have people with higher qualifications can relax their staffing ratios accordingly, but not many are attracting graduates, mainly because of the low pay relative to the long hours and emotional strain, even for women (it is a 95% female sector) who love young children.

In most European countries, by contrast, they have more relaxed ratios but more highly qualified staff, with many having degree-level qualifications. When a few years ago Sweden required all new pre-school staff to have a degree it did seem to help raise the status of the occupation, more so than with nursing. 'There was a noticeable

---

* At the time of writing in early 2024 there was some doubt about whether the expanded childcare provision could attract suitable staff at such short notice. There was an experiment in 20 local authorities with a £1,000 'golden handshake' to try to attract more recruits into, or back into, the sector.

change. When I came to pick up my little girl, I would often get earnest explanations from her main carer of what stage of language development she was at, or whatever the focus had been that day,' one Swedish friend told me. Nurseries should be looking to move in this direction, but without becoming a graduate-only sector. The model should be a two-tier one (as with the registered nurse/care assistant or teacher/teaching assistant model), with higher- and lower-qualified streams. The option of moving from the lower to higher stream, after appropriate experience and assessment, should always be kept open.

The best model for early years qualifications – which could also be the model for upgrading adult social care work – is, oddly enough, the accountancy profession. Accountants, unlike lawyers or doctors, do not require a degree but can move up the qualification ladder with a combination of experience and professional exams, from level 2 (GCSE) to level 7 (Masters). Trainee accountants can also branch off and take specialist modules in something like auditing, usually at level 4 or 5. Those with accountancy degrees can skip some of the exams but not the work experience. Similarly, people with a relevant degree in child development could skip some of the exams but not the on-the-job learning from more experienced nursery carers.

Nurseries should aim for a mix of people: some with no qualifications but the right temperament, others with a variety of mid-range qualifications rising to degree or master's level for some of the most senior staff, with conversion courses for graduates from related disciplines such as nursing or social care. But this will only happen if qualified staff are paid salaries commensurate with their skill, close to those in teaching or nursing, something that only becomes feasible with less onerous regulation.

The other means to reduce the cost of childcare is to rebuild the role of childminders, who were the biggest providers of formal childcare in the UK in the 1990s, especially for the youngest infants, for whom school preparation is least relevant. There are 25,000 childminders in the UK (down from 70,000 before the EYFS regulations kicked in), providing about 10% of the country's childcare for children under three; France, by contrast, has 256,000 *assistants maternels*, an exact equivalent, providing about 60%.

Childminders are often more flexible and, with lower overheads, normally cheaper than nurseries. Most childminders like the sense of professionalisation that the EYFS framework gives them, as it recognises their role as a great deal more than babysitting, but it should be applied in a more flexible way, especially when caring for children under three.*

Ruth Kelly, former Labour education secretary, has recommended two changes that could reverse the recent collapse.[9] First, taking regulation of childminders away from Ofsted and handing it to specialist childminder agencies that could strike a better balance between oversight and flexibility and promote a revival of the role. This is already happening on a small scale, but there are only three such agencies in operation and it is still cheaper for childminders to register with Ofsted. Second, creating childminder hubs, modelled on the *maisons d'assistants maternels* in France, that would allow childminders to work in groups and provide services outside domestic settings.

Currently, UNICEF ranks the UK 27th out of 41 rich countries for its support for young children.[10] Moreover, current childcare support is conditional on institutional arrangements that many parents don't

---

* A related problem is that when Ofsted took over the childminder inspection role from local authorities it was not tasked by the government with taking over the role of recruiting into the sector or promoting it.

want. But the introduction of a Home Care Allowance, along with the above reforms to childcare, could change the picture.

The arrival of a new baby, and in particular a first baby, is a profoundly stressful time for a couple's relationship. One simple way that the state can help is by providing a single online family hub with authoritative information about all manner of things: from nutrition, breastfeeding (including expressing and storing), sleep deprivation, dealing with the physical and sometimes mental scars of childbirth, reliable directions about child development and advice on how to protect the mother–father relationship. There is a huge amount of free advice already to be found online, but young mothers do not know who to trust and the imprimatur of the state would be a reassurance.

This is especially important for poorer families and single mothers with little support, but is potentially useful for all new parents. Labour's 3,000-plus Sure Start centres, focused initially on the poorest neighbourhoods, were designed to provide some of this support and advice in person. There is evidence that they did make a positive difference, but the debate continues about whether they were a cost-effective way of doing so.[11] As funding and management were gradually devolved to local authorities, most of them fell victim to post-2010 austerity budgets.

Sure Start centres have mainly been replaced by Family Hubs, which are now found in over half of the UK's local authorities. They deliver some but not all the family support available in a local authority area, and connect parents to the right people and places already delivering elsewhere. However, they are not the comprehensive one-stop shops that Sure Start centres aspired to be. Hubs are access points to the NHS, the welfare system, the charity sector or the private sector. Unlike Sure Start, they aim to cater for parents with children of all ages. But one important feature of the Family Hubs is their focus on relationships: through the government's Reducing Parental Conflict programmes they try to help couples deal with the inevitable conflict produced by the stress of early family life.

It is important that the Family Hubs (and the remaining Sure Start centres) take root and become part of the institutional infrastructure for all young families. But on current trends the Hubs will soon lack customers. The next section picks up the argument from Chapter 6 and considers whether anything can be done to stop plunging fertility rates.

CAN THE FALL IN FERTILITY BE STOPPED?

Having a child is a private matter with significant public benefits, as is all too evident from those countries like Japan and South Korea that have suffered the biggest drops in fertility. The physical and emotional cost of that private choice continues to be borne disproportionately by women. But thanks to birth control and shifting norms and expectations, the bearing of that cost is now optional for women in most countries. If we want more babies, the cost must be shared more fairly by society (taxpayers supporting decent childcare, maternity leave and so on) and fathers. Creating the conditions in which women have the number of children they say they want is the only way forward in both high-income and developing countries.

To recap from Chapter 6, around two thirds of the global population live in countries where the fertility rate is below the replacement rate of 2.1. Some parts of East Asia, Southern Europe and Central/Eastern Europe have reached an 'ultra low' of 0.8 to 1.3, which without unprecedented levels of immigration will lead to a population one sixth to one quarter the size in three generations. Yet even in countries with ultra-low fertility, or heading there, most women and couples still aspire to at least two children. This is one reason why the number of countries with explicitly pronatalist policies, aiming to raise the fertility rate, is rising and is now around 60 out of 195. This doesn't include the UK, where policies to encourage fertility have traditionally been regarded by progressives as conservative, if not nativist, yet most of the family policy tools – compensating parents, especially poorer ones, for the cost of children; reconciling motherhood with jobs and careers; supporting early childhood development – are also generally seen as enlightened.

It is sometimes said that you cannot 'bribe' parents to have more children with generous parental leave, cheap childcare, minimising the motherhood penalty in careers, rewarding bigger families with tax breaks, higher benefits, housing support and so on. This argument insists that culture is key and that individualistic high-income countries have lost, probably permanently, a natalist culture. The culture argument is not irrelevant but is too pessimistic. And it seems to be partly contradicted by the motherhood ambitions that most women still express.

We are adapting to lower fertility by raising retirement ages and running down infrastructure in regions with declining populations. Adaptation and pronatalist promotion are not alternatives, and although few countries have succeeded in raising fertility rates for a sustained period, pronatalist/family policies can be shown to have slowed decline and even produced temporary uplifts in several countries.

A paper by the United Nations Population Fund (UNFPA) found a strong correlation among OECD nations between high spending on families and high fertility, with France and the Nordic countries showing relatively strongly on both, and East Asian and Southern European countries doing poorly on both.

The UNFPA paper gives dozens of examples of short- and medium-term boosts to fertility provided by an array of incentives from improvements to childcare and parental leave to cash payments, including:

- After a fall in population in the 1990s and early 2000s, Estonia introduced Nordic-style parental leave and improved childcare and saw its fertility rate rise from 1.3 in 2003 to 1.7 in 2010.
- The Czech Republic in the 1990s implemented a family-friendly tax system and employer incentives to offer flexible working, further strengthened in 2017. Between 1999 and 2021 the country saw its fertility rise from 1.13 to 1.83.
- Australia introduced a baby bonus payment in 2004, rising to A25,000 in 2008, which is thought to have boosted the birth rate by more than 3%. There have been similar bonus schemes in Spain and Quebec, with similar results.
- Russia's 'maternity capital', a non-cash benefit that can be used for housing or pension support, raised the fertility rate from 1.28 in 2006 to 1.79 in 2016.
- Japan woke up to its baby bust, and 28% childlessness rate, in the early 2000s and has introduced several measures that have stopped the decline and slightly raised the fertility rate.
- West Germany used to have a male breadwinner model with poor childcare provision, unlike the old East Germany with a dual-earner assumption and free childcare, but in 2007 the unified Germany implemented a Nordic-style family policy which stopped fertility decline and boosted it slightly among the highly educated.[12]

There are many other such examples from the past 20 years. Most of them provided only a temporary boost that faded, in some cases because the incentive was withdrawn. Some of the incentives have also been very expensive. Hungary, for example, which introduced generous pro-family policies when the Orbán government returned to power in 2011 – with the declared priority of 'procreation, not immigration' – spends almost 6% of GDP on its package of well-paid parental leave, free IVF and loans which are partly forgiven as more children are born and written off on the birth of a third child.

Hungary's ethnonationalist framing of pronatalism is unlikely to win majority support in most European countries, and the Orbán package has been criticised by American family researcher Lyman Stone for not being cost-effective.[13] But it raised Hungary's fertility from the lowest in Europe at 1.2 in 2010, partly driven by high emigration, to 1.6 in 2020, though the rate has now fallen back to around 1.5.

However, the progressive-egalitarian Nordic approach is also expensive. Swedish parents get 480 days of parental leave per child to share (aside from the three months reserved only for the mother or father), at 80% of full pay. This is often topped up to 100% by employers. They then have access to heavily subsidised childcare for infants from the age of one, costing at most £150 a month, as well as the right to reduce their working hours by 25% for the first eight years of a child's life. Something similar is offered in Iceland, Finland, Sweden, Norway and Denmark, yet fertility is still heading downwards, led by Finland. Nevertheless, average fertility is still somewhat above the European average.

The Nordic model is an attractive mix of a parent-at-home, domesticity-supporting system, thanks to long and flexible parental leave and, on the other hand, a maternal work/career promoting system thanks to the heavily subsidised childcare starting at the end of parental leave or even earlier. They also now have significant 'use it or lose it' paternal leave of at least three months which, after a slow start in which only the highly educated took this leave, is now taken by most men.

This is, at least potentially, the twin-track approach this book has been advocating. Still, some home-focused women in Sweden complain that the system often forces them to hand over their children to formal nursery care much earlier than they want. Only Finland actively supports one parent to stay at home after the parental leave period is over, with around 40% using the Home Care Allowance for children under five.

France has the most pronatalist arrangements in Western Europe, though currently with much less generous parental leave than the Nordics, and is the only big country in Europe to come close to replacement, with a fertility rate of just under 1.7. Like Hungary, France has big tax breaks and cash transfers that explicitly reward larger families and preschool childcare that is free and mandatory at the age of three, with heavily subsidised childcare options before that (with childminders playing the main part). In early 2024, President Macron announced a 'demographic rearmament' policy consisting of a much more generously subsidised shareable six-month parental leave to replace the current three-year parental leave paid at only about £100 a week, for most of the period, and used by only a small minority of parents.

There are a couple of countries on the edge of Europe – Georgia and Israel – that have defied the trend and have above replacement fertility, and Georgia is a very rare example of recovering from sub-replacement fertility. The Georgia case, rising from 1.5 in 2003 to 2.2 in 2015, is sometimes attributed to the promise by the Patriarch of the Georgian Orthodox Church to personally baptise every third and subsequent child.* The more prosaic explanation is the sense of optimism and rapid economic growth following the peaceful revolution of 2003. Economic growth also seems to be driving the recovery from sub-replacement fertility in Kazakhstan and Mongolia.

The case of Israel, with fertility around 3, is unusual partly because it spends little on childcare. It makes up for this with the high fertility of the ultra-Orthodox but also because of a sense of threat both from Jewish history and from its exposed geographical position, which means that even secular Israelis have high fertility compared with people in comparable countries.

So what are the pronatalist lessons from this brief *tour d'horizon*? The case of Israel seems to point to the importance of a strong cultural presumption in favour of perpetuating the nation. This is hard to replicate in increasingly post-national high-income countries, and only 11% of British people think there is a duty to have children.[14] The celebrated 'Do it for Denmark' campaign was not promoted by the Danish government but was a light-hearted attempt by a travel company to encourage people to book an amorous holiday to stem population decline.[15]

In the absence of Israel's existential motivation there are clearly several necessary but not sufficient preconditions for higher fertility in high-income countries. These include the obvious ones of a sense of economic security, reconciling motherhood and work, having somewhere affordable to live, and having confidence in the durability of your relationship as parents. Pronatalist tax and welfare

---

* We may have no equivalent of the Patriarch of the Georgian Church, but the fact that the British royal family has been relatively fertile – and, maybe more important, that Victoria and David Beckham have four children – helps to normalise high fertility.

inducements should be generous and long-term, not regarded as short-term fixes.

Reversing Tolstoy's famous adage about families, it is probably harder to isolate the causes of happy fertility stories than it is to pinpoint the causes of the unhappy ones. The most unhappy Far Eastern and Southern European stories both feature relatively traditional gender norms, meaning a demanding second shift for women trying to combine career and motherhood, and a continuing taboo on children outside marriage. The Far East compounds the problem, with its long-hours work culture, very intensive parenting traditions and highly status-conscious societies that mean, for example, that educated South Korean women are reluctant to partner with men who are not at least equal with them in the educational and professional pecking order.

The argument that having two or more children is a public good, justifying a high level of public subsidy, is not yet part of the national conversation in the UK as it is in France, Italy and other European countries, and it may require further falls in fertility, towards the Japanese level of 1.3, to act as a wake-up call. Where France encourages large families, the UK still explicitly discourages them, both through lack of support in the tax system, the modest support for parental leave and high cost of childcare, the recent cuts to family welfare benefits, and since 2017 through limiting most benefits to two children.[*]

Since the UK fell below replacement fertility in 1973 – when Richard Nixon was in the White House – it has not occurred to any

---

[*] Typical of elite opinion in the UK, *The Economist* ran a cover story dismissing the idea that governments can incentivize higher birth rates saying countries will just have to adapt. 'Why Paying Women to Have More Babies Won't Work', *The Economist* (25 May 2024).

British government to do or say anything about the issue. Merely stating that the falling birth rate is a problem could make a big difference. And given what we know about unintentional childlessness, especially among women, there is a strong case for using sex education in schools to spell out how quickly fertility declines for a woman in her 30s and a man in his 40s. And ideally reproductive healthcare would start with an optional gynaecological check-up for women in their mid 20s, with a chance to discuss future fertility issues, something President Macron has recently proposed in France.

Many of us have become disconnected from our own physicality, especially the younger generations raised in a digital age of lightness and fluidity, and we need re-anchoring. Anna Rotkirch, the Finnish demographer, puts it like this: 'At the heart of the current fertility malaise there appears to lie a cultural ambivalence about care, dependency, and what it takes to make a new human being. We should relearn how to talk and teach about bodies, ovulation, biological differences between the sexes, how fecundity varies with age, and about voluntary and involuntary childlessness and the many shades in between.'[16]

Even with such a culture change, the challenge of bringing down the opportunity cost of motherhood for an educated woman is still a big one. Which is why, as mentioned in Chapter 6, it is sensible for policy to focus on making it easier for those who already *want* children to have as many as possible. For that reason, I recommend more generous public funding of IVF, as in countries like Israel and Hungary. Although it is recommended that three cycles of IVF should be offered on the NHS, it is usually much less than that, and about 75% of IVF treatments in the UK now take place in the private sector, at a cost of £6,000 to £12,000 per cycle. In Denmark 10% of children are born with the help of assisted reproduction, in Israel the figure is 4.3%, and in the UK it is 2.6%. More public support would make some difference, but there is also the danger of providing false hope for those who leave it late, and the small numbers will not move the dial much on overall fertility.

Another idea is redesigning higher education, as well as jobs, to fit around the reproductive desires of young women. Louise Perry has suggested making it easier to complete a degree or a further degree part-time over several years while having and looking after one or more children. At the other end of working life, we should consider rewarding the hard work of parenting by allowing a primary carer parent, woman or man, to draw their state pension two years earlier.

These ideas, along with a family tax allowance and Home Care Allowance, would be expensively privileging parents over non-parents, something that would not, as things stand today, be popular. But non-parents benefit in many ways from the taxpayers, carers, soldiers and so on that other people have raised. And if enough influential people become sufficiently alarmed at the consequences of the baby bust, the idea will take root that having babies is in the public as well as private interest. As taxes and public debt rise inexorably and growth stutters, it is possible to imagine a shift in concern and consciousness, somewhat akin to what has happened over climate change.

The corporate sector needs future workers and consumers and needs to play its part too, in, for example, thinking about how product design might help or hinder larger families. When, a few years ago, children's car seats became larger and it became impossible to fit more than two in the back seat of a car, it was suggested that this had persuaded some couples to stop at two.

Given the disproportionate influence of progressive opinion, regardless of which political party is in power, it may require a section of that opinion to at least stop being actively hostile to pronatalism to win this argument. Historically, parties of the centre-left have often been family-friendly: the founders of the Swedish welfare state, Roosevelt's New Deal, President Mitterand in France in 1981. And there are several points that can be made to appeal to today's progressive mind.

First, the simple idea that an ageing society is a more sclerotic one, lacking the fluid intelligence and innovative spirit needed to solve many of our biggest problems, including environmental ones. Second, as noted, many of the incentives required to make motherhood more attractive, especially to highly educated women, chime with the goals of sex equality. Third, most pronatalists are natural anti-discrimination liberals, meaning that as families become more diverse – including same-sex couples, blended families, and women having babies on their own – pronatalists (or most of them) want them all to have as many children as they want. Fourth, we may be heading for a low-fertility bottleneck, and if liberal-minded people do not have children society will be dominated by religious conservatives of various kinds when we emerge from this bottleneck.

In this regard there might be one glimmer of hope. Historically, as education goes up, fertility goes down, and in most rich countries non-graduate women still have more babies than graduates. But the gap has narrowed, and in the Nordic countries childlessness is now more common among the least well educated. Moreover, the most highly educated women, at least in the US, are starting to have more children than the somewhat less well educated. US women with a bachelor's degree average 1.3 children each, those with a master's degree average 1.4, and those with a doctorate average 1.5.[17]

If a section of the political, media and academic class did embrace pronatalism it would not only provide influential role models but also generate useful policy ideas, and one of those ideas could be to encourage more people to get and stay married. Many of the countries that have seen improvements in fertility, including Georgia and Hungary, have also seen increases in marriage. Couples who are married have more children than those who are not. Does that mean marriage should be promoted and encouraged alongside having babies?

IS MARRIAGE THE KEY?

Most people still like the idea of marriage, but fewer people are getting around to it, even when they have children. As noted, more than half of children in the UK are now born to unmarried parents. The UK is a European outlier in single parenthood but not in births outside marriage: the European average is over 50%, while in France the figure is 63%, though most couples are in a civil partnership and receive the generous family support in full. For those who do marry the story in the UK has improved somewhat, in that only about 36% of people who are marrying today are likely to end up divorced, down from a high of 44% in 1986.

In the UK, about 70% of the affluent and educated are still marrying, compared with less than one quarter of those in the bottom 30% of the income spectrum. In the US it is estimated that more one third of America's Gen Z will never marry. (And that is not just because of the expense of the typical modern wedding, though that is not helping.*)

Marriage has moved in my lifetime from being practically compulsory, to optional but mainstream, to a lifestyle choice for the better

---

* One Pew study in the US found that 73% of people thought that fulfilment came through having a good career and only 23% through marriage.

off. The pendulum has swung too far. Marriage sceptics will generally acknowledge the clear evidence of the far better outcomes in married families both for married people themselves and for their children. But they will claim that it is the characteristics of the population getting married – older, richer, better educated – that create the better outcomes, not the institution itself.

It is true that it is easier to create conditions of ongoing stability for children (which is the main point of marriage) if you have a good professional job than if you are living in a low-income area of town and doing two low-paid jobs. But a tough life is less tough if you have a companion who has committed to you in a public ceremony and who can share the stressful burden of child-rearing. Marriage is in fact *most* beneficial for those whose lives are toughest.

The evidence shows that the institution does matter, if you look at poorer young people who are raised in stable, married households and richer young people who are not. The stresses of single-parent life and the psychological distress of parental break-up when children are young are no respecter of class or income.

Marriage is not for everyone, and those of a certain temperament are likely to be more drawn to it than others. It is also true that there are plenty of cohabiters who have produced stable and happy family environments, but there is simply a higher risk of that stability ending than in married families. The public promise to 'forsake all others' made in the marriage ceremony in front of friends and family may be less sacred than a few generations ago, but it still counts for something. Around 60% of parents who never married split up in the UK, compared to 21% of those who married before their first child was born. And the evidence continues to stack up on the negative impact of family disruption on children's outcomes and mental health, as we saw in Chapter 3. Yet politics and legal reform continue to make divorce easier while doing nothing to prevent marriage from becoming an ever-receding ambition for almost half the population. Even around two thirds of divorced British adults think that it is too easy to get divorced.[18]

According to marriage experts, what has led to the epidemic of less secure partnerships in recent decades, even those involving children, is overhasty cohabitation, which often leads to getting relationship sequencing wrong. Cohabitation before marriage went from being almost non-existent in the early 1960s to the norm by the 1980s. In many cases the trial marriage led to a healthy, long-term real one, but in others drifting into the constraints of cohabitation, and maybe even children, preceded full dedication and then felt like a trap. According to Harry Benson of the Marriage Foundation, the divorce surge of the 1970s and 1980s, driven by unhappy wives, was partly a consequence of higher rates of cohabitation that was still combined with the strong social pressure to marry, pushing less committed men into half-hearted marriages.[19] As marriage has become more optional since the 1990s, it is only more committed men who go through with it, and divorce is now both lower and more equally initiated by both men and women.

If marriage used to signify dependence for women, it now provides protection for both men and women. Those who stick with long-term cohabitation in quasi-marriages are often surprised to discover that it does not confer the same rights as a real marriage or civil partnership. If the couple split up or one partner dies, there is no right to inheritance or financial support.

What is stopping cohabiters in their 20s and 30s today taking the step? Maybe seeing so many of their parents make a mess of their marriages. The wedding industry, too, has inflated the cost of a socially acceptable wedding out of many people's reach. According to the UK Wedding Report the average cost of a wedding, plus ring and honeymoon, is now £20,000.[20]

Over a third of marriages still end, mainly between years three and seven. I was married for more than 20 years but did not manage to stay the course, though I remain friendly with my ex and we communicate regularly about our four children. I do not advocate that marriage should always be forever (how could I?), though when children are still young couples should surely think harder than some of them appear to be doing before chucking it in.

The Marriage Foundation, as noted in Chapter 3, has produced some shocking data on how casually people leave marriages. An analysis of the authoritative Understanding Society survey found that 9% of couples could be categorised as high-conflict in the year before they split. Around 60% of married couples and 80% of cohabiting couples were low-conflict and reported some degree of happiness in the year before a split.[21] A YouGov survey of 3,500 divorced people found 'drifting apart' to be the main reason for divorce.[22]

This suggests that many more marriages would be salvageable if they were entered into with a greater appreciation of the inevitable troubles ahead and if more help was on hand, inexpensively, when those troubles start being experienced. The high-divorce society is both a cause and consequence of a surrounding culture that does more to encourage people to pursue their desires and autonomy than it does to sacrifice some short-term freedom for a longer-term reward.

People do sometimes make a mistake and end up in an impossible marriage. Long relationships are not easy to sustain, and people grow and change. Today, sexual infidelity carries less social stigma yet is often less tolerated by partners. Younger people face the extra stress of shifting gender norms, and more fluidity in sexual preferences, which might make solid relationships harder to establish in the first place. A recent survey by the American Enterprise Institute of 5,000 young Americans found that half of university-educated women and one third of similar men couldn't find someone who met their expectations.[23]

Maybe those expectations are too high. Mary Harrington complains about Big Romance and the difficulty of sustaining the inward-focused, self-expressive marriage. She prefers to regard the institution, especially where children are involved, as a joint enterprise based on mutual support and affection, rather than a romantic journey.[24]

And what is wrong with keeping up appearances for the good of the children? A university friend of mine told me recently that he lived separately from his wife at home for seven years while they shared parental responsibility for their two children. The youngest has just finished her A levels and they are now getting divorced.

The UK tax and welfare system is currently an active obstacle to marriage in the UK, despite all of the costs that this book has spelt out of the low-marriage, weaker family society. The legalisation of gay marriage is the one spectacular exception to this, but one that was not built on to promote heterosexual marriage.

What would help both to encourage people to get married in the first place, and then maybe to make a greater effort to stay together, is more public recognition and reward for the institution. Money does make a difference, especially for poorer people who are the ones mainly forsaking the institution, and so does the public approbation of elites and opinion-formers for whom marriage is generally a revealed, though less often stated, preference.

When the UK does eventually join most of the rest of the developed world in properly recognising families in the tax system, maybe it should be a reward only for those who commit for the longer term by being married or in a civil partnership? And perhaps the Home Care Allowance, too, with its front-ending of child benefit and direct payment of childcare subsidies to parents, should only be available to those who make some kind of public commitment.

Single parents and cohabiting parents with children should continue to receive their current support. Indeed, as noted earlier, to encourage single parents to create stable new couple relationships it should be possible to retain some or all of single-parent benefits for a period after forming a new relationship (as suggested in a Department of Work and Pensions paper) or have a new partner's income only counting against benefits above a certain threshold.[25] It is crucial to make state support less undermining of marriage, as it currently is, and the only decent way to do this is to provide extra rewards, as above, to those who make the commitment.

One other way that the public realm can support marriage, and couples more generally, is through more partnership *and* parenting counselling, preferably for free (at least for people on low incomes). Counselling should be available through Family Hubs and GPs with such a routine, universal offer helping to reduce any stigma or embarrassment. This is also useful for people parenting alone. Lone parents can overcompensate with parenting that is either too authoritarian or too affectionate and laissez-faire, rather than the authoritative 'love and boundaries' style that is usually associated with the best outcomes for children.

It is hard to tell how effective couple relationship counselling is in general, but specific programmes, such as the Reducing Parental Conflict programme directed at high-conflict families since 2018, are said to be making a difference.[26] Counselling services such as OnePlusOne and Relate have a strong online presence and a decent track record.

One minor but welcome proposal, floated by Gloria De Piero when she was Labour's shadow Culture Secretary, would be to waive the £70 marriage licence fee. A 2016 Conservative family manifesto took up the idea but said it should be conditional on couples agreeing to see a counsellor *before* marriage, perhaps in the way that people used to see a priest, to test their seriousness and prepare them for what can be a bumpy ride. Scotland's recent move to give cohabiting couples many of the same rights as married couples could help to blur the line between marriage and living together, though it is too early to tell whether this will contribute to more solid cohabitations.

Neither marriage nor pronatalism are yet popular ideas. But married people are on average happier, live longer and have more children, fewer of whom are depressed and struggling, and they are less dependent on the state.* By staying together they are also contributing to climate responsibility: it has been estimated that US households that experience separation use 42% to 61% more resources than they did before separation.[27]

Stay together and have babies for the planet, for your children's mental health, and for an innovative future that does not bankrupt your state! The state in most high-income countries, including the UK, needs citizens to take more responsibility for themselves and their family members both to prevent public spending running out of control and also to pay the taxes to better reward the everyday caring jobs that so many of us will either be working in or using in the coming decades. Improving the funding and image of the social care system is the main theme of the next chapter.

---

* According to the US 2022 General Social Survey, women aged 18–55 who are married are almost twice as likely to be 'very happy' (37%) compared to their single peers (19%), and married men aged 18–55 are also more likely to be 'very happy' (34%) compared to unmarried peers (13%).

9

RAISING STATUS AND SHARING RESPONSIBILITY

Care visits were often emotionally draining. It was challenging enough cleaning up the bodily fluids... but it would take a heart of stone not to be moved by some of the situations you encountered. I saw instances of elderly customers being left on their own by relatives with no food in the house, necessitating an unscheduled trip to the local shops... On one occasion I gave a blind man a bath, which took more than 20 minutes – the entire scheduled length of the visit. If you were late... a customer could be left sitting in a urine-soaked pad for hours, causing nasty sores.

James Bloodworth, *Hired: Six Months
Undercover in Low-Wage Britain*

The quote above is from journalist James Bloodworth, who worked briefly as a domiciliary care worker as part of a book-length survey of low-paid jobs. It is a familiar story at the sharp end of the care system, dashing from house to house to fulfil 20-minute or half-hour slots helping frail older people with everyday tasks like cooking, washing and getting dressed. The care workers themselves are sometimes paid below the minimum wage because travel time is not fully remunerated.

Everybody recognises that the social care system is unfair and inefficient, and needs more money injected into it, ideally both public and private, with some kind of cap for those facing excessive costs (usually dementia related). The sector supports nearly 1 million people and remains plagued by chronic staff recruitment problems, extensive unmet needs, and fragile finances of both the local authorities that fund most of the public support (now about £27 billion a year) and the mainly small, family firms that deliver the services. A smaller number of people with complex, expensive needs, especially among the younger people needing care, suck up a growing proportion of the budget.

For the future of older people's care, the best general model is surely the pension system. We need a decent basic care entitlement, part-funded by an extra National Insurance levy for those over 40, but with people encouraged and incentivised to fund extra services through special savings vehicles or equity withdrawal. (Care for younger working-age adults, roughly half of all social care budgets, would be mainly covered by the basic care entitlement.)

Local authorities should continue to manage the system, but the funding for the basic universal service should come direct from central government. Such a reform would nudge adult social care closer to the taxpayer-funded model of the NHS, though mixing in private funding from better-off people who have benefited from the property value windfall of the past 50 years. It would still leave private companies providing the bulk of care in alliance with families and friends, who are often essential to keeping people in their own home and out of hospital or residential care.

The system has grown haphazardly from its origins in the 1950s, when fewer people survived severe conditions in childhood and less care for older people was needed, as people died younger. The current distribution of resources and prestige between the NHS and social care might have been justified 70 years ago but is now obsolete and, to make it worse, most of the changes to the NHS in recent decades, such as closure of geriatric wards, have placed more pressure on social care.

It is a matter of adjusting our relative priorities and putting social care spending on a new footing, at an ongoing cost of around 0.5% of GDP. As a society, we have made several such commitments in recent years: the interventions to save the banking system after 2008, the equally extraordinary steps to preserve jobs during the pandemic, or the extra funding for the NHS after 2019 and during the pandemic. If the funding of long-term social care were to be combined with an element of co-payment in the NHS, and an introduction of private health insurance in the limited areas where it could work, there would be a much better balance between social care and health, while some of the increases in social care spending would be offset by savings to future health spending.

All rich countries have seen rising costs of ageing and more demands on both health and social care systems, but most either pay for social care out of higher levels of general taxation (the Nordics and France), have imposed special ongoing levies (Germany, Japan), or keep elder care largely in the family (Spain, Italy).* The UK is an outlier in the messiness of its system, the extensive unmet needs, and the potentially crippling costs to older people of modest means.

The current system uses technology poorly, has rigid demarcation lines between professional and non-professional staff, and has seen

---

* Sajid Javid, when Secretary of State for Health, met with his Italian counterpart in 2022 and was describing the spending pressures he faced in social care for the elderly, assuming his counterpart experienced something similar, only to be told that this was not a state responsibility in Italy.

productivity fall in recent years. It also has no single voice speaking for it in Whitehall, with responsibility shared between the Department of Health and Social Care, the Department of Work and Pensions, the Department for Levelling Up, Housing and Communities, and local authorities.

It is hard for people to navigate the current system, with different entitlements overseen by different arms of the central or local state: domiciliary care, residential and nursing care, day centres, home improvements for an older or disabled person, and benefits for informal carers are all funded and managed in different ways. When you suddenly need support, some parts of the system can work well, but another part of the system doesn't work at all, or there is a long delay that means peace of mind is hard to achieve.

A relative of mine was diagnosed with motor neurone disease a few years ago and reports that the initial hospital-based diagnosis went smoothly enough, as did the arrangement, with the help of an occupational therapist, of his Personal Independence Payment. The fitting of handrails in the house and acquiring a hospital-style bed also happened swiftly.

But arranging the home care necessary as his condition deteriorated became a long-running challenge requiring endless phone calls and the chasing of multiple officials. His needs assessment was agreed at two and a half hours a day, in a morning and evening session. His local authority offers non-means-tested home care, free to most residents on the grounds that it will keep more people out of the more expensive residential system. But council wages aren't sufficient to pay carers who live locally and who can therefore turn up at predictable times. My relative had to get used to being out of bed, washed and dressed at any time between 8 a.m. and 10 a.m. He and his wife, a doctor, are educated and articulate but still found the system frustratingly unresponsive. In the end they opted for more expensive, predictable care for fewer hours from an agency not on the council list, and were fortunate that the council agreed to support it.

I will not attempt here to provide yet another blueprint for a macro reform of the social care system, beyond the outlines I have sketched.[1] Rather, I want to focus in this final chapter on two of the book's over-arching themes – recognising and rewarding the role of the family in the provision of care, and raising the status of non-professional care workers. I will also explain why neither immigration nor technology are the answer to the pressures on the care system, though both have some role to play.

The recruitment crisis in social care, especially home visit care, is not an unfortunate fact of life. It could easily be resolved. People must be paid what economists call the 'efficiency wage': the wage needed to recruit, reward and retain people of sufficient skill and motivation to do the job well in an era when there are fewer Nancys (see Chapter 7) who are willing to work for less. People do get high job satisfaction from care work, but the desire to help others is not an inexhaustible resource.

This is not just a matter of pay but of rethinking our responsibilities. Longevity and technology are creating a deluge of extra care needs rolling our way: there will be an additional 3.3 million people over 65 in the next 10 years, requiring an extra 500,000 care workers on top of the current 1.6 million. As noted, the OBR predicts that spending on people over 65 will rise from 10% to 21% of GDP in the next 50 years.

These enormous numbers are both hard to grasp and seem a long way off, but if the UK is to avoid becoming a giant health and care system with a country attached, people and their families will need to take more responsibility for their own health. And these trends, in turn, will provide social care with the narrative and vocation it needs – to become the *national care prevention service*. If the job of the NHS is to fix people and dispatch them out of the back door of the hospital as quickly as possible, the job of social care should be to prevent them entering through the front door in the first place.

The NHS Constitution asks people to recognise that 'you can make a significant contribution to your own, and your family's, good health and wellbeing, and take personal responsibility for it.' Yet it does little to promote this idea. For decades people have been talking about shifting more resources in the NHS from acute care to prevention and community care – but little has happened, nor looks like happening in the near future. The NHS is biased towards expensive, high-tech hospital care where lobbyists such as doctors and suppliers are hugely influential. It is biased against public health and primary care, where many conditions can be tackled much more cheaply. We spend a fortune on putting out fires that shouldn't have started in the first place. This is why we need a national prevention service.

If we are to change the status and public image of the adult social care sector, and make it worthy of proper public and private investment, we need not only a new, more attractive narrative but also a much higher visibility. Residential care and domiciliary care for both disabled adults and older people is a key part of the national infrastructure, is found in every corner of the country, and has a growing role in local economies as the number of older people grows. It is under our noses, everywhere, and yet almost invisible. Schools should have more links with local care homes, volunteering should be easier, short-term gap year-type jobs should be encouraged, and older professionals wanting a late-career challenge should be encouraged to consider working as care managers. The social care sector is on course to play a bigger part in all of our lives. It needs more of our money and our attention, and in return it must open its doors and find its voice.

THE PREVENTION ROLE: REFRAMING
AND RESKILLING SOCIAL CARE

The UK is ageing unhealthily. Not all of this can be prevented. But millions of people could enjoy many more years of healthy old age – or 'healthspan' – and the system could save tens of billions a year if we lived more healthily from middle age onwards. And as the NHS has neither the motivation nor the capability to meet this challenge, social care must try to pick up the prevention baton as well as it can.

The UK ranks 16th in the International Longevity Centre's global 'Healthy Ageing and Prevention Index', with a large proportion of the population living for more than a fifth of their lives in poor health. About one third of all deaths in the UK are classed as premature.[2] Many illnesses in old age – heart disease, cancer and dementia – are exacerbated by lifestyle choices associated with loneliness and stress that more social connection and a richer family life could help to prevent. A bigger role for families in care, with appropriate state support, dovetails with a resilience and preventative mission for social care built around keeping people independent and in their own homes as long as possible.

There is a big social division in healthy ageing. Among the most deprived decile of the UK population, a shocking 25% will die before the planned higher retirement age of 68, compared with just 10% among the richest decile. The latest ONS figures show a 19-year difference in healthy life expectancy between the least and most deprived areas of the country, while 54% of women and 38% of men aged over 65 in the most deprived local authorities need some form of adult social care compared to 26% of women and 15% of men in the least.[3] Many studies have shown that poverty, and the unstable family life with which it is often associated, produces a high level of stress that in turn leads to bad decisions about diet, a dependence on analgesics of various kinds to provide short-term hits, and little regular exercise, all of which raise susceptibility to the early onset of chronic illnesses. Added to which, in the famous words of Wendell Berry, 'People are fed by the food industry, which pays no attention to health, and are treated by the health industry which pays no attention to food.'[4]

How much the state can (and should) intervene to promote or even compel better decisions is a difficult question. But long before we might have to consider compulsory (and expensive) Ozempic injections for people who are clinically obese, or similarly draconian measures, there is much that can be done to prompt healthier ageing, borrowing from countries like Sweden, the Netherlands and Japan, and the ideas of public health experts like Atul Gawande, who promotes the practice of people being an active agent in their own care.[5]

According to the Health Foundation, about 40% of the burden on the health service is from preventable conditions. Both obesity and dementia are significantly preventable, or at least delayable in the case of dementia. There were about 1.2 million obesity-related NHS admissions in 2022–3, almost twice the number than in 2016–17, and the organisation spends about £20 billion a year on treating the condition. Around 26% of British adults are clinically obese, and 20% of 11-year-olds, mainly those in the bottom half of the income spectrum. In 1950, less than 1% of the population was clinically obese.[*]

---

[*] Another 38% of adults are overweight but not obese. About 90% of people suffering from Type 2 diabetes are obese, and their condition, in most cases, is intimately linked to poor diet and being overweight.

The pressure group Diabetes UK says that 50% of Type 2 diabetes is preventable – and that may be an underestimate, though there is also a genetic susceptibility to it for people from South Asian and African backgrounds. (Some of the highest concentrations of the illness are found in heavily South Asian areas like Bradford and East London.)

Dementia, which is now the leading cause of death in the UK (11% of all deaths), is also said to be about 40% preventable, according to Jonathan Schott, professor of neurology at University College London.[6] The incidence of dementia has been slowing in most high-income countries in recent years, probably related to improvements in cardiovascular health, but numbers are still expected to rise as more people live into their late 80s.[*] Obesity and Type 2 diabetes are also significant risk factors for dementia and cancer.

This high degree of preventability of two of the Four Horsemen, with somewhat lower levels for cancer and heart disease, was a revelation to me. I had no idea, until I looked at the numbers, that we collaborate so much in our own physical decline. Given the extraordinary potential for transforming the health of the nation through preventing some of this enormous quantity of illness, and the truncated lives it brings, it may seem a tall order to suggest that the overstretched social care sector should take the lead role. Of course, it should not do so alone: individuals and families and local authorities (which now have the main responsibility for public health) and the NHS itself have key roles to play. The NHS will continue to be a central conduit for prevention through GPs and the rehabilitation work of occupational

---

[*] The number of people with dementia in the UK is normally said to be a bit below 1 million, though only 500,000 have an official diagnosis. The dementia organisations are predicting 1.7 million by 2040.

therapists and physiotherapists, as well as specific preventative initiatives, such as the one for Type 2 diabetes.

But social care has an ongoing, and usually intimate, relationship with its users, older people or younger disabled people, that cuts with the grain of families and communities. The NHS, by contrast, has an episodic, transactional relationship with people at a GP surgery or an acute hospital (especially now fewer of us have a direct connection with a family doctor). Social care goes to where you are (whether at home or in a residential home), and, at its best, understands the human connections you are part of and harmonises with them to your advantage.

It is the underpaid, undervalued social care workforce who are in the best position to orchestrate the behavioural changes that so many people need if they are to enjoy a healthier lifespan and stay out of hospital or residential care. This is not just about preventing illness in the first place but about slowing deterioration and preventing chronic conditions becoming acute and requiring hospital admission. Most of the behaviour changes are obvious: drink less alcohol, lose weight, eat less highly processed food, sleep well. But top of the pile, and the new consensus in medical science, is *to take regular exercise.*

Exercise turns out to be key not only for physical healthspan but cognitive health too. Yet over 40% of UK adults fail to do even 30 minutes of somewhat intense exercise five times a week (which might include a brisk walk).[7] 'If they managed that relatively small amount, their risk of developing heart disease, stroke, dementia, diabetes, and some cancers could fall by at least 30%,' writes Camilla Cavendish in the *Financial Times.*[8]

Even modest improvements in fitness could save billions. For example, falling over and breaking a bone is often a devastating experience for an older person and can lead to a rapid decline and loss of independence. Falls are said to cost the NHS £3 billion a year. Canadian physician and longevity researcher Peter Attia says that 15–30% of people over 65 will be dead within a year after falling and breaking a hip, and half of those who survive will experience a serious reduction in mobility.[9] One Swedish study found even more dramatic numbers, with nearly 40% of old peole who enter hospital with a hip or femur fracture dying within a year.[10] Older women are especially vulnerable to osteoporosis (fragile bones) and incontinence, which is one reason, along with their greater longevity, that women are more likely to end up in residential care. The symptoms can be alleviated but have received insufficient attention. Simple exercise programmes to improve balance, even for people in their late 80s and early 90s, could easily be incorporated into domiciliary care packages, with care staff trained up to deliver them, but most packages simply focus on washing and dressing.

One of the other platitudinous truths of modern behavioural science is that changing people's bad habits is very difficult. But programmes can work if they are designed in the right way and reinforced by family and friends. So, along with exercise, care packages should have an explicit goal of building or maintaining networks of friends and neighbours, as they do in the Netherlands.

Social care, alongside the NHS's occupational therapists, should be a player in the so-called 'movement economy', a world of behavioural nudges rewarding exercise on a host of apps and websites. One such is Sweatcoin, a free app that counts a user's steps via their phone and rewards them with points (like Air Miles for walking) that can be redeemed online for products and vouchers.

Milton Keynes University Hospital is handing out 2,000 Apple watches to patients with Type 2 diabetes, which they will be able to keep if they exercise a certain amount per day. Many of these people will be people in receipt of domiciliary care packages that can rein-force the message. Apparently, the programme will pay for itself if a single amputation is avoided.[11]

The bigger role for prevention in the social care mission, especially in domiciliary care, needs to go hand in hand with a broader upskilling and reinvention of the role. First, though, a note of caution. It is one of the comforting illusions of the modern world that all problems can be solved by more training and qualifications. But many people, like my cousin's carer Nancy, like the job partly because it is part-time friendly, the formal qualification requirements are low, and the job satisfaction is high if you have the temperament and emotional intelligence to perform it well. There must continue to be a central role for such first-rung carers, who are the backbone of the system.

However, it seems likely that even if pay levels are raised above the minimum wage, recruitment to the sector will still struggle without a shift in image and status. Part of the answer is to create a new cate-gory of care worker, an Enhanced Care Practitioner (ECP), capable of doing more than basic care. This could both drive recruitment and save the system billions.

There are already experiments happening all over the country with versions of this idea. During the pandemic, many carers, after basic training from a nurse, undertook tasks normally reserved for a professional, such as injecting insulin, taking blood pressure/tem-perature, and dressing wounds. Yet after talking to many carers and recipients of care over the past year I was surprised to discover the persistence of so many demarcation lines between professional and non-professional staff, at least some of which seem to serve no useful purpose. For example, care workers are not allowed to cut the toe-nails of clients, and while they can wash and cream legs, they are not allowed to apply a bandage.

When you are dealing with frail older people, the competence is paramount of those taking sometimes life and death treatment decisions. Professional demarcation lines are usually there for a purpose. Sometimes, however, they outlive their original purpose and should be retired. Here is John Bryant, former head of strategy and development at Torbay Council, an area with a disproportionate number of older people requiring care: 'We have very high levels of turnover of domiciliary care workers and we need to make the role more attractive by upskilling it. This could include, for example, wound care. The NHS spends about £8 billion a year on wound care and while some of this is highly complex and requires a trained nurse, there are many lower-level wound care tasks that a suitably trained care worker could carry out.'[12] This would save the time of many NHS occupational therapists and community nurses.

Bryant helped to put this idea of the ECP into practice with a scheme called Kit4Care which, using Bluetooth technology, allowed care workers to take vital signs of clients – blood pressure, oxygen levels, temperature and pulse – and send them to a GP hub where they could be monitored. This is a good example of social care as a preventative service.*

---

* There are also plans in Torbay to rationalise the wasteful duplication in the routes used by the 16 different domiciliary care companies serving 800 clients across 75 square miles. The care companies, with help from the Health Foundation, have come up with a plan that would save nearly 40% of the 850,000 annual miles, still provide choice for clients, and provide an extra 20,000 hours a year for care workers that could be redirected to longer visits, more preventative work and training in low-level-medical skills. If the experiment in Torbay succeeds, it could be rolled out to other parts of the country, with big savings in time and fuel costs, some of which could be reinvested in the workforce. It would also allow more people without driving licences to take up the job of home care if cycling or walking between appointments became possible.

Care assessments, too, are often bogged down in the professional hierarchy. Does an occupational therapist need to decide whether someone needs incontinence pads? This is something an ECP could have the authority to decide. Similarly, in residential care, with GPs rarely visiting care homes and district nurses overstretched, the obvious answer is to give more functions to a higher-qualified care worker.

The NHS professions are strongly unionised and may be tempted to resist devolving some of their work to a new kind of care worker. What tends to happen in this situation is that change is not rejected out of hand but expert objections are raised that then take years to resolve. However, there is plenty of work to go round, and local experiments should reassure unions that their members will benefit by allowing others to take over some of their more routine work.

Technology is reinforcing the argument for a higher-qualified ECP role with the increase in remote monitoring of patients, as in the Kit4Care experiment, and the 'hospital at home' idea in which clinical staff visit you at home. This requires someone who sees the patient every day, but also has some medical knowledge, to act as a go-between.

The ECP role would also fit neatly into a British version of the much-admired Dutch Buurtzorg model, with its self-governing teams of a dozen nurses looking after 50–60 clients in an area. The same is true of the trend towards multidisciplinary teams combining the NHS, GP hubs and social care.

Not all domiciliary care workers, or residential care workers, will want to acquire the extra skills to become an ECP. But if it is associated with higher status and pay, thanks to saving on the expensive time of NHS professionals, many are likely to be tempted.

There is an existing qualification system for social care, NVQs level 1–5, and in the best homes most staff will have a basic NVQ level 2 and most managers at least NVQ level 4. But many front-line staff have no qualifications beyond a few weeks shadowing an experienced member of staff. In early 2024 Helen Whately, then social care minister, unveiled a relaunch of the NVQ Level 2 Care Certificate and talked up social care as a career choice with professional development. The Care Certificate has been around for some years but has not had a universally recognised accreditation so has been of little value to carers moving around the system. That is now, belatedly, being fixed.

It is now possible to imagine a three-tier qualification system in front-line care work, loosely analogous to the registered nurse/care assistant model in the NHS. The basic care worker would have the minimal initial training of most carers today, but all would now be working towards a Care Certificate. Senior carers would require a Care Certificate and a minimum number of years' experience. And the higher-level ECP would acquire the competencies that allow the individual to undertake minor medical interventions.

The extra training required of a senior carer and an ECP would not have to be long or arduous, but it would help transform the image of care work as a low-pay backwater and connect it to the wider world of nursing and medicine. Domiciliary and residential care could take its place as a proper vocation (with staff equivalent in status to 'everyday profession' support staff like teaching assistant or NHS care assistant), attracting people with a range of skills and ambitions.

There has recently been some movement on the other side of the medical fence, with social care work being built into the training of NHS doctors and nurses. This points to a possible future of much more flexibility across the whole health and care system, from the lowliest care worker to the mightiest medical consultant, with much greater ease of movement between sectors and up professional hierarchies. Why, for example, should an advanced nurse practitioner not become a doctor with some extra training? In the army you can become an officer from the ranks, and many sectors such as IT did away with rigid hierarchies decades ago.

The old vocational professions, with their long front-ended training, are becoming maladjusted to the modern world, with the decline of the job for life and AI taking over many routine professional functions. Moreover, the training of doctors gives too great a significance to the skills and attributes of being a clinical research scientist rather than a jobbing doctor.

That is for the future. In the short term, Cinderella care services need rebranding as resilience and prevention services and some of the care workers need to be upskilled to ECPs. Domiciliary and residential care contracts would have to be redrafted to reward private care companies for the reduced burden on the NHS. But before any such rebranding takes place, care workers need to be paid enough to fill the vacancies, reduce the high turnover and prevent the UK stripping poor countries of the care staff they badly need themselves.

Filling the vacancies means restoring the pay differential that used to exist with retail and hospitality jobs and bringing basic pay for a first-rung carer close to the level of the NHS care assistant. That would require at least a £1 premium above the national minimum wage, now standing at £11.44 an hour. It has also been partially implemented in Scotland, where recruitment problems have been less severe than in England. And the £1 premium is not expensive. According to the Homecare Association, it would cost £1.7 billion a year, though Ben Zaranko of the IFS has a lower estimate of £1 to £1.5 billion[13] – either way a bargain for a national priority. And if £1,000 'golden handshakes' are being considered to attract nursery carers, why not for social care too?

Skills for Care frames the extra money as payment for well-being outcomes. And it is true that care homes with better-trained and -paid staff achieve higher well-being for residents and so superior ratings from the CQC. Using a social care-related quality of life metric, the organisation argues, that the sector adds £50 billion of value each year in England alone, meaning about £35,000 per employee, far more than the gross pay for a front-line worker of £25,000 for a 40-hour week.

Labour in opposition committed itself to reintroducing collective bargaining – so-called Fair Pay Agreements – and proposed that the plan should be trialled in social care. It is not clear how that will work in a sector with so many small operators and low unionisation, nor how the aim of a £15 an hour minimum wage would be funded. But Keir Starmer's sister has worked as a carer, and there is a realistic chance of a special Carer's Minimum Wage, perhaps £13 an hour, which could maybe be funded by reforming council tax bands to bring in more income from higher-value properties, currently one of the biggest anomalies in the UK tax system. Labour has also, encouragingly, expressed an interest in upskilling some of the social care workforce.

BUILDING IN THE FAMILY

In the year before Rishi Sunak was elected to Parliament in 2015, he worked for the investment firm Catamaran Ventures, owned by his father-in-law N. R. Narayana Murthy, head of Infosys. He also found the time, alongside a colleague, to write a report for the think tank Policy Exchange, which included the observation that just 7% of Asian households consist solely of retirees, compared with 25% for the population as a whole.[14]

It was still considered normal in the 1950s and 1960s among the white majority in the UK for older parents to be living in a three-generation household supported by their adult children, mainly by daughters or daughters-in-law. This was not always a happy experience, for either side, and as people got richer it was one they often bought themselves out of. The trend among South Asians appears to be gradually moving in the same direction.

Family care nevertheless continued, and continues, but it is less likely to take place under the same roof. Indeed, the English Longitudinal Study of Ageing survey finds that 72% of the 1940s cohort of older people rely on their children 'a lot'.[15]

The care infrastructure is already heavily dependent on informal carers, usually children or spouses. About 12% of all British adults care for an older or disabled person either part-time or full-time, but numbers will be squeezed – not least because by 2030, 2 million of people over 65s will be childless. The state should do everything it can to encourage and incentivise the biggest possible continuing role for family members in care.*

According to analysts at the King's Fund, fewer people were receiving social care support in 2022 than in 2015, despite 11% more people requesting it.[16] Age UK puts the number not getting care who need it at 1.6 million.† And according to *The Economist* in 2016, 6%

---

* An LSE report has projected that by 2035 there will be demand for 8 million unpaid carers but only 6 million available. The report is cited in Ben Cooper and Andrew Harrop, 'Support Guaranteed: The Roadmap to a National Care Service', Fabian Society, Jun. 2023.

† Age UK says that 1.2 million people without a care package struggle to bath themselves and 930,000 have trouble getting in and out of bed. ('New Age UK Report Finds 1.6 Million Older People Have Unmet Needs', Disability Rights UK (13 Jul. 2023).

of over 65s received state funded care, but by 2023 this had fallen to 5%.[17] In order to qualify for state support you need to hit the sweet spot that combines a serious level of need with assets of less than £23,250: those with more than that who cannot afford private care are wholly reliant on family care. This is one of those areas of modern life where things have got worse rather than better: 'When my gran was in her eighties she had a home help from the council, who did her shopping, did her cleaning, got her pension, brought her sandwiches and gave her a hot meal a couple of times a week. The district nurse helped her with bathing and dressing her legs. There was a lot more help in those days and a lot more time for older people,' recalls Cathie Williams of the Association of Directors of Adult Social Services.[18]

Such recollections do raise the question of whether we are more grudging about and less respectful towards older people than previous generations, both as a society and as families. The World Values Survey, cited in earlier chapters, found that only 31% of British people believe that 'adult children have the duty to provide long-term care for their parents'.[19] Nevertheless, we often act as if we do acknowledge that duty. According to the ONS, only 20% of people over 85 are in receipt of formal care, compared with 43% receiving informal care mainly from families. Japan and Sweden, the two countries that came below us in the survey (where even fewer accept the idea of a duty of care), both invest heavily in care of older people and are often models of imaginative policy.

How best to keep and promote family involvement? The 5 million-plus who are already working as carers, one third for more than 50 hours a week, need more recognition and support. They save the state tens of billions a year through reduced demand for formal care, smoothing hospital discharge and reducing A & E visits. And what do these informal carers get in return? The 1.4 million who care for at least 35 hours per week qualify for a weekly Carer's Allowance of £81.90, the equivalent of just £2.20 an hour, and they must earn no more than £151 a week to qualify. The majority of informal carers who are also working, around 2 million employees, can, since the 2023 Carer's Leave Act, claim one week's unpaid leave a year for caring duties.

This is a welcome breakthrough but, as with other measures such as paternity leave, leaves us lagging behind many other countries. The Japanese allow two months a year. And the US, normally a laggard in welfare, has allowed three months' unpaid leave since 1993.

Making it easier for informal carers to combine work with care responsibilities in this way also prevents many of them giving up work completely. The UK government has recently been worrying away at the increase in economic inactivity since Covid, focusing on the rise in mental health conditions, but it would do as well to focus on the 400,000 who are estimated to have left the labour market partly because of caring duties in 2021–2. A further 41% of carers are thinking of abandoning full-time work because of their care duties, according to one poll.[20]

There is a strong case for at least one month's unpaid leave a year for carers, to make it easier to combine their two roles. The Carer's Allowance should also be increased to £100 a week, and the earnings threshold raised to £250, and noisily publicised.* In the longer run, caring should qualify for a paid career break in the same way that parenthood does. In France those in need of care get one month's free domiciliary or residential care each year to give their carer a break.

---

* The Department for Work and Pensions has recently been pursuing carers who, often accidentally, earned over the £139 threshold.

A lot of us are en route to becoming carers. Carers UK says that women have a 50:50 chance of being in a caring role by the time they are 46, and men by the time they reach 57. It can be a lonely business, and if the role had a more public identity, with places to meet both online and face to face, it could help to relieve some of the pressure.* Yet carers remain scarcely visible. In his 267-page annual report, *Health in an Ageing Society*, Chief Medical Officer Chris Whitty mentions family carers in just three paragraphs.[21]

Another suggestion for increasing the visibility for families in the care system, but also nudging those who are inclined to walk away, takes the form of a pledge signed by government, the local authority and the family of the person with social care needs. The family side of the pledge would commit them to do whatever is reasonably within their power to support their relative, including looking after them at home for as long as this is practical.[22] Similar pledges or contracts between schools and parents are used to promote higher attendance or improved homework records.

Making it easier for families to stay geographically close makes sense both for grandparent childcare duties and subsequent adult child–older parent support. More than half of us still live less than 30 minutes from our mothers, but this number is likely to be in sharp decline thanks in part to the rise of mass residential higher education, which means more than 70% of all students leave their hometown to study. Some return, but many don't.

There are a couple of ways of mitigating the family dispersal problem. One is to increase the supply of specialist housing for older

---

* The Centre for Social Justice report ('Creating a Britain that Works and Cares') recommends the creation of a 'one-stop-shop' for carers, to guide them through the social care maze.

people who are still independent but need some support: if there was a decent stock of specialist retirement housing, it would be easier for families to bring a semi-independent older relative closer to the family home. This would allow family members to keep the older person or couple active and connected, and could also have significant knock-on benefits in the housing market: around 9 million homes belonging to people over 65s have surplus bedrooms, yet older people move house at half the rate of other age groups – although as many as one third (around 4 million people) are said to be interested in downsizing.[23]

The recent Mayhew Review on housing for older people found that specialist retirement housing schemes help older people stay healthier for longer. Mayhew says that with the number of people over 65 rising to 17.2 million in 2040, with 6.2 million of these people living alone, governments should focus less on first-time buyers and more on last-time buyers.[24] Partly because of the vagaries of the planning system, the UK has been falling way behind many comparable countries since the boom years in retirement housing of the 1980s and 1990s.[25] Only 2.5% of the UK's 29 million dwellings are defined as retirement housing, and only 1% of people over 60 live in such housing, compared with 17% in the US and 13% in Australia.[*]

Only around 7,000 retirement homes were built in 2022 out of an annual total of around 200,000, and only 10% of Homes England grants to housing associations, charities, private developers and local authorities are allocated to retirement housing.[26] Yet 80% of people over 65 own their own homes, a wall of money that could help

---

[*] The three most common types of retirement housing in the UK are extra care (usually purpose-built retirement villages), sheltered housing (8–10 separate dwellings with a warden), and supported living (people living in the same dwelling and sharing care), all providing a mix of independent living and varied levels of support.

underpin the market for specialist retirement homes. And the NHS, which owns large tracts of land, mainly around hospitals, should think about building specialist housing for older people, or enabling developers to do so, both raising money and providing convenient accommodation for the NHS's biggest users.

The second way of mitigating the dispersal problem is to make it easier for families to live under the same roof during an older person's later years. As we saw at the start of this section, this is routine among some non-white communities but has largely disappeared among white people. Nevertheless, carving out spaces in existing properties that still allow the older person, and the host family, to retain a sense of their own independent space – often known as the granny annexe – is becoming more popular. The government should find ways of promoting and even subsidising such dwellings. It could start by removing the various planning obstacles and the obligation to pay extra council tax, perhaps modelled on the accessory dwelling unit in many US states.* A converted garage, or basement, or ground floor space, ideally with its own separate entrance, can belong to a returning 20-something child, and then an older parent, and, after the parent dies, a lodger. A friend of mine went through these three stages with an annexe which, he boasted, was one of the best property investments of his lifetime. And as he lives in the nice part of a provincial city, he has now converted it into an Airbnb.

Many old people do not want to live with their children or move into any kind of supported living. But there are other ways to incentivise the family role in care. In Japan, people earn tax breaks if they

---

* In the last UK government's 2023 Autumn Statement a consultation was announced 'on a new Permitted Development Right for subdividing houses into two flats without changing the façade'.

move to live near their parents. And local authority and social housing lists should prioritise flats for older people vacating a house and
moving closer to relatives who can care for them.

One quasi-replacement for family – which might still require
some family oversight – is the idea of providing accommodation
for a younger person to rent in an older person's home in return for
some domestic help with shopping and cleaning plus simple companionship. Many old people have spare rooms, and many younger
people cannot afford the rent where the good jobs are. There are a few
organisations springing up to coordinate this relationship.*

The final way that the family can play a bigger role in caring for
disabled and older people is by becoming more medically competent. This is not possible for everyone. Many family carers are often
almost as frail and the same age as those they are caring for and
would be intimidated if they had to administer a finger prick test to
monitor someone's blood sugar or similar. But there are many others,
especially adult children, who would be keen to know more about
a parent's condition and likely progression, partly to communicate
on their behalf about it to an often revolving cast of medical professionals. They may also be able to intervene in an appropriate way
in, say, the administering of medicines or giving injections. As with
upskilling domiciliary care workers, this could potentially save the
system billions.

---

* One such is called Homeshare UK, which describes itself as a national provider
matching older people with compatible companions who pledge 10–15 hours a
week of help around the home and companionship. The pitch seems to be aimed
mainly at the older people, with the strapline 'The affordable alternative to live-in
support.'

IMMIGRATION AND TECHNOLOGY AS SAVIOURS?

When people turn their attention to all those alarming statistics about the ageing population, the rising dependency rate, the continuing recruitment crisis in many care jobs and the sliding fertility rate, there are two *ex machina* solutions that are normally produced: immigration and technology. Both can help mitigate some aspects of the looming care crisis, but no more than that.

Immigration is not a solution, beyond the most short-term recruitment crisis palliative, because immigrants grow old too and even source countries are seeing sharp birth rate declines. Moreover, our dependence on it is exacerbating the problem as it encourages us to postpone the investment and culture changes required to mitigate ageing. This applies to the economy as a whole, as well as the health and care sector. The belief that it is economically rational and morally defensible to import around 250,000 health and care workers (plus more than 300,000 of their dependents) between 2021 and 2023, mainly from poorer countries with much greater needs, rather than paying people living here slightly higher wages (in the case of social care) or providing more training places (for nurses and doctors), is hard to understand.

High levels of immigration in the past twenty years have contributed to rapid demographic change and political polarisation, one reason for the Brexit vote in 2016. Yet it has continued to enjoy strong support among employers and much of the political class based on the assumption of economic benefit, partly replacing older assumptions about the cultural benefits of diversity.

We have been experimenting with the magical idea that immigration drives growth for more than 25 years, and the evidence is underwhelming. Since 1997, our per capita economic growth has been about average for comparable countries, even though our immigration rates have been significantly higher than most. Decent growth rates up to 2007 were indeed partly immigration-driven, especially by highly paid professionals in finance and related businesses, but the record since has been poor: the increase in the proportion of non-UK-born people in the workforce continued after 2008, rising from 7.3% in 1997 to almost 20% in 2023, but per capita growth and productivity have both flatlined or even declined. The median weekly pay in April 2023 was 8% lower than in 2008 after adjusting for inflation.[27]

Some immigration can be advantageous to the economy and the median citizen, especially if it is highly productive, provides skills that are in short supply, and contributes more in taxes than it takes out in public services and benefits. But not nearly enough of our recent immigration has passed any of these tests.[*]

The Treasury is always on the lookout for employment-boosting measures, and in recent times has settled on immigration and encouraging women back to work as soon as possible after childbirth. But more jobs do not automatically mean higher growth, as it depends on how productive the job is. There are several economies, including the US and France, that have lower labour market participation than the UK but higher growth and productivity.

If the demand for labour for a particular task outstrips the supply, the typical response of an employer would normally be to increase pay

---

[*] The economic establishment – the CBI, Bank of England, top economic think tanks and the *Financial Times* and *The Economist* – did regularly cite immigration as one of the drivers of growth in the first 10–15 years of this century. The same establishment also rejected the idea that high immigration was leading to lower wages or job displacement for British workers. It is hard to reconcile these two views in conventional economic analysis. For if the large growth in labour supply post-1997 was responsible for higher per capita GDP growth, then the standard explanation is that it was because it led to lower wages, higher profits and so higher investment in capital stock and improved productivity.

to attract more people or invest in automation to replace the job. But if, as in recent years, the immigration tap has been left on, first through EU free movement and then with a liberal post-Brexit work visa system, employers in certain sectors will simply reach for a foreign worker, one of the reasons why our capital investment, productivity and employer training record has been so poor. And immigration has not helped our skills shortage problem: between 2011 and 2022, when the UK added 3.6 million immigrants to its population, the proportion of vacancies characterised as skill shortage vacancies *rose*, from 16% to one third.[28]

It is often assumed that because immigrants tend to be young and healthy, and have often been educated abroad, they will contribute more in taxes than they take out in services and benefits. Again, this seems not to be the case, partly because, post-Brexit, most people come from poorer countries outside Europe and are more likely to work in low-skill jobs than people who are UK-born. That means they don't pay much in tax, send some of their income home in remittances, and end up being supported more in the benefit system while in work, before retiring – when they will depend on the pension system and health and social care system.

We know that fully 53% of all UK resident adults in 2022 paid less in taxes than they received in benefits and services. The UK government does not produce figures on net contribution by country of origin. The Danish government does, however – and, as one might expect, Danish-born residents there have the most favourable overall contribution record, closely followed by immigrants from comparable high-income countries, with non-Western immigrants and their immediate descendants coming nowhere close to a positive contribution over their lifespan.

The decision by the Department of Health and Social Care to recruit an unprecedented number of social care workers in 2022/3 therefore makes no long-term sense for UK plc. The recent surge in international recruitment, bigger even than in the early 2000s when Labour initiated a step change in NHS investment, consists of people coming in on health and care visas – 255,001 were issued between the beginning of 2021 and the end of 2023, bringing in a further 315,855 dependants.[29] Some are doctors and nurses, but the majority are carers or senior carers, and mainly to fill close to minimum-wage jobs: in the two years after February 2022, about 150,000 care workers came via this route, mainly from India, Nigeria, Zimbabwe and Pakistan.

Despite this big inflow, more or less matching the sector's vacancy number of 150,000, the overall vacancy *rate* in early 2024 only declined from around 10% to 8% – about 7% in care homes and 12% for domiciliary care. That seems to be partly because the sector has grown by around 50,000 workers, and partly because international recruits are replacing leaving or retiring UK staff. I do not, of course, blame the international carers themselves, some of whom have been treated like indentured labourers when they get here.[30]

But is it right for rich European countries to be sucking out people from the last outpost of global fertility, sub-Saharan Africa? There are currently said to be more Ghanaian health workers working in the UK than in Ghana, even though the UK has more than ten times more doctors per head than Ghana. Moreover, more than half of recent care visas have come from the 'red list' of poorer countries, where the UK has pledged not to actively recruit.

If there was no alternative, this would be understandable. But there is a very obvious alternative, discussed above, of spending less than £2 billion a year on raising pay levels significantly above the minimum wage – as has happened in Scotland. Care worker visa numbers have been significantly lower over the border, even allowing for the fact that Scotland has lower immigration overall, and according to the

Migration Advisory Committee the higher hourly pay rates are part of the reason. This is a story that should be far better known.

Care home and domiciliary care managers complain that they cannot recruit local staff at the wages on offer. The same story about no British people wanting to do the job was heard from the haulage industry when the chronic shortage of lorry drivers emerged after Covid. In that case the government refused to oblige with plenty of international visas, so instead the industry started paying big bonuses, training was expanded and fast-tracked, and the problem disappeared. The difference in social care is that the wages are, in effect, publicly funded through the central government grant to local authorities, and politicians are refusing to practice what they preach, leaving underfunded care homes no option but to recruit from poor countries.

Neil O'Brien, former Conservative minister for social care, says it is not the case that we can't get British people to do these jobs for any money: 'In fact, eight out of ten care workers are UK nationals. But when I was (briefly) the social care minister I was struck by how responsive to slight variations in pay people are. A new Amazon warehouse locally can spell trouble for the local care sector.'[31]

The UK is an outlier among rich countries in its dependence on international recruitment for doctors and nurses, with a staggering 50% of all current NHS hospital doctors trained abroad and 30% of nurses. And the NHS appears to have finally recognised that this must end, with its Long Term Workforce Plan explicitly aiming to reduce international recruitment to 10% by 2037. Social care, by contrast, is racing off in the other direction with international recruitment, though since the right to bring in dependants was withdrawn in spring 2024 the inflows have started to decline.

To keep the UK's age structure and dependency rate fixed at current levels, with sharply declining domestic fertility, it is not enough to import a few million immigrants, as we have done in the past few years – 9 million between 1996 and 2021, with an expected 9.5 million between 2021 and 2046. Because immigrants themselves grow old and end up converging on the fertility levels of the host country, you need to keep renewing the immigration injection. It is a permanent treadmill.

The UN did some famous projections back in 2000 on how much immigration would be required to keep the dependency pyramid at roughly its level at that time. For the UK, keeping the support ratio at the 1995 level of 4.09 would require 59.8 million migrants between 1995 and 2050, slightly more than 1 million migrants a year on average. The overall population would reach 136 million in 2050, of which 60% would be post-1995 migrants or their descendants.[32]

Less drastic versions of that scenario are imaginable. But there is another problem. Where are the people going to come from? When Poland joined the EU in 2004 and its people were free to work in the UK, wage levels in the former communist country were about one seventh of the UK's; they are now about half. Moreover, Poland is ageing even faster than the UK and has severe labour shortages. Even without Brexit and Covid, the number of Polish people in the UK was destined to fall sharply.

The final problem with the recent immigration response to low fertility is that it has not been planned for and thus exacerbates the pressure on public infrastructure, so lowering the quality of life. With net immigration of around 764,000 in 2022 and 685,000 in 2023, every aspect of the public infrastructure – from housing to public transport and the local A & E department – has more pressure on it. Nearly 50% of London's social housing households are headed by someone born outside the UK.[33] Making it easier for people already living here to have children, or more children, requires decent public infrastructure and affordable housing. And maybe, too, a more intangible sense of somewhere familiar and not too crowded to build a nest. All those things are made harder by immigration on its recent scale.

What about the role of technology in care work? Will robots and AI help care for Auntie Sybil, especially if she is one of the 1.2 million childless people over 65? It is a mixed picture. On the one hand, face-to-face care work is, rightly, regarded as one of the last bastions of irreplaceable human activity. On the other hand, technology is on the cusp of penetrating far deeper into health and social care in ways that could produce significant benefits for both carers and cared-for. And many of the changes cry out for the Enhanced Care Practitioner role, the carer with some medical expertise, to act as an enabler of more virtual care.

According to *The Economist*, technology is already acting as a constraint on those spiralling costs of longevity and chronic sickness, and the world spent $2 trillion less in the second decade of the 21st century on healthcare than it did in the first decade.[34] Yet while AI is starting to revolutionise medical diagnostics, most hospitals in the UK are still struggling with IT systems that don't talk to each other. In 2011 the government wrote off £11 billion on a failed attempt to build a computer system for the whole of the NHS.

Nevertheless, for those in the social care system, and others mainly dependent on informal family support, digital connectivity is generally making a big positive difference. The NHS App has simplified appointments and prescriptions, and there is an online world of medical apps and wearable technology that allows people, or their carers, to administer medical tests, track daily activity and monitor their vital signs.[35] Cameras, speakers and intelligent fridges also allow people to be monitored at a distance, making it easier for family carers to enter or re-enter the workforce. Alexa, the virtual assistant, has made life easier for the bed-bound.

The spread of apps and websites allows people to navigate the world of care homes and nursing homes from their front rooms. And inside care homes, the digitalisation of care records has ensured that all care workers are fully informed of the different requirements of residents. 'You have a single QR code that lays out Beryl's routine and all her likes and dislikes,' as one manager told me.

One problem here is that as many as one quarter of people over 65 do not have access to the internet in their home and many lack confidence with modern communication technologies – though this problem is declining as the pre-tech generations pass away. This is another potential role for the caring family, with tech-savvy younger people helping grandparents master the technology that can make life easier for them and their carers.

Technology is also enabling hospital-level treatment at home, sometimes called the 'virtual ward', which since Covid-19 has become more popular.[36] This only applies to certain kinds of treatments, such as fitting intravenous drips or oxygen therapy, and usually requires support from family or a domiciliary care worker. But one recent study showed that caring for people at home can improve patient outcomes as well as relieving pressure on hospitals.[37]

There are technology experiments happening all over the country, some of which are likely to be adopted nationally. The digital domiciliary care company Cera, for example, uses AI to predict and prevent hospitalisations, which it claims it can reduce by 70%. The Enhanced Care Practitioner role is, again, potentially the key link in many of these home-based technology possibilities, as we saw earlier in this chapter with John Bryant's Kit4Care.

Sometimes there is resistance to new technologies. A few years ago, a friend of mine was involved with ADL Smartcare, a Newcastle University spin-off that used AI to make need assessments of patients, so avoiding the need for a home visit from an occupational therapist in about 80% of cases. The AI was shown to be more accurate and consistent in its assessments, but was blocked by occupational therapists in several places. In Bradford it was adopted, and by safely handling the vast majority of simple assessments online, it freed up resources to reduce the waiting time to see an occupational therapist for a complex category visit from six months to one day.

Most of the technologies mentioned above, such as remote monitoring, can also be used in care and nursing homes. But most residential and nursing home companies are small – about 5,500 companies run around 17,000 homes – so the capacity for investment in technology is limited. Almost all homes will have lifting equipment to help staff get people in and out of baths or, in some cases, in and out of bed. But few will have the exoskeleton-type wearable devices that provide powered assistance to caregivers when moving people around. Given how much heavier many old people are today, such devices can save carers having to double up when manoeuvring people.

Japan, where 30% of the population is made up of people over 65 (and 11% under 15), is worth observing as a technologically sophisticated, robotics-friendly, ageing society with little immigration and huge demand for care work. The country is famous for its infrastructure of ageing. Silver Centres, where older people can socialise and also work, were established in 1975. Health clinics, too, often double up as day centres. There is also a time bank care system that enables people to look after somebody nearby in exchange for someone looking after a relative who lives far away.*

---

* The time bank is often cited admiringly by Western observers, but it is hampered by a highly bureaucratic screening process and by the fact that there are too few younger people in the rural areas where many older people live.

Japan makes extensive use of remote monitoring, including fall detection technology. Toilet design, too, means that an older person's toilet needs can be dealt with cleanly and easily from a carer's point of view. Yet the role of robotics in Japan in actively caring for older people – by feeding or bathing them, or engaging with them through exercise classes or conversation – has so far been more limited, though some commentators do not rule out a take-off in the next few years. Much of this infrastructure is worthy of emulation, though some of it, notably care time banks, do not work as well as is sometimes claimed by Western observers.[38]

According to one sceptical analysis of Japanese care robotics, a 2019 survey of 9,000 care homes found only 10% using robots.[39] The author also found that instead of freeing up staff to attend more closely to the needs of their residents they became assistants to the robots: a robot that was meant to lead exercise classes with a repertoire of music and moves could only attract residents' attention if a carer was standing next to it copying its movements.

More progress seems to have been made with robot pets providing companionship, particularly for people facing cognitive decline or lone-liness. OHaNAS is a talking sheep which engages users in conversation, plays word games and responds to touch in various ways. Similarly, Robi Jr is a compact communication robot that uses more than 2,000 phrases and is promoted with the slogan '*Motto nakayoshi*' (get closer).[40]

Robot pets of various kinds, some designed to look like cats or dogs, are being used in the UK, especially in dementia homes, and research by Plymouth University suggests that these help to reduce anxiety and depression.[41] But many people have what is some-times called 'skin hunger', meaning that they want to be touched by another human being regularly and suffer if this doesn't happen. And some commentators fear that if carebots are successful pacifiers and monitors of old people who are losing their faculties, it will allow their human relatives to pay less attention.[42]

There is no shortcut via immigration or technology to better cultivating, and rewarding, the human skills of care in the decades ahead. And that requires the sector to emerge from the shadows.

OPENING UP SOCIAL CARE

Social care needs a rebrand: it needs to become something that's respected as much as a career in the NHS is. That's a struggle in a culture that cleaves to youth and in which care reminds us of human frailty, disease and our own mortality. The small, multipurpose word *care* may even bring back unpleasant childhood memories of Grandmother's teeth in a glass of water and alarming older people making odd noises in a smelly, ill-lit care home.

I have argued in this chapter that one way for social care to capture the national imagination is to define itself as the preventative care service – not only by keeping older people out of hospitals, but also by leading the national debate on the lifestyle changes needed to reduce preventable illness. Do we need a Japanese-style 'fat tax' (Metabo Law) that fines employers if their workers are overweight? Should people be rewarded for taking exercise?

As noted, social care currently has no real national profile, with its funding and governance split across three departments of state and local authorities, and its army of small-scale providers lacking a high-profile employers' body, despite employing more people than the NHS. Several people at the top of the NHS might easily appear on *Question Time* to talk about the nation's health service: the chief executive of the NHS, the head of the NHS confederation, the heads of the various Royal Colleges, the head of the British Medical

Association or the Royal College of Nursing. And the chief executive of one of the 215 NHS trusts is a hugely significant figure in their locality. But who speaks for social care? Nobody, which is one of the reasons it has been possible for politicians to ignore multiple sensible reform proposals over the past two decades. The social care sector in relation to the NHS is a bit like the further education sector in relation to the university sector: a poor cousin.

The government needs to make a rod for its own back by creating a single voice for the sector – a chief executive with a small staff – whose job it is to find common ground between the various stakeholders and make an almighty din. The social care sector is a mixed economy, with private and public funding, and myriad centres of authority. A chief executive would have only as much authority as they could personally command. But there are so many things that could be achieved by someone with sufficient energy and imagination.

Top of the list should be to increase the visibility of social care. And that means opening it up. Most care and nursing homes are inspected by the CQC, but what keeps them on their toes is the regular visits of residents' relatives, the absence of which was so evident during the pandemic.

Another way of opening up the sector is to encourage more volunteering. In my admittedly limited experience, the sector is not friendly to volunteers. I tried to volunteer at the end of 2022. It was partly because I was thinking of writing this book and wanted to get a feel for a typical care home. It was also because I met a friend of a friend, a retired police officer who volunteers every week in his late mother's former dementia home and says that even doing things like cleaning the residents' spectacles brings him pleasure. He says that most of the people don't know where they are or who he is, but they take comfort in company and he feels useful.

To find a nearby place to volunteer, I consulted the CQC website, looking for a home that was struggling and in need of improvement. I found one in East Finchley, checked that it accepted volunteers, and went for an interview. The interview seemed to go well, and the manager guided me around the home, showing off his former SAS member and a woman who was 101 years old (though neither of them were any longer aware of their military or longevity achievements).

Several weeks later, after I had failed to get any responses to my many emails asking when I was going to receive the relevant DBS (Disclosure and Barring Service) form, I cycled round to the home to be told that the manager had left. I started the whole process again with the new manager, who seemed enthusiastic enough – partly, I suspect, because the home had been criticised by the CQC for not stimulating residents enough, surely a perfect job for a volunteer. Weeks, and many more emails later, I drew another blank.

My experience is not necessarily representative, but having spoken to several people who have volunteered in care homes I believe it is not unusual. There is not a culture of openness in homes in the way that there is in NHS hospitals with their surrounding ecosystem of charities and 'friends of...' organisations. It is true that care homes, unlike hospitals, are semi-permanent residential homes, so it is not a good idea to have strangers wandering around in them, but there are still plenty of ways to link homes to wider society. One of the larger municipal care homes in Copenhagen runs an attractive restaurant open to the public. It is mostly used by single, older men who go there to get a hot meal at a reasonable price in a convivial atmosphere.

Not only should volunteering be easier, perhaps with the help of a national campaign to get it started, but social care should sell itself as the perfect place for a *gap year job*. Why build a bridge in Madagascar when you could go up the road and entertain the last of the Second World War generation, get to know your neighbourhood and its history better, and get paid for it?*

Employers should look favourably on such work, either paid or voluntary. And universities are starting to do so, at least in China. If a top Chinese student is competing to get into one of the nation's elite academies, it is now more or less compulsory that they have done holiday volunteer work in an older people's care home. Maybe this should be the case for Russell Group university undergraduates too. Indeed, why not a social care equivalent of Teach First, in which graduates commit to at least two years working as a front-line care manager?

This is not only relevant for young people. People in later middle age (65–75) could be trained and supported to become volunteers to older people (80–90) who need the companionship. Social care should also borrow from Now Teach – the organisation set up to encourage professionals close to the end of their careers into teaching – by selling social care management as a second career in late middle age. Managerial posts in social care are often well paid, but are challenging and varied in a way that most knowledge economy jobs aren't.

We need social care to be more visible, because we want to open up ageing and dying and shed light on all the many ways that we can make the last two decades of life both healthier and more reward-ing. There are many good ideas on ageing that need an authoritative national platform – from a UK version of the Japanese Silver Centres, to how to stimulate more specialist sheltered housing for older people – that the social care sector is well placed to promote. And

---

* There are innovative agencies, such as the Tribe Project, which manage commercial micro-commissioning of care work as well as arranging volunteering.

why not a *Casualty*-type TV soap opera following the struggles of a domiciliary care worker?

Older people are often seen as grumpy and unlovable, but as author Arthur C. Brooks has observed, there are plenty of upsides to ageing: 'If you follow the typical development, you can expect to be nicer and kinder, and less depressed and anxious... People also tend to become less envious with age, especially of success in education, social standing, looks, and romance.'[43] Maybe the anxious teenagers of Generation Z could find some solace and wisdom by talking more to their grandparents. For the most part, as Brooks observes, Boomers really *are* OK.

CONCLUSION

A BETTER BALANCE

What then shall we choose? Weight or lightness?

Milan Kundera, *The Unbearable Lightness of Being*

Our current predicament sounds like a cautionary tale. In a kingdom long, long ago, the people became richer and freer, yet somehow could no longer afford to have children and no longer had the time to attend to their dependants, young and old.

In this actual kingdom, our demographic fate means we have many older people, thanks to longer life expectancy, and fewer young people to look after them, thanks to decades of sub-replacement fertility. With robotics and immigration offering only limited help, more of us, men and women, will *have* to start practising the care and attention that our society so often preaches.

We have prided ourselves on creating a civilised society with the establishment of the NHS and expanded welfare state in the 1940s, followed by the social reforms of the 1960s and 1970s. But we have also absent-mindedly allowed certain things to slip away that under-pinned that civilised society: the stable family; community and family support for young parents; the option to be a stay-at-home parent for a few years; extended family obligations, especially towards older people. And despite our greater wealth and technological sophistication, it is a more challenging time to be alive for many young and older people than a generation or two ago.

American journalist Inez Stepman eloquently describes how Anglo-American culture has got out of kilter. She says it has historically been grounded on an idea of freedom, of breaking away from the extended family, the culture of 'no limits' that landed an American on the moon. This lightness was once balanced by the heaviness of religion and moral stigma, and without that countervailing force it 'traps people in a permanent state of late adolescence, without any thought for what they will need when they are a dependent old person.'[1]

People say they still want the old things: marriage (or long-term partnership), family, children, companionship in old age. But then it turns out we want other things even more: autonomy, careers, nice holidays, constant novelty and stimulation. And we also discover that the old things are hard and require sacrifice. It is sometimes painful and difficult looking after young children, working at a struggling marriage, figuring out how to be a good parent to troubled teenagers, caring for an ungrateful parent with dementia. And there is no AI on hand to make those things easier.

On the first page of this book, I pointed to four big trends – the less stable family, the mental fragility epidemic among young people, the rapidly falling birth rate and the recruitment crisis in many face-to-face care jobs – that are symptoms of our current malaise. I have argued that these Four Horsemen of liberal modernity are connected, beneath the surface, to the devaluing of the domestic realm and of the aptitudes connected to it. They are the partly unintended consequence of the great experiment in freedom that accelerated in the 1960s. Some redesigning of the domestic sphere was necessary and welcome in the light of smaller families and the new freedoms, above all the big step forward in women's autonomy and earning power. Women no longer had to put up with errant husbands in the way that my mother had to, and domestic work began to be shared more equally.

But the care-devaluing form that equality has often taken has not, as I have shown, suited all women, nor all men, and has left what Mary Harrington has called 'a mother-shaped blind spot in modern feminism' that is implicitly anti-natalist.[2] In pursuit of equality with men in the public realm, women have had to devalue many traditionally female attributes and responsibilities, and compete on a more masculine playing field. Some have flourished on that playing field, but many haven't.

Women have experienced a step change in opportunities in the public realm, but also many things that have contributed to lower levels of contentment: involuntary childlessness, having to return to work sooner than desired after childbirth, the exhaustion of the second shift, a loss of the security that a long-term, companionate marriage can provide. And professional success for some comes alongside the continuing miserly pay for those 'prisoners of love' working in emotionally draining care jobs.

One of the most pressing questions for the quality of life in the UK in the next few decades is this: is sex equality now sufficiently entrenched to allow for a broader expression of women's interests so that the care balancer perspective may have its fair share of influence alongside the priorities of the egalitarians? And will men continue to step up sufficiently to make the new balance work?

The four big trends I have described are connected, and reinforce what looks like a doom loop for long-term well-being, with more insecure families creating more mental fragility, which in turn reinforces the baby bust and reduces the pool of potential carers. My own modest proposals for strengthening family life, promoting higher fertility, upgrading public economy care work and encouraging men to move into female-majority sectors are no more than nudges against what feels like the colossal economic and cultural forces favouring the GDP economy and the immediate rewards of lightness and autonomy.

But the outlook for the upward revaluing of the domestic realm in the equality era may not be quite that bleak. For a start, we are set to spend a lot more time at home in the next few years.

First, the arrival of AI, by providing a vast array of technical expertise almost for free, will surely lead to a shorter working week and more time at home for both women and men, and a further evolution in the gender division of labour.

Second, the post-pandemic embedding of working from home, for at least a few days per week, not only restores life to the home during the day but also makes it easier to combine work and parenthood for mothers and fathers. The 60%-plus of 'adaptive mothers' who want to combine part-time work and parenting when children are young – and who most surveys suggest are on average happier than either stay-at-home mothers or more work-focused mothers – will generally find it easier to do so with this institutionalisation of homeworking. (Conversely, those who cannot work from home, such as teachers, nurses, doctors, social care staff, factory, transport and construction workers, may in future require some compensation for their disadvantage.)

Third, there has been an uptick in multigenerational households (as many as 9 million, according to Eliza Filby, a researcher of generational divides), mainly driven by young adults living with their parents after college thanks to a decline in partnerships and the struggle to get on the housing ladder.[3]

More broadly, as Anne Fennell, chair of Mothers at Home Matter, argues, the disparaging narrative around the home as a place of seclusion and isolation bears little relationship to her reality, and modern digital connectivity makes it easier for a full-time parent to take part in social and community life outside the family.

This return of the domestic sphere may also be reinforced by a small-c conservative version of post-material/post-consumerist concerns – sceptical about GDP growth, individual wealth and high-stress living – often associated with the green movement. As MP Danny Kruger has written, 'It should not be assumed that the only valid career for a man or woman is a paid role far from home.'

The pandemic may have shifted the priorities of a few million people in this post-consumerist direction. Ipsos polling on the roots of happiness found only 4% equating success with working long hours, with 51% agreeing with the statement 'I am happy with what I have, even though I know some things could be better,' compared with just 30% signing up to the statement 'I want to get the best I can in life instead of settling for what I already have, even if that means more hard work.' Home ownership, financial security and independence are seen as the markers of success by a majority, more important than more possessions and luxury goods.[4]

This can be seen in a negative light as a loss of work ethic – perhaps for some it is, but for others it is about the search for something more meaningful to apply that work ethic to. That might be a hobby, children or grandchildren, or a community project.

As AI starts to eat into more middle-class jobs in the way that automation and globalisation have already done to working-class jobs, what will be left is creativity and caring in their many forms. And, fortunately, it turns out that caring is good for us. People who care about others are almost always happier than people who are preoccupied with themselves. And surely one of the causes of the mental fragility epidemic among young people is that not enough is asked of them, while at the same time they are expected to find their own way in a world of endless lightness and fluidity.

In her book about caring for her terminally ill mother, Emily Kenway talks about how it improved her as a person: 'I always struggled with regulating my emotions... My mother's illness required me to control myself, to learn when to display and when to mask emotions, to protect her needs and her wellbeing above my own strife... I've developed faculties that help me to live my life and will benefit those around me too, especially in hard times. I can see the same in many of the caregivers I have interviewed.'[5] What she describes are also some of the character traits of a good parent.

Advocating for pronatalist policies and a strengthened domestic sphere are normally seen as conservative, if not Conservative, goals. On the contrary, I believe that the cluster of ideas and policies spelt out in this book (see below for a non-exhaustive list)* offer an opportunity to transcend the usual political divides and provide a space

---

* The Home Care Allowance, making it easier for one parent to stay at home when children are of preschool age; a family tax allowance for those raising children and full transferability of tax allowance between married parents raising children; single parents able to retain some of their benefits for a transitional period when a new partnership is established; more generous maternity pay and one month paternity leave paid at the higher rate; the right for one parent to draw their state pension two years earlier for each child; more recognition of the role of grandparenting; salaries near teacher levels for childcare staff and more flexible regulation to keep costs down; redefining social care as the preventative care service and paying at least £1 above minimum wage and higher salaries to staff with some medical capabilities; student debt forgiveness for nurses who stay more than five years; more free IVF on the NHS and a fertility check at 25; higher carers' allowance and more time off for carers; making granny flats easier to build; and more specialist housing for older people.

where both conservative Somewhere and liberal Anywhere intuitions can be accommodated.

Raising the status of the domestic sphere, as I argued in Chapter 8, should be the culmination of Claudia Goldin's 'grand gender convergence'. State support to protect the family from the demands of the GDP economy when children are young, by making it feasible for one parent to stay at home, would reduce stress and also help more relationships survive the maelstrom.

Being a parent, especially a young mother, is harder than it used to be since old traditions such as lying-in have faded. The sudden loss of autonomy and career-derived status makes it more disorientating than in the past, and family dispersal means less support. Indeed, parenting has often come to be seen as something joyless and demanding. Journalist Janice Turner has noted how motherhood has come to be painted in the 'darkest hues' in popular culture. She compares the sitcom about family life *Motherland*, in which the lead is permanently on the verge of a nervous breakdown, with *Outnumbered*, from 15 years earlier, which covered the same ground but with humour and warmth.[*]

There is a growing consensus that the over-attentive helicopter parenting of the 1980s and 1990s has been a wrong turn. An influential recent paper in the *Journal of Paediatrics* concluded that the parenting focus shifted from an idea 'of children as responsible and resilient to the opposite', to the great detriment of those children.[6] But even the most apparently self-assured and educated parents need help in finding that 'love and boundaries' balance. And relationship stability makes it a great deal easier.

---

[*] Turner notes how *The Guardian*'s parenting columnist Rhiannon Lucy Cosslett writes about motherhood 'as if she's an inmate in Abu Ghraib – little but mental health crises, tears, tedium, arrogant fellow parents, "mum-shaming", dire maternity care and sleepless gloom'. 'Bye, Bye, Baby', *Saturday Times* magazine (30 Mar. 2024).

None of this stands in the way of a more equal division of labour in the home, nor of women reconciling motherhood with jobs and careers. Companies must adapt, and are adapting, to longer career breaks for women and, as Goldin argues, the institutionalisation of working from home is a potential game changer. Fathers are increasing their share of domestic labour and becoming more involved in childcare, something that longer paternity leave will reinforce. You can learn how to be a better father, too. A friend who led some parenting classes for young men told them to imagine listening to a speech by their soon-to-be child at their 18th birthday and thinking about what they would like them to say about their father. I wish someone had put that thought into my head when I was a father-to-be.

A list of mainstream equality demands – affordable childcare, more support in the tax and benefit system for the cost of raising children, men playing a bigger role in childcare – can happily sit alongside policies that communitarian Somewheres can embrace too, incentivising a bigger role for families, and extended families/grandparents, in looking after their young and old. One American Somewhere gave an account, a few years ago, of the case for such family involvement in a manner that today sounds excessively censorious: 'The day-care centers and nursing homes blossoming across the American landscape are monuments to our growing unwillingness to accept personal responsibility for those to whom we owe the most – our children, our parents, and our grandparents. If we continue to turn our backs on those who are closest to us, how long can we hope to meet any of our obligations as the great nation history intended us to be.'

This was Senator Joe Biden, writing in the *Daily Times* of Salisbury, Maryland, in 1981. It shows how quickly and completely moral fashions can change. Public opinion in the UK, however, remains consistently in favour of the kind of care balancer programme that this book has spelt out. More support for stay-at-home parents *as well as* making it easier to combine parenting and work; more support for the family to provide higher levels of care at both ends of life; a moderate pronatalist nudge in the tax and benefit system; promoting more involvement by fathers and the evolution – but not abolition – of the gender division of labour.

But elite opinion, represented by the Treasury, all the main political parties, academia, charities and most media commentary, is, for now, strongly pointed in the direction of more GDP and pumping up the labour supply, the well-being of families and infants be damned. Both main parties are committed to big expansions of formal childcare including for infants under two, despite the reservations of many child development experts. But this £4 billion-plus extra investment in childcare is estimated to create just 60,000 extra full-time equivalent jobs, and perpetuates the questionable idea that expanding the labour supply is the source of per capita economic growth.

The UK's employment rate of 75% is already close to its peak of 76% in 2019 and in the top third of the OECD rich country club of 38 nations, way ahead of the EU average. Several countries – including the US, France, Ireland, Belgium, France, Austria and Finland – have lower employment rates but higher productivity and per capita income. The route to intensive economic growth comes through public and private investment and innovation, and being able to build the houses, factories, laboratories and energy infrastructure where they are needed.* It does not come through adding to today's tally of 33 million UK workers yet more low-productivity immigrants, or a few

---

* A single Danish medical company, Novo Nordisk, was responsible for more than 2% of Danish GDP growth in 2022–3. Annual growth stood at 1.7%; without it, growth would have fallen by 0.3%.

tens of thousands of recent mothers, mainly working part-time in low-productivity service jobs, many of whom would prefer to be at home looking after children. Keir Starmer, however, has said he wants to raise the employment rate to 80%.

Politicians are also fixated on the UK's inactivity rate, which includes students (plus foreign students), stay-at-home parents and people with chronic illnesses and has hovered between 8.4 million and 9.5 million for the past 30 years. It currently stands at 9.2 million, somewhat higher than 8.6 million in October 2019, just before the pandemic. But as a percentage of the workforce, the inactivity rate (at 22%) is still well *below* the average of recent decades and the OECD average.

It is true, however, that the long-term chronically ill element of inactivity at 30% is the highest it has ever been, and at 2.7 million it is more than half a million higher than before the pandemic. Some of that will be related to the after-effects of Covid and NHS waiting lists, including the 400,000 who have left jobs to care for people in recent years. But with many more people leaving jobs due to depression and anxiety, perhaps we should be looking more carefully at where the trouble is coming from. And part of the answer will surely be the less stable family background experienced by many millions of people, along with the loneliness and lack of motivation experienced by those who have no supportive family. Is it too far-fetched to imagine some connection between the more than halving of the number of full-time parents in the past 30 years, and the almost 50% increase in people who are chronically ill and on long-term sick leave, from 1.8 million to 2.7 million?*

---

* It seems there is some sort of constant of economic inactivity. In the 1950s and 1960s it was the stay-at-home mother, in the 1980s and 1990s it was unemployed people, and now it is people who are sick and depressed.

The progressive mind has long dreamt of transcending the conventional family, holding it responsible for the subordination of women and the entrenchment of inequality. The first accusation is now mainly historic. The second accusation is not so easily answered: there *is* an inherent tension between family and equality, and if the family becomes more important, the genetic, behavioural and financial benefits of coming from a successful family could count for even more. From Engels and the early communists, via the kibbutz movement to the theorists of the redistributive welfare state, one of the main goals of the left has been to disrupt the family as a transmission belt of class advantage. This approach has had only limited success, partly because family ties and the impulse to hand on advantage is so strong. Besides, in recent decades, it is the poorest who are most likely to have abandoned the family, which has only accentuated their disadvantage.

The lesson of recent history is that it is better to *lean in* to family, especially for those at the bottom of the income and education hierarchy, rather than lean away from it, as the current public policy bias prefers. The work of economic equalisation can be done elsewhere, through the tax system and tilting public spending towards people on the lowest incomes – especially in education spending, with a higher pupil premium for the most disadvantaged.

Like the failure to develop an appealing humanist alternative to traditional religion, no real alternative has been found to the family, though it has evolved into many different shapes. From TV drama *Friends* to Harry Potter and his mates, the idea of alternatives to family has been prominently advocated but without yet producing any new institutions or ways of life. That could change in the near future, with the growth of what writer Anthony Costello calls 'sympathy groups'.[7]

This is Carol from South London: 'I looked after my mother, who had dementia. I managed every aspect of her everyday life, which was, at times, overwhelming. It also brought home to me that I was without children: who would do for me what I was doing for my mother? The answer was no one. I decided that I should become more pro-active about ageing... I live in a very tight-knit neighbourhood in South London. We are a lively, feisty group that has had to take on developers several times, and we have grown into a strong community. During Covid we were looking after our older residents, doing the shopping and picking up prescriptions. So I decided to tap into this pandemic spirit and set up what I call the 'Elders' group. The idea is to support one another into a healthy old age.'[8] The future may see many such groups springing up, but for now the main alternative to the family continues to be the individual interacting with the state or the market, the rather bleak, individualistic model that some Nordic countries are pioneering.[*]

Finally, what hope is there for the pro-family, pro-baby care balancer ideas I have described in this book? There is a constituency for these ideas in more socially conservative parts of the country and among family-orientated ethnic minorities, but they do not yet carry enough political weight to challenge the Anywhere consensus. The real hope lies, I think, in the economics. Over the next few years, it will become clearer to more people that we are feasting off the future. We are inflating the workforce, GDP and tax income of today and leaving people too busy and stressed to raise the workers of tomorrow. Ageing, low fertility societies require ever higher taxes on younger people. That cycle leads either to poverty and bankruptcy or a dramatic withdrawal of the state.

There is another, even more alarming prospect: we may turn against older people and leave them to fend for themselves. And it

---

[*] Pippi Longstocking springs to mind: the autonomous, motherless nine-year-old girl created by Swedish writer Astrid Lindgren in 1945.

may become tempting for governments to legalise euthanasia and then nudge more and more people towards the door, as some people claim is already happening in Canada. The right to die could become a duty to die.[9]

Avoiding such a bleak future requires shoring up the family to save the state from even more responsibilities. You cannot in the long run have small families and a small state, or even the size of state we currently have.[10] Some of my proposals do cost money – the Home Care Allowance, longer paternity leave, higher pay for nursery staff and adult social carers – but internally generated population growth similar to the baby boom years would restore the national balance sheet.

Such population growth will take time and money to generate, and our democracies are not designed for long-term decisions that create short-term costs for voters. Politicians will find it easier to try to mitigate worsening dependency ratios with more immigration and sending more mothers straight back to work. But at some point it will become clear that this won't be enough.

In the present, merely preserving current fertility levels, difficult though that seems with the apparently anti-natal bias of Gen Z, would avoid some of the worst economic scenarios. And our public discussion about these themes would be so much better informed if the supremacy of GDP output metrics were supplemented and challenged by numbers that gave us a truer picture of human activity, including in the non-money economy of the family, and captured more of the quality rather than the quantity of our economic lives.

A young father who decides to give up the low-paid job he does not enjoy and draws on the Home Care Allowance to look after his two preschool children would be subtracting from GDP. But he would be improving his quality of life and contributing to a less stressful background for raising his children and managing his partnership.* Well-being goes up, GDP goes down. It must be possible with modern survey techniques, already central to GDP data collection, to capture a broader sense of the quality of people's lives rather than having national economic management completely dominated by mere output data. We have spent years putting the cart before the horse, straining to raise GDP regardless of what it is doing to the quality of work or family life.

Reinvigorating the family, in the era of equality, would not increase GDP, at least in the short term. But it *could* help produce more resilient, well-balanced, productive children, keep more marriages and partnerships together, combat loneliness in old age, save the state hundreds of billions of pounds, and provide purpose and meaning in a post-religious age.

It is worth trying.

---

* Celebrated American economist Paul Samuelson, author of the bestselling textbook *Economics*, gave the now quaintly old-fashioned example of the pitfalls in GDP accounting by pointing out that if a man married his maid, GDP would fall. The example was dropped after the third edition.

ACKNOWLEDGEMENTS

I am a generalist, a journalist with an interest in political and social trends. In the past few years I have written big picture books that cover vast terrains of human life and I often stray into fields where I have little specialist knowledge. That means I am dependent on many others to provide me with expertise or insight drawn from their research or personal experience. I have also developed the habit of sending out chapters of a book, as I am writing, to relevant experts and/or friends. This helps to explain why my list of acknowledgements is so long.

First, a very special thanks to my partner, Kate, who lived with the book for two years and provided wise counsel on many of its themes. Thanks also to my publisher, Mark Richards, editor Jack Ramm and copy-editor Sarah Terry, for helping me to produce a much more polished and well-organised book, and my agent Toby Mundy for guiding me in their direction. Thanks to Richard Norrie and Ellen Pasternack for research help and a constant flow of good ideas. Then thanks to all my relatives who shared their experiences of the care system – my brother-in-law George and his carers, my uncle Charles, plus my cousin Alice and my cousin Frances's spouse Jim – plus all the other relatives, including most of my siblings and two of my children, Maud and Stan, who read parts of the book and approved (or sometimes disapproved) of my comments on life in the family I was born into and the one that I helped to raise. A special thanks to Sharon Rider and Sten Widmalm at Uppsala University in Sweden for a valuable month there in 2022 that got the book under way. Thanks to Dean Godson and Julia Mizen at Policy Exchange, where I work part-time, for agreeing to take an interest in family matters. And another special thanks to a select band of people who engaged with the book as it was being written and helped to shape it in important ways: John Bryant, Jess Butcher, Ken Charman, Robert Colvile, Manuela Grayson, Dorte Heurlin, Ruth Kelly, Iain Mansfield, Paul Morland, Cristina Odone, Catriona Olding, and Anna Rotkirch.

Finally, thanks too to a larger group of people who I interviewed or who commented on parts of the book or helped in some other way: Claire Ainsley, Harry Benson, Belinda Brown, Samantha Callan, Rachel Carrell, Joanne Cash, Miriam Cates, Melanie Chater, Daisy Christodoulou, George Cook, Anna Coote, Edward Davies, Pamela Dow, Michelle Dyson, Anne Fennell, Caroline Ffiske, Alun Francis, Nicola Gooch, Helen Goulden, Johan Hakelius, Sybille Hazward, Sian Hughes, Sarah Johnson, Lucy Kellaway, Tim Leunig, Leo Lewis, Warwick Lightfoot, John Lloyd, David Loyn, David Lucas, Gerard Lyons, Maria Lyons, Wade Newmark, Neil O'Brien, Sean Phillips, Hannah Preston, Robert Rowthorn, Sophia Russell-Cobb, Jean Seaton, Rupert Sheldrake, Oonagh Smyth, Patrick Spencer, Amanda Spielman, Madeleine Sumption, Carole Ulanowsky-Rose, Bobby Vedral, Simon Wessely, Brett Wigdortz, David Wild, Karl Williams, Alison Wolf, Rachel Wolf, Jessica Wren, Frank Young. Apologies to anyone I have forgotten.

NOTES

1. THE ROAD HOME

1 National Centre for Social Research, British Social Attitudes 40, 'Change and Continuity at Work and at Home', Sept. 2023.

2 Correspondence with the author.

3 Anne-Marie Slaughter, *Unfinished Business: Women Men Work Family* (Oneworld, 2015), 122–3.

4 See Kundera's obituary in *The Economist* (22 Jul. 2023).

5 See Stephen Bush, 'Liberalism's Problems Are Problems of Success', *Financial Times* (23 May 2023).

6 Arlie Russell Hochschild, *The Second Shift: Working Families and the Revolution at Home* (Viking Penguin, 1989).

7 Ellen Pasternack, 'Parenting as a Public Good', *Works in Progress* (21 Jan. 2022).

8 Mary Harrington, *Feminism Against Progress* (Forum, 2023), 16–17.

9 Mary Harrington, 'Peter Thiel on the Dangers of Progress', *Unherd* (30 Dec. 2022).

10 National Centre for Social Research, British Social Attitudes 40, 'Change and Continuity at Work and at Home', Sep. 2023.

11 Ellen Pasternack, 'Who Will Look After the Kids?', *The Critic* (Feb. 2023).

12 These figures are taken from ukpublicspending.co.uk.

13 Amy L. Wax, 'Caring Enough: Sex Roles, Work and Taxing Women', *Villanova Law Review*, 44/3 (1999), 495–523.

14 Jonathan Haidt, *The Anxious Generation: How the Great Rewiring of Childhood Is Causing an Epidemic of Mental Illness* (Allen Lane, 2024).

15 Louise Perry, 'The Dignity of Domestic Labour', *The Critic* (Jul./Aug. 2020).

2. A SHORT HISTORY OF THE POST-WAR FAMILY

1 Erika Bachiochi, 'Pursuing the Reunification of Home and Work', *American Compass* (15 Jul. 2022).

2 Erika Bachiochi, *The Rights of Women: Reclaiming a Lost Vision* (University of Notre Dame Press, 2021).

3 The full statement of purpose can be found on NOW's website at https://now.org/about/history/statement-of-purpose.

4 Mary Harrington, 'Surrogacy and Robots Won't Solve the Baby Bust', *Unherd* (31 Jul. 2023).

5 Letter to the editor, *The American Enterprise* (Jul./Aug. 1998).

6 Alan Macfarlane, *The Origins of English Individualism* (Wiley-Blackwell, 1978).

7 Peter Laslett, *The World We Have Lost: England Before the Industrial Age* (Methuen, 1971).

8 All figures on the family taken from Office for National Statistics reports.

9 Pat Thane, 'Happy Families? History and Family Policy' [PDF publication], British Academy (Oct. 2010), 37.

10 Harry Benson, *What is the Divorce Rate?*, Marriage Foundation, Nov. 2023.

11 Thanks to Professor John Curtice for this observation: 'Britain's Baby Bust', *Trendy* [podcast] (25 Jan. 2024).

12 Harry Benson, *Sources of Family Breakdown*, Marriage Foundation, Jul. 2023, https://marriagefoundation.org.uk/research/source-of-family-breakdown/

13 Stephanie Spencer,' Girls at Risk. Early School-Leaving and Early Marriage in the 1950s', *Journal of Educational Administration and History*, 41/2 (2009), 179–92.

14 National Centre for Social Research, British Social Attitudes 40, 'Change and Continuity at Work and at Home', Sep. 2023.

15 Tina Miller, *Making Sense of Parenthood: Caring, Gender and Family Lives* (Cambridge University Press, 2017), 43.

16 Catherine Hakim, 'Work-Lifestyle Choices in the 21st Century: Preference Theory' (Oxford University Press, 2001).

17 Miller, *Making Sense of Parenthood*.

18 Pierre Walthery and Heejung Chung, 'Sharing of Childcare and Well-being Outcomes: An Empirical Analysis', Government Equalities Office, Jan. 2021.

19 Claudia Goldin, *Career and Family: Women's Century-Long Journey Toward Equity* (Princeton University Press, 2021), 15.

20 Alison Wolf, *The XX Factor: How Working Women Are Creating a New Society* (Profile Books, 2013), 2.

21 This statement is based on statistics at https://explore-education-statistics.service.gov.uk/find-statistics/childcare-and-early-years-survey-of-parents.

3. THE FALLOUT: INSECURE CHILDREN
AND MISERABLE MOTHERS

1 Trevor Phillips, 'My Daughter's Death Gave Us a New Mission to Speak up on Mental Health', *The Times* (3 Jun. 2023).

2 Anthony Giddens, *The Transformation of Intimacy: Sexuality, Love and Eroticism in Modern Societies* (Polity Press, 1992), 96.

3 The figures quoted are taken from a Marriage Foundation research briefing paper, which can be downloaded at https://marriagefoundation.org.uk/research/source-of-family-breakdown.

4 Adrienne Burgess, 'Separated Fathers: How Often Do They See Their Children?', Dad.info, Feb. 2018.

5 Kathleen Kiernan, Sam Crossman and Angus Phimister, 'Families and Inequalities', IFS Deaton Review of Inequalities, 2022. Unless otherwise stated, the data and judgements in this chapter are taken from this paper.

6 Sumi Rabindrakumar, 'Family Portrait: Single Parent Families and Transitions over Time', University of Sheffield, 2018.

7 Alessandro Di Nallo and Daniel Oesch, 'How Social Class Influences Family Breakdown' [blog], Understanding Society: The UK Household Longitudinal Study (23 Oct. 2023).

8 Jamie Lennox, '37% of Parents Not Complying With Child Maintenance Payments', Today's Family Lawyer, Sep. 2022.

9 Harry Benson and Spencer James, 'Out of the Blue: Family Breakdown in the UK', Marriage Foundation, 2015.

10 Anna Garriga and Fulvia Pennoni. 'The Causal Effects of Parental Divorce and Parental Temporary Separation on Children's Cognitive Abilities and Psychological Well-Being According to Parental Relationship Quality', *Social Indicators Research*, 161/2–3 (2022), 963–87.

11 NHS, 'Mental Health Bulletin, 2022–23: Annual Report', Feb. 2004.

12 Charlie McCurdy and Louise Murphy, 'We've Only Just Begun: Action to Improve Young People's Mental Health, Education and Employment', Resolution Foundation, Feb. 2024.

13 See Benji Waterhouse, *You Don't Have to Be Mad to Work Here: A Psychiatrist's Life* (Jonathan Cape, 2024).

14 The survey can be found at https://digital.nhs.uk/data-and-information/publications/statistical/mental-health-of-children-and-young-people-in-england/2022-follow-up-to-the-2017-survey/introduction.

15 Matthew Lelii, Lucy O'Brien and Lucy Hancock, 'Rising Ill-Health and

Economic Inactivity Because of Long-Term Sickness, UK: 2019 to 2023', Census 2021.

16 Bart Shaw et al., 'Special Educational Needs and Their Links to Poverty', Joseph Rowntree Foundation, Feb. 2016.

17 Quoted in Eleanor Hayward, 'NHS Taskforce to Investigate Surge in ADHD Diagnoses', *The Times* (29 Mar. 2024).

18 GL Assessment, Children's Wellbeing, Feb. 2017.

19 'Mental Health of Children and Young People in England', NHS Digital, 2017, 18.

20 'Mental Health and Wellbeing Plan: Discussion Paper and Call for Evidence – Results', Department of Health and Social Care, May 2023.

21 'Mental Health of Children and Young People in England 2021 – Wave 2 Follow up to the 2017 Survey', NHS, Sep. 2021.

22 Harry Benson, 'Family Breakdown and Teenage Mental Health', Marriage Foundation, Nov. 2017.

23 Once separation or divorce has taken place, most children endorse their parents' decision, with 82% of 14- to 22-year-olds supporting the change, according to a 2015 survey by the family law organization Resolution. The survey was reported in Owen Bowcott, 'Children of Divorce: 82% Rather Parents Separate than "Stay for the Kids"', *The Guardian* (22 Nov. 2015).

24 Jeremy Holmes, *John Bowlby and Attachment Theory* (Routledge, 2014).

25 Allan N. Schore, 'Attachment and the Regulation of the Right Brain', *Attachment and Human Development*, 2/1 (2000), 23–47.

26 Shelley E. Taylor, 'Mechanisms Linking Early Life Stress to Adult Health Outcomes', *Proceedings of the National Academy of Sciences*, 107/19 (2010), 8507–12.

27 Maria Lyons, 'Universal Childcare: Is It Good for Children?', Civitas, Feb. 2024.

28 Critical Science, 'Childcare: What the Science Says', *Medium* (2 May 2021).

29 Michael Baker, Jonathan Gruber and Kevin Milligan, 'Universal Child Care, Maternal Labor Supply, and Family Well-Being', Working Paper, National Bureau of Economic Research, Dec. 2005.

30 The full results can be read at https://explore-education-statistics.service.gov.uk/find-statistics/childcare-and-early-years-provider-survey/2022.

31 The 2020 Study of Early Education and Development (SEED), funded by the Department for Education.

32 Correspondence with the author.

33 Ben Shaw et al., 'Children's Independent Mobility: An International Comparison and Recommendations for Action', Policy Studies Institute, Jul. 2015.

34 Mary Harrington, *Feminism Against Progress* (Forum, 2023), 126.

35 *Sunday Times* book review, 'Why We're Still Trapped in Housework Hell' (6 Aug. 2023).

36 Killian Mullan, 'Chapter 10: Technology in the Daily Lives of Children and Teenagers', in Jonathan Gershuny and Oriel Sullivan, *What We Really Do All Day: Insights from the Centre for Time Use Research* (Pelican, 2019) 209–36.

37 Children's Commissioner, 'Family Review: A Positive Approach to Parenting, Part 2 of the Independent Family Review', Dec. 2022.

38 Roberts is quoted in Sally Weale and Caelainn Barr, 'Number of Working Mothers in England Rises by a Million in 20 Years', *The Guardian* (29 Sep. 2017).

39 Eliane Glaser, *Motherhood: Feminism's Unfinished Business* (4th Estate, 2022), 4.

40 Jeanette Milgrom et al., 'Antenatal Risk Factors for Postnatal Depression: A Large Prospective Study,' *Journal of Affective Disorders*, 108/1–2 (2008), 147–57.

41 Donald W. Winnicott, The Baby as a Going Concern, Collected Works Volume 3 (Oxford Academic, 2016).

42 Shira Offer, 'The Costs of Thinking About Work and Family: Mental Labor, Work–Family Spillover, and Gender Inequality Among Parents in Dual-Earner Families, *Sociological Forum*, 29/4 (2014), 916–36.

43 Glaser, *Motherhood*, 216.

44 Carole Ulanowsky, 'Women as Mothers: Changing Role Perceptions. An Intergenerational Study', PhD thesis, Open University, 2008.

45 Laura Tiehen, 'Has Working More Caused Married Women to Volunteer Less? Evidence from Time Diary Data, 1965 to 1993', *Nonprofit and Voluntary Sector Quarterly*, 29/4 (2000), 505–29.

4. POLITICS OF THE FAMILY

1 'Parents Report Stronger Relationships with Their Children During Lockdown, Understanding Society (5 Jul. 2020), https://www.understandingsociety.ac.uk/news/2020/07/05/parents-report-stronger-relationships-with-their-children-during-lockdown/.

2 Eliza Filby, 'When the State Fails, Family Steps In', *Unherd* (1 Dec. 2020).

3 Aviva Newsroom, '1 in 3 Homes Are Multi-Generational' (11 Sep. 2020).

4 See almost all the recent reports on expanding formal childcare that take this position, including those from the IFS, Nesta, the Fawcett Society, and childcare lobby Pregnant then Screwed. See also chapter 4 of the 2023 Economic Report of the US President (which can be found at https://www.whitehouse.gov/wp-content/uploads/2023/03/erp-2023.pdf).

5 Bridget Phillipson, Speech to the Onward think tank, 9 Mar. 2023, see https://www.bridgetphillipson.com/speeches/2023/03/09/speech-onward/.

6 See IFS, 'Still a Man's World? Gender Inequalities, Parenthood and the Workplace' [podcast] (23 Aug. 2023); and IFS, 'Men and Women at Work: The More Things Change the More They Stay the Same?' [webinar] (6 Dec. 2021).

7 Alison Andrew et al., 'Women Much More Likely than Men to Give up Paid Work or Cut Hours After Childbirth Even When They Earn More', IFS, March 2023.

8 Alison Andrew et al., 'The Careers and Time Use of Mothers and Fathers', IFS, March 2023.

9 Zaimal Azad, Alesha De-Freitas and Lizzie Ville, 'Transforming Early Childhood Education and Care: Sharing International Learning', Part 1, Fawcett Society, Dec. 2023.

10 Yanna Weisberg, 'A Gender Difference in Personality Traits in Terms of Big Five', *Occupational Medical Health*, 10/4 (2022), 400.

11 Claudia Goldin, interview with Tyler Cowan, 'Claudia Goldin on the Economics of Inequality', *Conversations with Tyler* [podcast] (1 Sep. 2021).

12 Gijsbert Stoet and David C. Geary, 'The Gender-Equality Paradox in Science, Technology, Engineering, and Mathematics Education', *Association for Psychological Science*, 29/4 (2018).

13 Claudia Goldin, interview with Alice Evans, 'Career and Family', *Rocking Our Priors* [podcast] (15 Oct. 2021).

14 Anna Rotkirch, 'What Are Couples Made Of? Union Formation in High-Income Societies', in Oskar Burger, Ronald Lee and Rebecca Sear (eds), Human Evolutionary Demography (Open Book Publishers, 2024), 575–98.

15 Inez Stepman, interview with Louise Perry, 'Episode 33: Why I'm an Anti-Feminist' *Maiden, Mother, Matriarch* [podcast] (1 Oct. 2023).

16 Eliza Filby, 'Why Gen Z Daughters Won't Follow in Their Mums' Career Footsteps', *CityA.M.* (24 Oct. 2023).

17 Jess Butcher, 'Is Modern Feminism Starting to Undermine Itself?', TEDx Talk, (5 Sep. 2018).

18 Victoria Richards, 'The Truth About Maternity Leave: It Can Be Desperately, Achingly Lonely', *HuffPost* (29 Nov. 2018)..

19 Ruby Warrington, interview with Louise Perry, 'Episode 52: 'Women Without Kids', *Maiden, Mother, Matriarch* [podcast] (11 Feb. 2024).

20 Louise Perry, *The Case Against the Sexual Revolution: A New Guide to Sex in the 21st Century* (Polity, 2022), 172.

21 Christine Emba, interview with Chris Williamson, 'Episode 664: Talking to a Feminist About Masculinity', *Modern Wisdom* [podcast] (7 Aug. 2023).

22 MaryEberstadt, interview with Chris Williamson, 'Did the Sexual Revolution Actually Benefit Women?', *Modern Wisdom* [podcast] (26 Oct. 2023).

23 Caroline Davies and agency, 'Number of Abortions in England and Wales Hits Record Levels', *The Guardian* (24 May 2018).

24 Valerie Elliott and Ian Gallagher, 'Being Home with the Children and Doing the Housework Made Me Feel Like a Drudge, said Margaret Thatcher in a Long-Last Article', *Daily Mail* (27 Apr. 2019).

25 David Cameron speech to the Relationships Alliance Summit, 18 Aug. 2014.

26 Robert Rowthorn and David Webster, 'Male Worklessness and the Rise of Lone Parenthood in Great Britain', *Cambridge Journal of Regions, Economy and Society*, 1/1 (2008), 69–88. Leading UK publication *The Economic Journal* turned down the paper without sending it out to referees, on the grounds that the subject was not of interest.

27 Melissa Kearney, *The Two-Parent Privilege: How the Decline in Marriage Has Increased Inequality and Lowered Social Mobility, and What We Can Do About It* (University of Chicago Press, 2023).

28 Anne Case and Angus Deaton, *Deaths of Despair and the Future of Capitalism* (Princeton University Press, March 2020).

29 David Willetts, *The Pinch: How the Baby Boomers Took Their Children's Future – and Why They Should Give It Back* (Atlantic Books, 2010), 26.

30 Danny Kruger, *Covenant: The New Politics of Home, Neighbourhood and Nation* (Forum, 2023).

31 Robert Whelan, *Broken Homes and Battered Children: A Study of the Relationship Between Child Abuse and Family Type* (Family Education Trust, 1994).

32 Correspondence with the author.

33 Centre for Social Justice, 'Why Family Matters: A Comprehensive Analysis of the Consequences of Family Breakdown', Mar. 2019.

34 'The Saturday Read Conversation', *New Statesman* (14 Sep. 2023).

35 Jennifer Dixon, 'An Election Manifesto for the NHS – and a Healthy Economy', *Financial Times* (18 Apr. 2024).

36 Sebastian Millbank, 'Whataboutmeism', *The Critic* (3 Oct. 2023).

37 Andrea Mrozek, 'Nobel Laureate James Heckman: "The Family is the Whole Story"', Institute for Family Studies, Mar. 2021.

38 Peter Wilby, 'The Expert in Social Mobility Who Says Education Cannot Make It Happen, *The Guardian* (17 Mar. 2020).

39 'Why Family Matters', Centre for Social Justice.

40 National Centre for Social Research, British Social Attitudes 40, 'Change and Continuity at Work and at Home', Sep. 2023.

41 The full survey can be found at https://explore-education-statistics.service.gov.uk/find-statistics/childcare-and-early-years-survey-of-parents.

42 Office for Budget Responsibility, 'Economic and Fiscal Outlook', Mar. 2023, 21.

5. WHAT ABOUT MEN?

1 See IFS, 'Still a Man's World? Gender Inequalities, Parenthood and the Workplace' [podcast] (23 Aug. 2023).

2 Jude Winter, 'Stuart Broad: Why the Retired England Great Doesn't Like to Use the "R-Word"', BBC Sport (16 Nov. 2023).

3 Anna Machin, 'In Praise of Fathers', *Observer* (20 Jun. 2021).

4 Oriel Sullivan and Evrim Altintas, 'Chapter 5: Dividing Domestic Labour and Care', in Jonathan Gershuny and Oriel Sullivan, *What We Really Do All Day: Insights from the Centre for Time Use Research* (Pelican, 2019), 105–28.

5 'Time Use in the UK: March 2023', Census 2021, https://www.ons.gov.uk/peoplepopulationandcommunity/personalandhouseholdfinances/incomeandwealth/bulletins/timeuseintheuk/march2023.

6 Wendy Wang, 'American Dads Are More Involved Than Ever – Especially College-Educated or Married Dads', Institute for Family Studies, Oct. 2023.

7 Pierre Walthery and Heejung Chung, 'Sharing of Childcare and Well-being Outcomes: An Empirical Analysis', Government Equalities Office, Jan. 2021.

8 Richard Fry, 'Almost 1 in 5 Stay-at-Home Parents in the US are Dads', Pew Research, Aug. 2023.

9 Stephanie H. Murray, 'The Problem with Splitting Parental Leave Down the Middle', *The Atlantic* (12 Jun. 2023).

10 Anna Langseth, 'Women Take Parental Leave More Than Previously Known', *Svenska Dagbladet* (10 Nov. 2023).

11 Patrick Jack, 'Women Outnumber Men on UK PhDs for First Time', *Times Higher Education* (17 Nov. 2022).

12 Cory Clark, interview with Chris Williamson, 'Episode 665: 5 Forbidden Topics That Psychology Won't Discuss', *Modern Wisdom* [podcast], 10 Aug. 2023.

13 Michael Schaerer et al, 'On the Trajectory of Discrimination: A Meta-Analysis and Forecasting Survey Capturing 44 Years of Field Experiments on Gender and Hiring Decisions', *Journal of Organizational Behaviour and Human Decision Processes*, 179 (2023).

14 'Is HR Really a Woman's World?', *Personnel Today* (24 Feb. 2011).

15 Noam Gidron and Peter A. Hall, 'The Politics of Social Status: Economic and Cultural Roots of the Populist Right', *British Journal of Sociology*, 68/1 (2017), 57–84.

16 National Centre for Social Research, British Social Attitudes 39, 'Culture Wars', 2022.

17 Original analysis by Richard Norrie based on 'Understanding Society: Waves 1–13, 2009–2022 and Harmonised BHPS: Waves 1–18, 1991–2009' [data

collection], 18th edition, UK Data Service. SN: 6614. doi: 10.5255/UKDA-SN-6614-19.

18 Original analysis by Richard Norrie based on World Values Survey: Round Seven – Country-Pooled Datafile. Madrid, Spain & Vienna, Austria: JD Systems Institute & WVSA Secretariat, C. Haerpfer et al. (eds), 2020. doi: 10.14281/18241.1.

19 'Masculinity and Women's Equality: Study Finds Emerging Gender Divide in Young People's Attitudes', Kings College London, Feb. 2024. An outlier Ipsos survey for International Women's Day in March 2024 found 47% of British people (59% of these men and 35% women) agreeing that equal rights for women have gone far enough.

20 Manoel Horta Ribeiro et al., 'The Evolution of the Manosphere Across the Web', Proceedings of the International AAAI Conference on Web and Socia Media, 15/1 (2021), 196–201.

21 See 'Understanding the Young Male Syndrome', *Rob Henderson's Newsletter* [blog] (22 Oct. 2023).

22 John Burn-Murdoch, 'How Disadvantage Became Deadly in America', *Financial Times* (13 Oct. 2023).

23 Roy F. Baumeister, 'Stalking the True Self Through the Jungles of Authenticity: Problems, Contradictions, Inconsistencies, Disturbing Findings – and a Possible Way Forward', *Review of General Psychology*, 23/1 (2019), 143–54.

24 Brigid Francis-Devine and Georgina Hutton, 'Women and the UK Economy' [research briefing], House of Commons, Mar. 2024.

25 Martin Seager and John A. Barry, 'Cognitive Distortion in Thinking About Gender Issues: Gamma Bias and the Gender Distortion Matrix', in John A. Barry et al. (eds), *The Palgrave Handbook of Male Psychology and Mental Health* (Palgrave Macmillan, 2019), 87–104.

26 'The Rise of Childlessness', *The Economist* (29 Jul. 2017).

27 Marianne Bertrand et al., 'Social Norms, Labor Market Opportunities, and the Marriage Gap for Skilled Women' [working paper], US National Bureau of Economic Research, Feb. 2016.

28 Ingvild Almas et al., 'The Economics of Hypergamy', IZA Institute of Labour Economics, Feb. 2019.

29 Geoff Dench, *Transforming Men: Changing Patterns of Dependency and Dominance in Gender Relations* (Transaction Publishers, 1998).

30 Nicholas Eberstadt, *Men Without Work: America's Invisible Crisis* (Rutgers University Press, 2022).

31 Robert Colvile, 'We Need to Talk About the Family', *Sunday Times* (8 Aug. 2021).

32 Raj Chetty et al., 'Childhood Environment and Gender Gaps in Adulthood', *American Economic Review*, 106/5 (2015), 282–8.

33 Mary Eberstadt, interview with Chris Williamson, 'Did the Sexual Revolution Actually Benefit Women?', *Modern Wisdom* [podcast], (26 Oct. 2023).

34 Megan Lim, Elise Carrotte and Margaret Hellard, 'The Impact of Pornography on Gender-based Violence, Sexual Health and Well-Being: What Do We Know?', *Journal of Epidemiology and Community Health*, 70/1 (2016), 3–5.

35 Daniel A. Cox, 'American Men Suffer a Friendship Recession', American Enterprise Institute (6 Jul. 2021).

36 'Is There a Crisis of Masculinity?', *The Economist* [podcast] (12 May 2023).

37 Kim Parker, Pew Research, 1 Oct. 2015.

38 Melissa Kearney, *The Two-Parent Privilege: How the Decline in Marriage Has Increased Inequality and Lowered Social Mobility, and What We Can Do About It* (University of Chicago Press, 2023).

39 Correspondence with the author.

40 Nicholas Eberstadt, interview with Chris Williamson, 'Episode 614: Why Do Millions of Men Not Want to Work?', *Modern Wisdom* [podcast] (13 Apr. 2023).

41 Richard Reeves, 'Getting More Men to Teach in Early-Years Education', *The Bulwark* (5 Dec. 2022).

42 Daniel Susskind, *A World Without Work* (Allen Lane, 2020).

43 Claire Cain Miller, 'Why Men Don't Want the Jobs Done Mostly by Women', *New York* Times (4 Jan. 2017).

6. SLEEPWALKING INTO LOW FERTILITY

1 Charlie Gowans-Eglinton, 'I Would Have a Baby If I Could Afford It, but for Women Like Me the Costs Are Too High', *The Times* (7 Oct. 2023).

2 'A Third of New Parents Can Not Afford to Have Children', Pregnant Then Screwed (15 Nov. 2022).

3 John Burn-Murdoch, 'The Housing Crisis Is Still Being Underplayed', *Financial Times* (13 Jan. 2024).

4 'Housing: The Unintended Contraceptive' [briefing note], Land Promoters and Developers Federation, Jan. 2023.

5 The poll of 1,000 young people, carried out by OnePoll, was reported in *The Times* on 26 July 2023 ('Young Put Off Having Children by Global Fears'). An even more dramatic poll by the Generations and Gender programme, reported by *The Times* on 19 Jan. 2024, found that just 20% of 26- to 35-year-olds in the UK definitely wanted children.

6 Caroline Hickman et al., 'Climate Anxiety in Children and Young People and Their Beliefs About Government Responses to Climate Change: A Global Survey', *The Lancet*, 5/12 (2021), E863–73.

7 Anvar Sarygulov and Phoebe Arslanagic-Wakefield, 'Understanding the Baby Boom', *Works in Progress* (7 Sep. 2023).

8 Ezra Klein, 'The Deep Conflict Between Our Work and Parenting Ideals', *The Ezra Klein Show* [podcast] (22 Mar. 2024).

9 Wolfgang Lutz, Vegard Skirbekk and Maria Rita Testa, 'The Low-Fertility Trap Hypothesis: Forces that May Lead to Further Postponement and Fewer Births in Europe,' *Vienna Yearbook of Population Research*, 4 (2006), 167–92.

10 Jac Thomas, Francisco Rowe and Eric S. Lin, 'Declining Fertility in Taiwan: The Deterring Impact of Housework Imbalance', *Asian Population Studies*, 19/3 (2023), 270–88.

11 Jill Filipovic, 'Women Are Having Fewer Babies Because They Have More Choices', *New York Times* (27 Jun. 2021).

12 Eva Beaujouan and Caroline Berghammer, 'The Gap Between Lifetime Fertility Intentions and Completed Fertility in Europe and the United States: A Cohort Approach', *Population Research and Policy Review*, 38 (2019), 507–35.

13 Maria Rita Testa, 'Family Sizes in Europe: Evidence from the 2011 Eurobarometer Survey', European Demographic Research Papers, 2012.

14 Steve Smallwood and Julie Jeffries, 'Family Building Intentions in England and Wales: Trends, Outcomes and Interpretations', Population Trends, 112 (2003), 15–28.

15 New Social Covenant Unit poll, 'Closing the Birth Gap', Nov. 2023.

16 Renske Keizer, 'Remaining Childless: Causes and Consequences from a Life Course Perspective', dissertation, Utrecht University, 2010.

17 Ann Berrington, 'Perpetual Postponers? Women's, Men's and Couple's Fertility Intentions and Subsequent Fertility Behaviour', *Population Trends*, 117 (2004), 9–19.

18 The leading advocate of this position is Stephen Shaw, at Birthgap.org.

19 Germaine Greer, *The Whole Woman* (Penguin, 2007).

20 Amelia Hill, '"I Just Assumed It Would Happen": The Unspoken Grief of Childless Men', *The Guardian* (28 Aug. 2023).

21 David M Buss, 'Sex Differences in Human Mate Preferences: Evolutionary Hypotheses Tested in 37 Cultures', *Behavioral and Brain Sciences*, 12/1 (1989), 1–14.

22 Marcia Inhorn, interview with Tina Miller, 'What's Changing About Childbirth', BBC Radio 4(19 Jun. 2023).

23 Yolien De Hauw, André Grow and Jan Van Bavel, 'The Reversed Gender Gap in Education and Assortative Mating in Europe', *European Journal of Population*, 33/4 (2017), 445–74.

24 Correspondence with the author.

25 Jennifer Glass, Robin W. Simon and Matthew A. Andersson, 'Parenthood and Happiness: Effects of Work-Family Reconciliation Policies in 22 OECD Countries', National Library of Medicine (Nov. 2016)..

26 Viviana Zelizer, *Pricing the Priceless Child: The Changing Social Value of Children* (Princeton University Press, 1985).

27 Filipovic, 'Women Are Having Fewer Babies Because They Have More Choices'.

28 K. Modig et al., 'Payback Time? Influence of Having Children on Mortality and Old Age', *Journal of Epidemiology & Community Health*, 71/5 (2017), 424–30; 'How Children Influence the Life Expectancy of Their Parents', Max Planck Institute (23 Oct. 2019).

29 Colin Brazier, *Sticking up for Siblings: Who's Deciding the Size of Britain's Families?* (Civitas, 2013).

30 'Understanding Society: Waves 1–13, 2009–2022 and Harmonised BHPS: Waves 1–18, 1991–2009' [data collection], 18th edition, UK Data Service. SN: 6614, doi: 10.5255/UKDA-SN-6614-19.

31 Robert Waldinger, 'What Makes a Good Life? Lessons from the Longest Study on Happiness', TED Talk (Nov. 2015).

32 Darell Bricker and John Ibbitson, *Empty Planet; The Shock of Global Population Decline* (Robinson, 2019), 3–4.

33 Paul Morland, *Tomorrow's People: The Future of Humanity in Ten Numbers* (Picador, 2022), 249–53.

34 See Post-Liberal Pete, 'The Low Fertility Trap', *Posting Alone* [blog] (7 Feb. 2024).

35 Scott Corfe and Aveek Bhattacharya, 'Baby Bust and Baby Boom: Examining the Liberal Case for Pronatalism' [briefing paper], Social Market Foundation, Sep. 2021.

36 'It's Not Just a Fiscal Fiasco: Greying Economies Also Innovate Less', *The Economist* (30 May 2023).

37 'It's Not Just a Fiscal Fiasco', *The Economist*.

38 Valentina Romei, Eleni Varvitsioti and Arjun Neil Alim, 'Has Europe's Population Peaked?', *Financial Times* (24 May 2024).

39 Neil O'Brien, 'Something's Got to Give', *Neil's Substack* [blog] (8 Apr. 2024).

40 'Britons in Their Thirties Are Stuck in a Dark Age', *The Economist* (5 Jan. 2023).

41 Ben Ansell, 'Generation Games', *Political Calculus* [blog] (2 Jan. 2023).

7. BIGGER, NOT BETTER: WHY THE CARE ECONOMY IS STRUGGLING

1 Neil O'Brien, 'Something's Got to Give', *Neil's Substack* [blog] (8 Apr. 2024).

2 Paul Johnson, *Follow the Money: How Much Does Britain Cost?* (Abacus Books, 2023), 166–7.

3 Johnson, *Follow the Money*, 167.

4 Neil O'Brien, 'Welfare Spending and Mental Health', *Neil's Substack* [blog] (9 May 2024).

5 Sean Phillips and Stuart Carroll, 'Not Fit for Purpose: An Appraisal of the "Fit Note" and Assessments of Fitness for Work', Policy Exchange, Apr. 2024.

6 Charlie McCurdy and Louise Murphy, 'We've Only Just Begun', Resolution Foundation, Feb. 2024.

7 Matthew Smith, 'Public Services Are in Bad Shape Across the Board', YouGov (3 Oct. 2023).

8 James Lloyd, 'The State of Intergenerational Relations Today', International Longevity Centre, Oct. 2008.

9 Dominic Lawson, 'What the Union Leaders Don't Want to Talk About', *Sunday Times* (4 Dec. 2022).

10 Camilla Cavendish, *Extra Time: 10 Lessons for an Ageing World* (Harper Collins, 2019), 97.

11 Simon Bottery, 'Where's the Z in Social Care Workforce?', The King's Fund, Dec. 2023.

12 Asaf Levanon, Paula England and Paul Allison, 'Occupational Feminization and Pay: Assessing Causal Dynamics Using 1950–2000 U.S. Census Data', *Social Forces*, 88/2 (2009), 865–91. 2

13 Nancy Folbre, 'Should Women Care Less? Intrinsic Motivation and Gender Inequality', *British Journal of Industrial Relations*, 50/4 (2012), 597–619.

14 'Workplace Employee Relations Survey', Department for Business, Innovation and Skills, Advisory, Conciliation and Arbitration Service and National Institute of Economic and Social Research, 2011.

15 Nancy Folbre, '"Holding Hands at Midnight": The Paradox of Caring Labour', *Feminist Economics*, 1/1 (1995), 73–92.

16 These figures are not precise and are drawn from King's Fund and Department for Health and Social Care estimates.

17 Laura Schlepper and Emma Dodsworth, 'The Decline of Publicly Funded Social Care for Adults', Nuffield Trust (13 Mar. 2023).

18 Madeleine Bunting, *Labours of Love: The Crisis of Care* (Granta, 2020), 4.

19 'The Feinstein Graph', *Life Chances Across the Life Course* [blog] (16 Aug. 2016).

20 Christine Farquharson, Robert Joyce and Tom Waters, 'Early Years and Childcare in England: Public Spending, Private Costs, and the Challenges Ahead', IFS, Mar. 2023.

21 Christine Farquharson speaking at the Civitas childcare panel, 22 Apr. 2024.

22 Richard Layard et al., 'What Predicts a Successful Life? A Life-Course Model of Well-Being'. *Economic Journal*, 124/580 (2014), F720–F738.

8. BRINGING IT ALL BACK HOME

1 Claudia Goldin, 'A Grand Gender Convergence: Its Last Chapter', *American Economic Review*, 104/4 (2014), 1091–1119.
2 Erika Bachiochi, *The Rights of Women: Reclaiming a Lost Vision* (University of Notre Dame, 2021).
3 Correspondence with the author.
4 Mike Brewer and Alex Clegg, 'Ratchets, Retrenchment and Reform: The Social Security Ssystem Since 2010', Resolution Foundation briefing, Jun. 2024, 29.
5 Erika Bachiochi, 'Pursuing the Reunification of Home and Work', *American Compass* (15 Jul. 2022).
6 Hannah Barnes, 'The Trauma Ward', *New Statesman* (12 Apr. 2024).
7 Ellen Pasternack and George Cook, 'Back to Basics: What Is Childcare Policy for?', Civitas, Apr. 2024.
8 Frank Young, 'Why Can't Mums Choose? Rethinking Child Benefit and Childcare Spending', Civitas, Oct. 2022.
9 Ruth Kelly and Connor MacDonald, 'Better Childcare: Putting Families First', Policy Exchange, Aug. 2022.
10 'UNICEF Warns of "Looming Children's Crisis" and Urgent Need for UK to Take Action to Improve Lives of Children', UNICEF (2 Sept. 2020).
11 Paul Johnson, 'Sure Start Achieved Its Aims, Then We Threw It Away', *The Times* (15 Apr. 2024), republished by the IFS at https://ifs.org.uk/articles/sure-start-achieved-its-aims-then-we-threw-it-away.
12 Tomáš Sabotka, Anna Matysiak and Zuzanna Brzozowska, 'Policy Responses to Low Fertility: How Effective Are They?', UNFPA, May 2019.
13 Lyman Stone, 'Is Hungary Experiencing a Policy-Induced Baby Boom?', Institute for Family Studies (10 Jul. 2018).
14 'Parenting Priorities: International Attitudes Towards Raising Children', The UK in the World Values Survey, Kings College London, Sept. 2023.
15 For a brief overview of the campaign, see https://en.wikipedia.org/wiki/Do_it_for_Denmark.
16 Anna Rotkirch, 'Low Birth Rates: Ten Steps Towards More Baby-Friendly Policies for 2024 and Beyond', Population Europe, 2022.
17 Laurie DeRose, 'Do the More Educated Want Fewer Children?', Institute for Family Studies (31 Jan. 2024).
18 'Why Family Matters: A Comprehensive Analysis of the Consequences of Family Breakdown', Centre for Justice, 2019.
19 Harry Benson, 'Divorce Rates Have Halved for New Brides. Why?', Marriage Foundation, Sep. 2012. f

20 Sarah Bridge, 'How Much Do British Weddings Cost in 2024?', *Good Housekeeping* (12 Jun. 2024). /

21 Harry Benson and Spencer James, 'Out of the Blue: Family Breakdown in the UK,' Marriage Foundation, 2015.

22 Lucy Ward, 'Drifting Apart Blamed for 47% of Divorces', *The Guardian* (9 Mar. 2005).

23 Daniel A. Cox, 'From Swiping to Sexting: The Enduring Gender Divide in American Dating and Relationships', American Enterprise Institute (13 Feb. 2023).

24 Mary Harrington, 'Is There Hope for Marriage? On Big Romance and Other Myths of the Modern Age', *The Hedgehog Review*, 24/3 (2022).

25 'Are Household Formation Decisions and Living Together Fraud and Error Affected by the Living Together as a Married Couple Policy? An Evidence Review', Department for Work and Pensions, Jul. 2023.

26 Lorna Adams et al., 'Reducing Parental Conflict Programme Evaluation: Third Interim Report: Findings from the Second and Third Years of Delivery', UK Government, Apr. 2023.

27 'The Sustainability Implications of Single Occupancy Households', *Buildings and Cities* (9 Feb. 2021), https://www.buildingsandcities.org/insights/commentaries/sustainability-single-households.html.

9. RAISING STATUS AND SHARING RESPONSIBILITY

1 The best summary can be found in Damien Green MP, 'Fixing the Care Crisis', Centre for Policy Studies, Apr. 2019.

2 'Chapter 6: Public Health, Prevention and Patient Responsibility', Select Committee on the Long-Term Sustainability of the NHS and Adult Social Care, UK Parliament, Apr. 2017.

3 Sarah Bedford and Daniel Button, 'Universal Quality Social Care: Transforming Adult Social Care in England', New Economics Foundation, Jan. 2022.

4 Wendell Berry, *Sex, Economy, Freedom and Community: Eight Essays* (Pantheon, 1993).

5 Atul Gawande, *Being Mortal: Illness, Medicine and What Matters in the End* (Profile Books, 2015).

6 Jonathan M. Schott, 'How Preventable Is Dementia?', Dementia Research Centre UCL, 2021.

7 According to the Academy of Royal Colleges.

8 Camilla Cavendish, 'Prevention is Always Better than Cure', *Financial Times*, 27 December 2019.

9 Peter Attia, *Outlive: The Science and Art of Longevity* (Vermilion, 2023).

10 Olof Wolf et al., 'How Deadly Is a Fracture Distal to the Hip in the Elderly? An Observational Cohort Study of 11,799 Femoral Fractures in the Swedish Fracture Register', *Acta Orthopaedica*, 92/1 (2021), 40–6.

11 Rachel Sylvester, 'New Technology Can Revolutionise the NHS, If Only Staff Will Let It', *The Times* (2 Dec. 2023).

12 Conversation with the author.

13 Millie Cooke, 'Hidden Cost of Labour's Social Care Plans Laid Bare as Experts Warn of Funding Gap Worth Billions', *GB News* (8 Apr. 2024).

14 Rishi Sunak and Saratha Rajeswaran, 'A Portrait of Modern Britain', Policy Exchange, May 2014.

15 'Ageing Better? Life Over 50 in the 21st Century', English Longitudinal Study of Ageing, 2023./

16 Simon Bottery and Saoirse Mallorie, 'Social Care 360', The King's Fund, Mar. 2024.

17 'The Silence of the Bedpans', *The Economist*, 22 Jun. 2024.

18 See Emma Duncan, 'Social Care: The Time Bomb No Political Party Wants to Touch', *The Times* (29 Jul. 2023).

19 'Parenting Priorities: International Attitudes Towards Raising Children', The UK in the World Values Survey, Kings College London, Sept. 2023.

20 'Creating a Britain that Works and Cares', Centre for Social Justice, Feb. 2024.

21 As noted in 'Creating a Britain that Works and Cares', Centre for Social Justice.

22 This idea comes from Danny Kruger MP, in his report 'The Care Commitment: A New Model of Social Care for England', Demos, Feb. 2021.

23 See Mark Hammond, Stefan White and Stephen Walsh, 'Rightsizing: Reframing the Housing Offer for Older People', Centre for Ageing Better, Oct. 2018; and https://committees.parliament.uk/committee/17/levelling-up-housing-and-communities-committee.

24 Les Mayhew, 'Future-Proofing Retirement Living: Easing the Care and Housing Crises', International Longevity Centre UK, Nov. 2022./

25 See Camilla Cavendish, 'Making Downsizing Easier Could Help Britain's Financial Crisis', *Financial Times* (24 Jun. 2023).

26 See 'Creating a Britain that Works and Cares', Centre for Social Justice.

27 Brigid Francis-Devine, 'Research Briefing: Average Earnings by Age and Region', House of Commons Library, Dec. 2023.

28 See 'Five Myths about Immigration and Economic Growth', *Pimlico Journal* [blog] (30 Nov. 2023).

29 Home Office, 'Vis_Do2', entry clearance visa applications and outcomes detailed datasets, year ending December 2023 (29 Feb. 2024).

30 'Migration Committee (MAC) Advisory Report, 2023', UK Government, Dec. 2023.

31 Neil O'Brien, 'The Grammar School of the Western World', *Neil's Substack* [blog] (23 Nov. 2023).

32 'Replacement Migration: Is it a solution to declining and ageing populations?', Population Division, Department of Economic and Social Afffairs, UN Secretariat, Mar. 2000.

33 Will Grimond, 'Most Social Housing Residents in London Were Born in the UK', PA Media (18 Dec. 2023).

34 'How Health-Care Costs Stopped Rising', *The Economist* (26 Oct. 2023).

35 Jennifer Thomas, 'A Review of Digital Technology Solutions to Support Caregivers, Digital Health and Care Institute, Mar. 2020.

36 Richard Sloggett, 'Care Closer to Home: The Role of Clinical Homecare in the Revolution of Patient Care', Future Health, Mar. 2022.

37 'Reducing Length of Stay', NHS England, see https://www.england.nhs.uk/urgent-emergency-care/reducing-length-of-stay.

38 Author interview with Leo Lewis, *Financial Times Asia* business editor.

39 James Wright, 'Inside Japan's Long Experiment in Automating Elder Care,' *MIT Technology Review* (9 Jan. 2023).

40 See 'Creating a Britain that Works and Cares', Centre for Social Justice.

41 Chris Tate, 'New Study Finds Care Home Residents Benefit from Robot Pets', University of Plymouth (29 Sep. 2022).

42 Emily Kenway, *Who Cares: The Hidden Crisis of Caregiving, and How We Solve It* (Wildfire, 2023), 117.

43 Arthur C. Brooks, 'How to Be Happy Growing Older', *The Atlantic* (28 Dec. 2023).

CONCLUSION

1 Inez Stepman, interview with Louise Perry, 'Episode 33: Why I'm an Anti-Feminist', *Maiden Mother Matriarch* [podcast] (1 Oct. 2023).

2 Mary Harrington, 'How Motherhood Put an End to My Liberalism', *Unherd* (9 Oct. 2019)./

3 Eliza Filby, 'When the State Fails, Family Steps In', *Unherd* (1 Dec. 2020).

4 See 'Signs of Success', Ipsos, Dec. 2023.

5 Emily Kenway, *Who Cares: The Hidden Crisis of Caregiving, and How We Solve It* (Wildfire, 2023), 119.

6 See Matthew Syed, 'No Pain, No Gain – What Weights Taught Me About Raising Children', *Sunday Times* (7 Jan. 2024).

7 Anthony Costello, *The Social Edge: The Power of Sympathy Groups For Our Health, Wealth and Sustainable Future* (Thornwick Ltd, 2018).

8 'Creating a Britain That Works and Cares', Centre for Social Justice, Feb. 2024.
9 See Sonia Sodha, 'When the Right to Die Becomes the Duty to Die, Who Will Step in to Save Those Most at Risk?', *Observer* (7 Apr. 2024).
10 Paul Morland and Philip Pilkington, 'Small State or Small Families?', Policy Exchange, Sep. 2024.

INDEX